U•X•L Encyclopedia of Weather and Natural Disasters

U·X·L Encyclopedia of Weather and Natural Disasters

Humans, Weather, and Natural Disasters VOLUME 5

Anaxos, Inc., Editors

U·X·L
An imprint of Thomson Gale,
a part of The Thomson Corporation

THOMSON
™
GALE

Detroit • New York • San Francisco • New Haven, Conn. • Waterville, Maine • London

U·X·L Encyclopedia of Weather and Natural Disasters

Anaxos, Inc., editors

Project Editor
Melissa Hill

Editorial
Julie Carnagie, Paul Lewon, Lemma Shomali

Indexing Services
Factiva, a Dow Jones & Reuters Company

Rights and Acquisitions
Margaret Abendroth, Margaret Chamberlain-Gaston, Tracie Richardson

Imaging and Multimedia
Lezlie Light, Robyn V. Young

Product Design
Pamela A. Galbreath, Jennifer Wahi

Composition
Evi Seoud, Mary Beth Trimper

Manufacturing
Wendy Blurton, Dorothy Maki

LIBRARY OF CONGRESS CATALOGING-IN-PUBLICATION DATA

UXL encyclopedia of weather and natural disasters / Anaxos, Inc., editors.
    p. cm.
    Includes bibliographical references and index.
    ISBN 978-1-4144-1879-7 (set : alk. paper) -- ISBN 978-1-4144-1880-3 (vol. 1 : alk. paper) --
ISBN 978-1-4144-1881-0 (vol. 2 : alk. paper) -- ISBN 978-1-4144-1882-7 (vol. 3 : alk. paper) --
ISBN 978-1-4144-1883-4 (vol. 4 : alk. paper) -- ISBN 978-1-4144-1884-1 (vol. 5 : alk. paper) --
    1. Meteorology--Encyclopedias, Juvenile. 2. Natural disasters--Encyclopedias, Juvenile.
I. Anaxos, Inc.
    QC854.U95 2008
    551.503--dc22
                                                                          2007011300

ISBN-13:

978-1-4144-1879-7 (set)	978-1-4144-1882-7 (vol. 3)
978-1-4144-1880-3 (vol. 1)	978-1-4144-1883-4 (vol. 4)
978-1-4144-1881-0 (vol. 2)	978-1-4144-1884-1 (vol. 5)

ISBN-10:

1-4144-1879-5 (set)	1-4144-1882-5 (vol. 3)
1-4144-1880-9 (vol. 1)	1-4144-1883-3 (vol. 4)
1-4144-1881-7 (vol. 2)	1-4144-1884-1 (vol. 5)

This title is also available as an e-book.
ISBN-13 978-1-4144-1885-8, ISBN-10 1-4144-1885-X
Contact your Gale sales representative for ordering information.
Printed in China
10 9 8 7 6 5 4 3 2 1

Table of Contents

Reader's Guide

Weather in all its manifestations—from peaceful blankets of mountain fog to ferocious hurricanes—fascinates most humans. Young children wonder why the sky is blue. Busy professionals wonder whether ice storms will cause flight delays. Backyard gardeners wonder whether their plants will survive a hot, dry summer. *The U•X•L Encyclopedia of Weather and Natural Disasters* presents a comprehensive, up-to-date survey of weather, weather-related topics, and natural disasters that gives readers the science behind the weather events that affect us all every day.

Scope and format

Each of the chapters in this five-volume series presents its topic in clear, nontechnical language. The topics are arranged in alphabetical order. The material is enlivened with eyewitness descriptions of recent weather phenomena, historical accounts of famous past weather events and disasters, biographies of famous figures in meteorology, practical information on handling extreme weather situations, relevant book and film recommendations, and hundreds of photographs, illustrations, and charts. Each chapter also presents step-by-step experiments, suitable for home or classroom, that allow students to have hands-on experiences with the foundations of weather and meteorology. Additionally, *The U•X•L Encyclopedia of Weather and Natural Disasters* provides a "Words to Know" section in each chapter, with key terms clearly defined. A cumulative index and a comprehensive "Where to Learn More" section at the back of each volume give readers easy access to material both within the series and in outside resources.

Volume 1 of this series serves as a general introduction to the topic of weather and natural disasters, and includes chapters on climate, clouds, and precipitation.

Volume 2 presents the first six of the alphabetically arranged chapters on weather and natural disaster topics: Avalanche, Blizzard, Drought, Dust Storm, Earthquake, and El Niño.

Volume 3 presents the fo!lowing seven chapters: Flood, Fog, Hurricane, Landslide, La Niña, Local Winds, and Monsoon.

Volume 4 wraps up the alphabetically arranged chapters with six more chapters: Optical Effects, Thunderstorm, Tornado, Tsunami, Volcano, and Wildfire.

Volume 5 examines human involvement with weather and natural disasters, offering chapters on forecasting, climate change, and the influence of humans on weather.

Acknowledgements

The development of *The U•X•L Encyclopedia of Weather and Natural Disasters* was a collaborative effort by the staff of Anaxos, Inc., but several key members of the team require special acknowledgement and appreciation. Many thanks are owed to Dr. Elliot Richmond for his broad meteorological expertise and good humor. Special thanks also to Emily Baker-Falconer and Russ Falconer, for their organizational vigor and editorial acumen, and to Liza Banks, for her copyediting prowess.

The staff of Anaxos would also like to thank Gale content project editor Melissa Hill and content product manager Debra Kirby for their guidance, insight, and inspiration.

Also, Melissa Hill would like to thank Lou Camp for additional review of the Climate Change and Global Warming entry. His knowledge of the topic and candid insights contribute much to the final product.

Timeline

c. 1650 B.C.E. The Mediterranean island of Thera is destroyed by a volcanic eruption. The event possibly gives rise to the legend of the lost civilization of Atlantis.

218 B.C.E. Carthaginian leader Hannibal's army is decimated by avalanches as he attempts to cross the Alps with tens of thousands of soldiers and a multitude of war elephants.

350 B.C.E Greek philosopher Aristotle writes *Meteorology*.

79 Eruption of Mount Vesuvius destroys Pompeii and Herculaneum in Italy.

1281 A Chinese fleet of around 4,000 warships is destroyed by a typhoon during an attempted invasion of Japan. The relieved Japanese called the typhoon *kamikaze,* or "divine wind," believing it came from the gods for their protection.

1375 An earthquake destroys the famous lighthouse of Alexandria, Egypt, one of two remaining wonders of the ancient world (the other being the great pyramids of Egypt).

1441 Invention of standardized rain gauge by King Sejong and Prince Munjong of Korea.

1450 Leone Battista Alberti invents first anemometer.

1606 Galileo invents the thermometer.

1643 Evangelista Torricelli invents the barometer.

1657 King Ferdinand II of Tuscany establishes the Accademia Del Cimento of Florence, which develops many early meteorological tools.

1686 English astronomer Edmund Halley publishes a ground-breaking study of trade winds and monsoons.

1707 Mount Fuji in Japan erupts for the last time.

1714 Gabriel Fahrenheit invents the first mercury thermometer.

1742 Swedish astronomer Anders Celsius outlines the centigrade temperature scale. This would lead to what is now the Celsius scale.

1752 Benjamin Franklin performs his famous "kite" experiment, flying a kite that dangled a metal key during a thunderstorm to determine the relationship between lightning and electricity.

1783 Iceland's Mount Laki erupts, spewing massive clouds of ash into the atmosphere and killing up to one fifth of the population of Iceland.

1784 Benjamin Franklin theorizes that the abnormally cold European winter of 1783–1784 was due to the eruption of Mount Laki, becoming one of the first scientists to note the relationship between volcanic eruptions and climate cooling.

1786 Benjamin Franklin publishes an accurate map of the Gulf Stream.

1820 The U.S. Army begins making and recording formal weather observations.

1841 Elias Loomis creates the first synoptic weather map.

1842 James P. Espy is appointed first official U.S. government meteorologist.

1846 Irish astronomer and physicist John Thomas Romney Robinson invents the cup anemometer.

1849 The Smithsonian Institution establishes a national weather observation network using information relayed via telegraph from 150 observers across the country.

1860 As head of the newly established British Meteorological Office, Robert FitzRoy uses the new telegraph system to gather daily observations from across England to make "weather forecasts," a term he coined.

1863 Robert FitzRoy publishes *Weather Book*, an important meteorological text.

1870 President Ulysses S. Grant establishes a national weather warning service under the Secretary of War.

1873 International Meteorological Organization founded.

1875 Benito Vines, the director of the Meteorological Observatory at Belen in Havana, Cuba, issues an accurate hurricane warning two days before a hurricane hits Cuba. His warning saves many lives.

1876 A cyclone in Bangladesh kills more than 200,000.

1883 Eruption of Krakatau causes massive tsunamis that kill 36,000 in Java and Sumatra.

1887 The Yellow River in China floods, killing an estimated one million people.

1889 A dam bursts in Johnstown, Pennsylvania, causing a flood that kills 2,000 people.

1890 U.S. Weather Bureau is founded.

1892 Captain Camilo Carrilo tells the Geographical Society of Lima, Peru, of "El Niño," his term for a warm northerly current and associated climate noticeable around Christmas.

1897 Belgian Adrien de Gerlache sets off for the Antarctic (with a crew that included first-mate Roald Amundsen) to make geographical and meteorological observations of Antarctica. It is the first expedition to spend an entire winter in the Antarctic.

1898 U.S. Weather Bureau establishes a hurricane warning network at Kingston, Jamaica.

1900 A hurricane strikes Galveston, Texas, killing more than 6,000 people.

1902 Stratosphere is discovered. Two scientists, working independently, share credit for the discovery: Richard Assmann and Léon Teisserenc de Bort.

1906 Earthquake in San Francisco kills approximately 3,000.

1919 Introduction of the Norwegian Cyclone Model, a revolutionary method of weather map analysis and interpretation.

1921 Sakuhei Fujiwara publishes a paper on the "Fujiwara Effect," the rotation of two cyclones around each other.

1924 Sir Gilbert Walker coins the term "Southern Oscillation" to describe the current and climate shifts popularly known as El Niño.

1925 The so-called Tri-State Tornado ravages Missouri, Illinois, and Indiana, killing nearly 700 people.

1930 Russian scientist Pavel Mochanov successfully launches his radiosonde, a balloon-borne device that can take weather measurements and relay them by radio, into the stratosphere.

1934 The "Dust Bowl," a severe drought in southern plains states that lasted several years, begins.

1938 Guy Steward Callendar publishes "The Artificial Production of Carbon Dioxide and Its Influence on Temperature," considered the first description of global warming caused by carbon dioxide emissions.

1943 Pilot J. B. Duckworth intentionally flies into a hurricane off the coast of Texas for the purpose of weather reconnaissance.

1948 First correct tornado prediction made in Oklahoma.

1948 Pacific Tsunami Warning System is established in Honolulu, Hawaii.

1951 The World Meteorological Association, operating as a specialized agency of the United Nations, replaces the International Meteorological Association.

1954 The U.S. National Weather Service begins naming each season's hurricanes alphabetically using female names.

1956 F. K. Ball publishes his theory of the generation of Antarctic katabatic winds.

1959 World's first weather satellite, Vanguard 2, is launched.

1969 The Saffir-Simpson Hurricane Scale is created. The scale rates the strength of hurricanes on a scale of 1 to 5.

1969 Hurricane Camille hits the Gulf Coast of the U.S., killing several hundred people.

1970 The National Oceanic and Atmospheric Administration (NOAA) is established.

1971 Ted Fujita introduces the Fujita scales for rating tornadoes.

1978 Record-breaking blizzard hits northeastern U.S.

1980 Mount St. Helens in Washington State explodes.

1985 Discovery of the Antarctic ozone hole.

2004 Massive tsunami kills nearly 300,000 people in Thailand, India, and Indonesia.

2005 Hurricane Katrina pummels New Orleans and the Mississippi Gulf Coast, killing nearly 2,000 people and forcing millions of people from their homes.

2006 The U.S. experiences a record-breaking wildfire season, with nearly ten million acres burned.

2007 The Enhanced Fujita Scale replaces the Fujita scale as a system for rating tornadoes.

Words to Know

absolute humidity: the amount of water vapor in the air, expressed as a ratio of the amount of water per unit of air.

accretion: the process by which a hailstone grows larger, by gradually accumulating cloud droplets as it travels through a cloud.

acid precipitation: rain and snow that are made more acidic when carbon, sulfur, and/or nitrogen oxides in the air dissolve into water. Also known as acid rain.

acid rain: rain that is made more acidic when carbon, sulfur, and/or nitrogen oxides in the air dissolve into water. Also known as acid precipitation.

active solar collector: system for gathering and storing the Sun's heat that uses pumps and motors. Often used for heating water.

active volcano: a volcano that continues to erupt regularly.

adiabatic process: a process by which the temperature of a moving air parcel changes, even though no heat is exchanged between the air parcel and the surrounding air.

advection: the horizontal movement of a mass such as air or an ocean current.

aftershock: ground shaking that occurs after the main shock of an earthquake.

agricultural report: a specialized weather report tailored to the needs of farmers that includes current temperature, precipitation, and wind speed and direction, as well as frost warnings and predictions of temperature and precipitation for the days to come.

air mass: a large quantity of air throughout which temperature and moisture content is fairly constant.

air pollutant: any harmful substance that exists in the atmosphere at concentrations great enough to endanger the health of living organisms.

air pressure: the pressure exerted by the weight of air over a given area of Earth's surface. Also called atmospheric pressure or barometric pressure.

Air Quality Index (AQI): measurement of air quality, based on concentrations of surface ozone averaged over an eight-hour period for specific locations.

Alps: mountain system composed of more than fifteen principle mountain ranges that extends in an arc for almost 660 miles (1,060 kilometers) across south-central Europe.

anabatic wind: winds caused by warm air close to Earth's surface. The air is less dense than the surrounding air and travels upward along a slope.

Andes: mountain range extending more than 5,000 miles (8,045 kilometers) along the western coast of South America.

anemometer: an instrument that measures wind speed.

aneroid barometer: a type of barometer that consists of a vacuum-sealed metal capsule, within which a spring expands or contracts with changing air pressure.

anvil: the flattened formation at the top of a mature cumulonimbus cloud.

aquifer: an underground layer of spongy rock, gravel, or sand in which water collects.

arid: describes a climate in which almost no rain or snow falls.

ash: very small, fine fragments of lava or rock that are blasted into the air during volcanic explosions.

asthenosphere: region of the mantle below the lithosphere, composed of partially melted rock.

aurora: a bright, colorful display of light in the night sky, produced when charged particles from the Sun enter Earth's atmosphere.

avalanche: a large mass of snow, ice, rocks, soil, or a combination of these elements that moves suddenly and swiftly down a mountain slope, pulled by the force of gravity.

avalanche path: the course an avalanche takes down a slope, composed of a starting zone, a track, and a runout zone.

avalanche wind: a cloudlike mixture of snow particles and air pushed ahead of a slab avalanche as it races downward.

aviation report: a specialized weather report tailored to the needs of pilots that provides information on the height of the clouds, visibility, and storm systems.

backfire: a small fire set by firefighters in the path of an oncoming wildfire to burn up the fuel before the main fire arrives, thus blocking it.

backing wind: a wind that shifts direction, rotating counterclockwise higher in the atmosphere.

barchan dune: a sand dune that, when viewed from above, resembles a crescent moon, with the tips of the crescent pointing downwind. Also called barchane dune, barkhan dune, or crescentic dune.

barograph: an aneroid barometer that records changes in air pressure over time on a rotating drum.

barometer: an instrument used to measure air pressure.

basalt: a type of rock that forms from hardened lava.

blizzard: the most severe type of winter storm, characterized by winds of 35 miles (56 kilometers) per hour or greater, large quantities of falling or blowing snow, and low temperatures.

blocking system: a whirling air mass containing either a high-pressure system (a blocking high) or a low-pressure system (a blocking low), that gets cut off from the main flow of upper-air westerlies.

caldera: a large depression, usually circular or oval shaped, left behind when a volcano's summit collapses.

calvus: "bald"; describes when the upper part of a cloud is losing its rounded, cauliflower-like outline and becoming diffuse and fibrous.

capillatus: "having hair"; a cloud with a cirriform, streaky structure on its upper edges.

castellanus: "castlelike"; used to describe clouds with vertical extensions.

Cenozoic era: the historical period from sixty-five million years ago to the present.

chaos theory: the theory that the weather, by its very nature, is unpredictable. Every time one atmospheric variable (such as heat, air pressure, or water) changes, every other variable also changes—but in ways that are out of proportion with the first variable's change.

chinook: a dry, warm katabatic wind in North America that blows down the eastern side of the Rocky Mountains, from New Mexico to Canada in winter or early spring.

chinook wall cloud: a solid bank of wispy, white clouds that appears over the eastern edge of the Rocky Mountains in advance of a chinook wind.

chlorofluorocarbons (CFCs): compounds similar to hydrocarbons in which one or more of the hydrogen atoms are replaced by fluorine or chlorine.

cinder: a small piece of material thrown from a volcano during an eruption.

cinder cone: a volcanic cone made of lava fragments.

cirriform: a wispy, feathery fair-weather cloud formation that exists at high levels of the troposphere.

cirrostratus: a thin layer of high-altitude clouds that cover most of the sky, but are semitransparent.

cirrus: clouds at high levels of the troposphere, created by wind-blown ice crystals, that are so thin as to be nearly transparent.

Clean Air Act: set of environmental regulations limiting pollutants emitted by cars, factories, and other sources. First enacted by the U.S. Congress in 1970 and updated several times since then.

clear-cutting: the logging practice of harvesting all trees from vast forest tracts.

climate: the weather experienced by a given location, averaged over several decades.

coalescence: the process by which an ice crystal grows larger. The ice crystal collides and sticks together with water droplets as the ice crystal travels down through a cloud.

coastal flood: an overflow of water onto a coastal area caused by a storm surge, strong winds, or tsunami.

cold front: the leading edge of a moving mass of cold air.

cold-phase ENSO (El Niño/Southern Oscillation): another name for La Niña; colder-than-normal eastern Pacific waters.

composite volcano: a volcano with steep sides made of layers of lava and ash.

compressional warming: an adiabatic process by which an air parcel warms as it descends. The descending parcel is compressed by the increasing pressure of the surrounding air, which adds kinetic energy to the molecules. Also called compressional heating.

condensation: the process by which water changes from a gas to a liquid.

condensation nucleus: a tiny solid particle around which condensation of water vapor occurs.

conduction: the transfer of heat by collisions between moving molecules or atoms.

cone: the sloping outer sides of a volcano (not all volcanoes have cones).

conelet: a small cone on the side of a large volcano.

congestus: "congested"; describes clouds with upper parts that are piled up and sharply defined; resembles a head of cauliflower.

conservation tillage: the practice of leaving vegetation on fields during idle periods to protect the soil from erosion and trap moisture.

continental drift: geologic theory that all continents were part of a single, original landmass before they slowly separated and gradually drifted apart.

convection: the upward motion of an air mass or air parcel that has been heated.

convection current: circular movement of a gas or liquid between hot and cold areas.

convective cell: a unit within a thunderstorm cloud that contains updrafts and downdrafts.

convective zone: the region of warm tropical water over which thunderstorms form; the ocean under the Intertropical Convergence Zone.

conventional radar: instrument that detects the location, movement, and intensity of precipitation, and gives indications about the type of precipitation. It operates by emitting microwaves, which are reflected by precipitation. Also called radar.

convergence: the movement of air inward toward a central point, such as the trade winds blowing from the north and south near the equator.

Coriolis effect: the apparent curvature of large-scale winds, ocean currents, and anything else that moves freely across Earth, due to the rotation of Earth around its axis.

corona: a circle of light centered on the Moon or Sun that is usually bounded by a colorful ring or set of rings.

cosmic rays: invisible, high-energy particles that bombard Earth from space.

crater: the bowl-shaped area around the opening at the top of a volcano.

crepuscular rays: bright beams of light that radiate from the Sun and cross the sky.

crest: the highest point of a wave.

critical angle: the angle at which sunlight must strike the back of the raindrop in order to be reflected back to the front of the drop.

crown fire: a fire that spreads through the treetops, or crown, of a forest.

crust: the outermost layer of Earth, varying in thickness from 3.5 miles (5 kilometers) under the ocean to 50 miles (80 kilometers) thick under the continents.

cumuliform: a puffy, heaped-up cloud formation.

cumulonimbus: a tall, vertically developed cloud reaching to the top of the troposphere or above, and capable of producing heavy rain, high winds, and lightning.

cumulus: fluffy, white, mid-level clouds that look like white or light-gray cotton balls of various shapes.

cyclone: a weather system characterized by air that flows inward and circulates around a low-pressure area.

dart leaders: the series of dim lightning strokes that occur immediately after the original lightning stroke, that serve to discharge the remaining buildup of electrons near the base of the cloud.

debris avalanche: a downward slide of loose, earthen material (soil, mud, and small rocks) that begins suddenly and travels at great speeds;

similar to a snow avalanche. It builds into a fearsome mass of mud, trees, and rocks that can cause much damage.

debris slide: a slide of small rocks and shallow layers of loose soil that commonly follows volcanic eruptions.

deforestation: the removal of all or most of the trees from an area.

dendrochronology: the study of the annual growth of rings of trees.

deposition: the process by which water changes directly from a gas to a solid, without first going through the liquid phase.

derecho: a destructive, straight-line wind, which travels faster than 58 mph (93 kph) and has a path of damage at least 280 miles (450 kilometers) long. Also called plow wind.

desert climate: the world's driest climate type, with less than 10 inches (25 centimeters) of rainfall annually.

desert pavement: hard, flat, dry ground and gravel that remain after all sand and dust has been eroded from a surface.

desertification: the process by which semiarid lands turn to desert (also called land degradation). It is caused by prolonged drought, during which time the top layers of soil dry out and blow away.

dew point: the temperature at which a given parcel of air reaches its saturation point and can no longer hold water in the vapor state.

diffraction: the slight bending of sunlight or moonlight around water droplets or other tiny particles.

dispersion: the selective refraction of light that results in the separation of light into the spectrum of colors.

divergence: the movement of air outward, away from a central point.

Doppler radar: a sophisticated type of radar that relies on the Doppler effect, the change in frequency of waves emitted from a moving source, to determine wind speed and direction as well as the direction in which precipitation is moving.

dormant volcano: a volcano that has not erupted for many years.

downburst: an extremely strong, localized downdraft beneath a thunderstorm that spreads horizontally when it hits the ground, destroying objects in its path.

downdraft: a downward blast of air from a thunderstorm cloud, felt at the surface as a cool wind gust.

drizzle: precipitation formed by raindrops between 0.008 inches and 0.02 inches in diameter.

drought: an extended period when the amount of rain or snow that falls on an area is much lower than usual.

dry adiabatic lapse rate: the constant rate at which the temperature of an unsaturated air parcel changes as it ascends or descends through the atmosphere. Specifically, air cools by 5.5°F for every 1,000 feet (1.0°C for every 100 meters) it ascends and warms by 5.5°F for every 1,000 feet (1.0°C for every 100 meters) it descends.

Dust Bowl: the popular name for the approximately 150,000 square-mile-area (400,000-square-kilometer-area) in the southern portion of the Great Plains region of the United States. It is characterized by low annual rainfall, a shallow layer of topsoil, and high winds.

dust devil: a spinning vortex of sand and dust that is usually harmless but may grow quite large. Also called a whirlwind.

dust storm: a large cloud of dust blown by a strong wind.

earthflow: a landslide that consists of material that is moist and full of clay, yet drier than the material in mudflows.

earthquake: a sudden shifting of masses of rock beneath Earth's surface, which releases enormous amounts of energy and sends out shock waves that cause the ground to shake.

eccentricity: the alternating change in shape of Earth's orbit between a circle and an ellipse.

ecosystem: a community of plants and animals, including humans, and their physical surroundings.

effusive eruption: the type of eruption in which lava spills over the side of a crater.

El Niño: Spanish for "the Christ child;" an extraordinarily strong episode (occurring every two to seven years) of the annual warming of the Pacific waters off the coast of Peru and Ecuador.

El Niño/Southern Oscillation (ENSO): the simultaneous warming of the waters of the eastern Pacific and the accompanying shifts in air pressure over the eastern and western Pacific.

electromagnetic spectrum: the array of electromagnetic radiation, which includes radio waves, infrared radiation, visible light, ultraviolet radiation, x rays, and gamma rays.

ENSO: stands for El Niño/Southern Oscillation. It describes the simultaneous warming of the waters in the eastern Pacific Ocean and the shifting pattern of air pressure between the eastern and western edges of the Pacific.

entrainment: the process by which cool, unsaturated air next to a thunderstorm cloud gets pulled into the cloud during the mature stage of a thunderstorm.

Environmental Protection Agency (EPA): government agency charged with implementing the provisions of the Clean Air Act.

epicenter: the point on Earth's surface directly above the focus of an earthquake, where seismic waves first appear.

equinoxes: the days marking the start of spring and fall. Also the two days of the year in which day and night are most similar in length and the Sun appears to cross Earth's equator in its yearly motion.

erosion: the wearing away of a surface by the action of wind, water, or ice.

eruption: the release of pressure that sends lava, rocks, ash, and gases out of a volcano.

evaporation: the process by which water changes from a liquid to a gas.

evaporation fog: fog that is formed when water vapor evaporates into cool air and brings the air to its saturation point.

extinct volcano: a volcano that is never expected to erupt again.

extratropical cyclones: a storm system that forms outside of the tropics and involves contrasting warm and cold air masses.

eye: an area of clear sky and warm, dry, descending air at the center of a hurricane.

eye wall: a vertical area of thick clouds, intense rain, and strong winds marking the outer boundary of the eye.

F

fair-weather waterspout: relatively harmless waterspout that forms over water and arises either in conjunction with, or independently of, a severe thunderstorm. Also called nontornadic waterspout.

fall: the downward motion of rock or soil through the air or along the surface of a steep slope.

Fata Morgana: a special type of superior mirage that takes the form of spectacular castles, buildings, or cliffs rising above cold land or water.

fault: crack in Earth's surface where two plates or sections of the crust push and slide in opposite directions against one another.

fault creep: slow, continuous movement of plates along a fault, allowing pressure to be released.

fibratus: "fibrous"; describes clouds with hairlike strands with no hooks or curls at the end.

fire line: a strip of ground, cleared of all combustible material, that is dug by firefighters to stop the advance of a wildfire. Also called control line.

fire triangle: the combination of three elements required for any fire: fuel, oxygen, and heat.

firestorm: also called a blowup, it is the most explosive and violent type of wildfire.

fissure: a crack in Earth's surface through which volcanic materials can escape.

flash flood: a sudden, intense, localized flooding caused by persistent heavy rainfall or the failure of a levee or dam.

floccus: "flock of wool"; describes clouds with small tufts with ragged undersides.

flood: an overflow of water on land that is normally dry.

flood basalt: high temperature basaltic lava that flows from a fissure in Earth's crust and covers large areas of the landscape. Also known as plateau basalt.

focus: the underground starting place of an earthquake, also called the hypocenter.

fog: a cloud that forms near or on the ground.

food chain: the transfer of food energy from one organism to another. It begins with a plant species, which is eaten by an animal species; it continues with a second animal species, which eats the first, and so on.

foreshock: ground shaking that occurs before the main shock of an earthquake.

fossil fuels: coal, oil, and natural gas—materials composed of the remains of plants or animals that covered Earth millions of years ago and are today burned for fuel.

fractus: "fractured"; describes clouds with broken up, ragged edges.

freezing nuclei: a tiny particle of ice or other solid onto which super-cooled water droplets can freeze.

front: the dividing line between two air masses of different temperatures.

frontal system: a weather pattern that accompanies an advancing front.

frostbite: the freezing of the skin.

fuel cell: device that generates electricity by combining hydrogen and oxygen; it emits water vapor as a by-product.

Fujita Intensity scale: scale that measures tornado intensity, based on wind speed and the damage created.

fumarole: a vent in Earth's surface that releases steam and other gases, but generally no lava.

funnel cloud: cone-shaped spinning column of air that hangs well below the base of a thunderstorm cloud.

gale-force wind: any wind whose sustained speed is between 39 and 54 mph (63 and 87 kph).

geologist: a scientist who studies the origin, history, and structure of Earth.

geostationary satellite: weather satellite that remains above a given point on Earth's equator, traveling at the same speed as Earth's rotation about 22,300 miles (35,900 kilometers) above the surface.

geyser: a regular spray of hot water and steam from underground into the air.

glacier: slowly flowing masses of ice created by years of snowfall and cold temperatures.

global warming: the theory that average temperatures around the world have begun to rise, and will continue to rise, due to an increase of certain gases, called greenhouse gases, in the atmosphere. Also called enhanced greenhouse effect and global climate change.

global water budget: the balance of the volume of water coming and going between the oceans, atmosphere, and continental landmasses.

glory: a set of colored rings that appears on the top surface of a cloud, directly beneath the observer. A glory is formed by the interaction of sunlight with tiny cloud droplets and is most often viewed from an airplane.

Great Depression: the worst economic collapse in the history of the modern world. It began with the stock market crash of 1929 and lasted through the late 1930s.

green flash: a very brief flash of green light that appears near the top edge of a rising or setting Sun.

greenhouse effect: the warming of Earth due to the presence of greenhouse gases, which trap upwardly radiating heat and return it to Earth's surface.

greenhouse gases: gases that trap heat in the atmosphere. The most abundant greenhouse gases are water vapor and carbon dioxide. Others include methane, nitrous oxide, and chlorofluorocarbons.

ground blizzard: the drifting and blowing of snow that occurs after a snowfall has ended.

ground fire: a fire that burns beneath the layer of dead plant material on the forest floor.

gust front: the dividing line between cold downdrafts and warm air at the surface, characterized by strong, cold, shifting winds.

haboob: a tumbling black wall of sand that has been stirred up by cold downdrafts along the leading edge of a thunderstorm or cold front. It occurs in north-central Africa and the southwestern United States.

hail: precipitation comprised of hailstones.

hailstone: frozen precipitation that is either round or has a jagged surface, is either totally or partially transparent and ranges in size from that of a pea to that of a softball.

hair hygrometer: an instrument that measures relative humidity. It uses hairs (human or horse) that grow longer and shorter in response to changing humidity.

halo: a thin ring of light that appears around the Sun or Moon, caused by the refraction of light by ice crystals.

harmattan: a mild, dry, and dusty wind that originates in the Sahara Desert.

haze: the uniform, milky-white appearance of the sky that results when humidity is high and there are a large number of particles in the air.

heat cramps: muscle cramps or spasms, usually afflicting the abdomen or legs, that may occur during exercise in hot weather.

heat exhaustion: a form of mild shock that results when fluid and salt are lost through heavy perspiration.

heat stroke: a life-threatening condition that sets in when heat exhaustion is left untreated and the body has spent all its efforts to cool itself. Also called sunstroke.

heat wave: an extended period of high heat and humidity.

heating-degree-days: the number of degrees difference between the day's mean (average) temperature and the temperature at which most people set their thermostats. The total number of heating-degree-days in a season is an indicator of how much heating fuel has been consumed.

heavy snow: snowfall that reduces visibility to 0.31 mile (0.5 kilometer) and yields, on average, 4 inches (10 centimeters) or more in a twelve-hour period or 6 inches (15 centimeters) or more in a twenty-four-hour period.

hollow column: a snowflake in the shape of a long, six-sided column.

Holocene: the most recent part of the Cenozoic era, from ten thousand years ago to the present.

horse latitudes: a high-pressure belt that exists at around 30° latitude, north and south, where air from the equatorial region descends and brings clear skies.

hot spot: an area beneath Earth's crust where magma currents rise.

hotshot: a specialized firefighter who ventures into hazardous areas and spends long hours battling blazes.

humilis: "humble" or "lowly"; describes clouds with a small, flattened appearance.

humiture index: an index that combines temperature and relative humidity to determine how hot it actually feels and, consequently, how stressful outdoor activity will be. Also called temperature-humidity index or heat index.

hurricane: the most intense form of tropical cyclone. A hurricane is a storm that forms in the northern Atlantic Ocean or in the eastern Pacific Ocean. It is made up of a series of tightly coiled bands of thunderstorm clouds, with a well-defined pattern of rotating winds and maximum sustained winds greater than 74 mph (119 kph).

hurricane warning: hurricane landfall is imminent.

hurricane watch: hurricane landfall is possible.

hurricane-force wind: sustained winds greater than 74 mph (119 kph).

hygrometer: an instrument used to measure relative humidity. It consists of a dry-bulb thermometer and a wet-bulb thermometer. Also called psychrometer.

hypothermia: a condition characterized by a drop in core body temperature from the normal 98.6°F (37°C) to 95°F (35°C) or lower.

ice age: a period during which significant portions of Earth's surface are covered with ice.

igneous rock: rock made of solidified molten material that made its way from the interior of the planet to the surface.

incus: "anvil" or "fan-shaped"; describes a cloud with a spreading, smooth or fibrous mass at the top.

induction: the process whereby excess electrical charges in one object cause the accumulation by displacement of electrical charges with the opposite charge in another nearby object.

inferior mirage: a mirage that appears as an inverted, lowered image of a distant object. It typically forms in hot weather.

insulator: a substance through which electricity does not readily flow.

intensity: description of the physical damage caused by an earthquake.

interglacial period: a relatively warm period that exists between two ice ages.

Intertropical Convergence Zone: a belt of warm, rising, unstable air formed from the inward-flowing trade winds from north and south of the equator.

intortis: "intertwined"; describes clouds with entangled, fibrous strands.

inversion, atmospheric: a stable reversal of the normal pattern of atmospheric temperature, formed when a warm air mass sits over a cold air mass near the surface.

ion: an atom that has lost or gained an electron, thereby acquiring a positive or negative electrical charge.

iridescence: an irregular patch of colored light on a cloud.

isobar: an imaginary line that connects areas of equal air pressure, after the air pressure measurements have been adjusted to sea level.

isotherm: an imaginary line connecting areas of similar temperature.

jet stream: the world's fastest upper-air winds. Jet streams travel in a west-to-east direction, at speeds of 80 to 190 miles (130 to 300 kilometers) per hour, around 30,000 feet (9,150 meters) above the ground. Jet streams occur where the largest differences in air temperature and air pressure exist. In North America, jet streams are typically found over southern Canada and the northern United States, as well as over the southern United States and Mexico. The northern jet stream is called the polar jet stream, and the southern jet stream is called the subtropical jet stream.

katabatic wind: a strong wind that travels down a mountain under the force of gravity, and is stronger than a valley breeze.

khamsin: a hot, dry, southerly wind that originates on the Sahara and produces large sand and dust storms.

kinetic energy: the energy of motion.

La Niña: Spanish for little girl, a period of cooler-than-normal water temperatures in the eastern Pacific near the coast of Peru and Ecuador. It often follows an El Niño.

lahar: a mudflow of volcanic ash and water that sometimes occurs after a volcanic eruption.

lake breeze: a wind similar to a sea breeze that can be felt at the edge of a large lake.

landfall: the point on a coast where the center of a hurricane first crosses.

landslide: the movement of large amounts of soil, rocks, mud, and other debris downward and outward along a slope.

latent heat: the heat that must be removed from a quantity of water vapor to cause it to turn into a liquid, or that must be added to a quantity of liquid water to cause it to turn into a vapor; called latent because the temperature of the quantity of water or water vapor does not change.

latitude: an imaginary line encircling Earth, parallel to the equator, that tells one's position north or south on the globe.

lava: molten rock that erupts from a fissure or a vent (*see* magma).

lava domes: volcanic formations built up from layers of viscous lava that does not flow far from its source.

lava tube: a tube formed when an outer layer of lava is cooled by the air and hardens and molten lava then flows out of the middle of the tube, leaving it hollow.

leeward: the opposite direction from which the wind is blowing. Also the slope of a mountain opposite to the direction of local or prevailing winds down which cold air descends, producing dry conditions.

lenticularis: "lens-shaped"; describes clouds that are elongated, or almond-shaped with well-defined outlines.

lightning: a short-lived, bright flash of light during a thunderstorm that is produced by a 100-million-volt electrical discharge in the atmosphere.

liquefaction: the transformation of water-saturated soil into a liquidlike mass, usually by the action of seismic waves.

lithosphere: the rigid outermost region of Earth, composed of the crust and the upper part of the mantle.

local winds: winds that blow across surface areas ranging from a few miles to about 100 miles (about 160 kilometers) in width. Also known as mesoscale winds or regional winds.

loose-snow avalanche: avalanche composed of loosely packed snow that begins at a single point and slides down a slope, fanning out in the shape of an inverted V.

M

magma: molten rock containing dissolved gas and crystals that originates deep within Earth. When it reaches the surface it is called lava.

magma chamber: a reservoir of magma beneath Earth's surface.

magnitude: the power of an earthquake, as recorded by a seismograph, or seismometer.

mammatus: round, pouchlike cloud formations that appear in clusters and hang from the underside of a larger cloud.

mantle: the thick, dense layer of rock that lies beneath Earth's crust. The mantle is about 1,800 miles (2,900 kilometers) thick and accounts for about 84 percent of Earth's volume.

marine forecast: a specialized weather forecast of interest to coastal residents and mariners, which gives projections of the times of high and low tide, wave height, wind speed and direction, and visibility.

Maunder minimum: a period of time from 1645 to 1715, during which sunspot activity was almost nonexistent.

mediocris: "mediocre"; describes clouds of moderate vertical development with lumpy tops.

mesocyclone: region of rotating updrafts created by wind shear within a supercell storm; it may be the beginnings of a tornado.

mesoscale winds: winds that blow across surface areas ranging from a few miles to about 100 miles (about 160 kilometers) in width. Also known as local winds or regional winds.

Mesozoic era: the historical period from 225 million years ago to 65 million years ago, best known as the age of the dinosaurs.

meteorologist: a scientist who studies weather and climate.

meteorology: the scientific study of the atmosphere and atmospheric processes, namely weather and climate.

middle latitudes: the regions of the world that lie between the latitudes of 30° and 60° north and south. Also called temperate regions.

Milankovitch theory: the theory stating that the three types of variation in Earth's orbit, taken together, can be linked with warm and cold periods throughout history. These variations include: the shape of Earth's orbit, the direction of tilt of its axis, and the degree of tilt of its axis.

mirage: an optical illusion in which an object appears in a position that differs from its true position, or a nonexistent object (such as a body of water) appears.

modified Mercalli scale: scale developed by Italian seismologist Giuseppe Mercalli to measure the intensity of an earthquake based on the amount of vibration felt by people and the extent of damage to buildings.

moist adiabatic lapse rate: the variable rate at which the temperature of a saturated air parcel changes as it ascends or descends through the atmosphere.

monsoon: a name for seasonal winds that result in a rainy season occurring in the summer on tropical continents, when the land becomes warmer than the sea beside it.

monsoon climate: a climate that is warm year-round with very rainy (flood-prone) summers and relatively dry winters. It encompasses much of southern and southeastern Asia, the Philippines, coastal regions of northern South America, and slices of central Africa.

mountain breeze: a gentle downhill wind that forms at night as cold, dense, surface air travels down a mountainside and sinks into the valley. Also called gravity wind or drainage wind.

mud slide: a landslide of mostly mud mixed with debris, often caused by heavy rains on steep land with sparse vegetation.

mudflow: a landslide consisting of soil mixed with water. It is wetter than the material in an earthflow.

multi-cell thunderstorm: a thunderstorm system that contains several convective cells.

multi-vortex tornado: tornado in which the vortex divides into several smaller vortices called suction vortices.

nebulosus: "nebulous"; describes clouds that are a thin, hazy veil.

NEXRAD: acronym for Next Generation Weather Radar, the network of high-powered Doppler radar units that cover the continental United States, Alaska, Hawaii, Guam, and South Korea.

nor'easter: a strong, northeasterly wind that brings cold air, often accompanied by heavy rain, snow, or sleet, to the coastal areas of New England and the mid-Atlantic states. Also called northeaster.

Northern Hemisphere: the half of the Earth that lies north of the equator.

numerical prediction model: a computer program that mathematically duplicates conditions in nature. It is often used to predict the weather.

obliquity: the angle of the tilt of Earth's axis in relation to the plane of its orbit.

occluded front: a front formed by the interaction of three air masses: one cold, one cool, and one warm. The result is a multi-tiered air system, with cold air wedged on the bottom, cool air resting partially on top of the cold air, and warm air on the very top.

ocean currents: the major routes through which ocean water is circulated around the globe.

oceanography: the study and exploration of the ocean.

Organized Convection Theory: a widely accepted model of hurricane formation.

orographic lifting: the upward motion of warm air that occurs when a warm air mass travels up the side of a mountain.

orographic thunderstorm: a type of air mass thunderstorm that's initiated by the flow of warm air up a mountainside. Also called mountain thunderstorm.

orographic uplift: the forcing of air upward, caused by the movement of air masses over mountains.

oxidation: a chemical reaction involving the combination of a material with oxygen.

ozone days: days on which the smog threshold is surpassed.

ozone hole: the region above Antarctica where the ozone concentration in the upper atmosphere gets very low at the end of each winter.

ozone layer: the layer of Earth's atmosphere, between 25 and 40 miles (40 and 65 kilometers) above ground, that filters out the Sun's harmful rays. It contains a higher concentration of ozone, which is a form of oxygen that has three atoms per molecule.

paleoclimatologist: a scientist who studies climates of the past.

Paleozoic era: the historical period from 570 million years ago to 225 million years ago.

particulates: small particles suspended in the air and responsible for most atmospheric haze. Particulates can irritate the lungs and cause lung disease with long exposure.

passive solar collector: system for collecting and storing the Sun's heat that has no moving parts and is generally used for home heating.

period: the time between two successive waves.

permafrost: a layer of subterranean soil that remains frozen year-round.

photochemical smog: a hazy layer containing ozone and other gases that sometimes appears brown. It is produced when pollutants that are released by car exhaust fumes react with strong sunlight.

photovoltaic cell: light-sensitive device containing semiconductor crystals (materials that conduct an electric current under certain conditions) that convert sunlight to electricity. Also called solar cells.

phytoplankton: tiny marine plants that occupy the lowest level of the food chain.

pileus: "felt cap"; small cap- or hood-shaped formation perched above or attached to the top of a cloud.

pipe: a narrow passageway that leads from a magma reservoir to a vent.

plate: a large section of Earth's crust.

plate tectonics: the geologic theory that Earth's crust is composed of rigid plates that are in constant motion with respect to each other, creating the major geologic features on the planet's surface.

Plinian eruption: a volcanic eruption that releases a deadly cloud of gas, dust, and ash.

polar easterlies: cold, global winds that travel across the polar regions, from the northeast to the southwest in the Northern Hemisphere and from the southeast to the northwest in the Southern Hemisphere.

polar front: the region or boundary separating air masses of polar origin from those of tropical or subtropical origin.

polar jet stream: a North American jet stream, typically found over southern Canada or the northern United States.

polar orbiting satellite: a weather satellite that travels in a north-south path, crossing over both poles just 500 to 625 miles (800 to 1,000 kilometers) above Earth's surface.

precession of the equinoxes: the reversal of the seasons every thirteen thousand years. This occurs because Earth spins about its axis like a top in slow motion and wobbles its way through one complete revolution every twenty-six thousand years.

precipitation: water particles that originate in the atmosphere (usually referring to water particles that form in clouds) and fall to the ground as rain, snow, ice pellets, or hail.

prescribed burn: a planned, controlled fire that clears flammable debris from the forest floor.

pressure gradient: the difference in air pressure between a high and low pressure area relative to the distance separating them.

psychrometer: an instrument used to measure relative humidity. It consists of a dry-bulb thermometer and a wet-bulb thermometer. Also called hygrometer.

Pulaski: a combination ax and hoe that is used by firefighters to clear brush and create a fire line. It was invented by forest ranger Edward Pulaski in 1903.

pumice: volcanic rock formed during the explosive eruption of magma; it has numerous gas bubbles and may float on water.

pyroclastic flow: a rapid flow of hot material consisting of ash, pumice, other rock fragments, and gas ejected by an explosive eruption.

radar: an instrument that detects the location, movement, and intensity of precipitation, and gives indications about the type of precipitation. It operates by emitting microwaves, which are reflected by precipitation. It is an abbreviation for **Ra**dio **D**etection **a**nd **R**anging. Radar may be called conventional radar to distinguish it from Doppler radar.

radiational cooling: the loss of heat from the ground upward into the atmosphere.

radioactive dating: a technique used to determine the age of rocks that contain radioactive elements, which works on the principle that radioactive nuclei emit high-energy particles over time.

radiosonde: an instrument package carried aloft on a small helium- or hydrogen-filled balloon. It measures temperature, air pressure, and relative humidity from the ground to a maximum height of 19 miles (30 kilometers).

rain band: a band of heavy thunderstorms forming a tightly coiled spiral around the center of a tropical storm.

rain gauge: a container that catches rain and measures the amount of rainfall.

rain shadow effect: the uneven distribution of precipitation across a mountain, with most of the precipitation falling on the windward side and very little falling on the leeward side.

rainbow: an arc of light, separated into its constituent colors, that stretches across the sky.

research buoy: a tethered or drifting buoy placed in the open ocean capable of recording atmospheric and ocean conditions and transmitting them to a satellite.

reflection: the process by which light both strikes a surface, and bounces off that surface, at the same angle.

refraction: the bending of light as it is transmitted between two transparent media of different densities.

regeneration: the process of making or starting anew.

relative humidity: a measure of humidity as a percentage of the total moisture a given volume of air, at a particular temperature, can hold.

Richter scale: the scale developed by American seismologist Charles Richter that describes the amount of energy released by an earthquake on a scale from 1 to 10. Each whole number increase in value on the scale indicates a ten-fold increase in the energy released. Earthquakes measuring 7 to 7.9 are major and those measuring 8 or above cause widespread destruction.

ridge: a northward crest in the wavelike flow of upper-air westerlies, within which exists a high pressure area.

Ring of Fire: the name given to the geologically active belt that surrounds the Pacific Ocean and is home to more than 75 percent of the world's volcanoes.

river flood: a flood caused when a river spills over its banks.

rock slide: a cascade of rocks (of any size) down a steep slope at high speeds.

roll cloud: a cloud that looks like a giant, elongated cylinder lying on its side, that is rolling forward. It follows in the wake of a gust front.

Saffir-Simpson Hurricane Damage Potential scale: a scale devised by Herbert Saffir and Robert Simpson intended to be used to predict a hurricane's destructive potential.

saltation: the wind-driven movement of particles along the ground and through the air.

saturated: air that contains all of the water vapor it can hold at a given temperature; 100 percent relative humidity.

saturation point: the point at which a given volume of air contains the maximum possible amount of water vapor.

scattering: multidirectional reflection of light by minute particles in the air.

sea breeze: the gentle wind that blows from over the sea to the shore during the day, due to differences in air pressure above each surface.

season: a period of the year characterized by certain weather conditions, such as temperature and precipitation, as well as the number of hours of sunlight each day.

sector plate: a star-shaped snowflake.

seismic waves: vibrations that move outward from the focus of an earthquake, causing the ground to shake.

seismograph: instrument used to detect and measure seismic waves. Also known as a seismometer.

semiarid: a climate in which very little rain or snow falls.

semipermanent highs and lows: the four large pressure areas (two high-pressure and two low-pressure), situated throughout the Northern Hemisphere, that undergo slight shifts in position, and major changes in strength, throughout the year.

severe blizzard: a blizzard in which wind speeds exceed 45 miles (72 kilometers) per hour, snowfall is heavy, and the temperature is 10°F (−12°C) or lower.

severe thunderstorm: a thunderstorm with wind gusts of at least 58 mph (93 kph); hailstones at least 3/4 inch (2 centimeters) in diameter; or tornadoes or funnel clouds.

shamal: a hot, dry, dusty wind that blows for one to five days at a time, producing great dust storms throughout the Persian Gulf.

shelf cloud: a fan-shaped cloud with a flat base that forms along the edge of a gust front.

shield volcano: a volcano with long, gentle slopes, built primarily by lava flows.

shower: a brief spell of localized rainfall, possibly heavy, that only occurs in warm weather.

simoom: a hot, dry, blustery, dust-laden wind that blows across the Sahara and the deserts of Israel, Syria, and the Arabian peninsula.

sinkhole: a natural, steep depression in a land surface caused by collapse of a cavern roof.

skin cancer: a disease of the skin caused primarily by exposure to the ultraviolet rays in sunlight.

slab avalanche: avalanche that begins when fracture lines develop in a snowpack and a large surface plate breaks away, then crumbles into blocks as it falls down a slope.

sling psychrometer: an instrument that measures relative humidity. It consists of a dry-bulb thermometer and a wet-bulb thermometer mounted side by side on a metal strip, which rotates on a handle at one end.

slump: the slow downhill movement of large portions (called blocks) of a slope. Each block rotates backward toward the slope in a series of curving movements.

smog: common name for photochemical smog—a layer of hazy, brown air pollution at Earth's surface comprised of ozone and other chemicals.

smog threshold: the level of smog allowed by law and set by the Environmental Protection Agency at 80 parts per billion (ppb) of surface ozone.

smokejumper: a specialized firefighter who parachutes to strategic locations from airplanes to battle wildfires.

snow fence: a device placed in fields and along highways that slows the wind and reduces the blowing and drifting of snow.

solifluction: the most rapid type of earthflow, occurring when snow or ice thaws or when earthquakes produce shocks that turn the soil into a fluid-like mass.

Southern Oscillation: shifting patterns of air pressure at sea level, between the eastern and western edges of the Pacific Ocean.

spissatus: "tightly packed"; describes icy formations at the top of a vertical cloud that are dense enough to block out the Sun.

spotting: the starting of new fires, called spot fires, by sparks and embers that drift ahead of an advancing wildfire.

squall line: a moving band of strong thunderstorms.

stable air layer: an atmospheric layer through which an air parcel cannot rise or descend.

stationary front: a boundary between two air masses at different temperatures which are not moving or are moving slowly.

steam eruption: a violent eruption that occurs when water comes in contact with magma, rapidly turns to steam, and causes the mixture to explode.

stepped leader: an invisible stream of electrons that initiates a lightning stroke. A stepped leader surges from the negatively charged region of a cloud, down through the base of the cloud, and travels in a stepwise fashion toward the ground.

storm surge: an abnormal rise of the sea over and above normal tides and due to strong winds and low pressure accompanying a storm or hurricane.

stratiformis: "covering" or "blanket"; describes clouds that form a thick layer.

stratosphere: the second-lowest layer of Earth's atmosphere, from about 9 to 40 miles (15 to 65 kilometers) above ground.

stratus: gloomy, gray, featureless sheets of clouds that cover the entire sky, at low levels of the atmosphere.

subduction zone: a region where two plates come together and the edge of one plate slides beneath the other.

subsidence: a gradual sinking of the land surface relative to its previous level.

subtropical jet stream: a North American jet stream, typically found over the southern United States or northern Mexico.

suction vortices: small vortices within a single tornado that continually form and dissipate as the tornado moves along, creating the tornado's strongest surface winds.

sunspot: an area of magnetic disturbance on the surface of the Sun, sometimes referred to as a sun storm.

supercell storm: the most destructive and long-lasting form of a severe thunderstorm, arising from a single, powerful convective cell. It is characterized by strong tornadoes, heavy rain, and hail the size of golf balls or larger.

supercooled water: water that remains in the liquid state below the freezing point.

superior mirage: a cold-weather mirage that appears as a taller and closer, and sometimes inverted, image of a distant object.

surface fire: a fire with a visible flame that consumes plant material and debris on the forest floor.

thermal: a pocket of rising, warm air that is produced by uneven heating of the ground.

thermograph: an instrument consisting of a thermometer and a needle that etches on a rotating drum, continually recording the temperature.

thermometer: an instrument used to measure temperature. It consists of a vacuum-sealed narrow glass tube with a bulb in the bottom containing mercury or red-dyed alcohol. Also called dry-bulb thermometer.

thunderstorm: a relatively small but intense storm system resulting from strong rising air currents; characterized by heavy rain or hail along with thunder, lightning, and sometimes tornadoes.

tidal station: a floating instrument center in the ocean that records water levels.

topography: the shape and height of Earth's surface features.

tornadic waterspout: tornado that forms over land and travels over water. Tornadic waterspouts are relatively rare and are the most intense form of waterspouts.

tornado: rapidly spinning column of air that extends from a thunderstorm cloud to the ground. Also called a twister.

tornado cyclone: spinning column of air that protrudes through the base of a thunderstorm cloud.

tornado family: a group of tornadoes that develop from a single thunderstorm.

tornado outbreak: emergence of a tornado family. Tornado outbreaks are responsible for the greatest amount of tornado-related damage.

trade winds: dominant surface winds near the equator, generally blowing from east to west and toward the equator.

translucidus: "translucent"; describes clouds that form a transparent layer covering a large part of the sky, through which the Sun or Moon shines.

transpiration: the process by which plants emit water through tiny pores in the underside of their leaves.

transverse dune: a series of connected barchan dunes, which appear as tall, elongated crescents of sand running perpendicular to the prevailing wind.

tropical cyclone: any rotating weather system that forms over tropical waters.

tropical depression: a storm with rotating bands of clouds and thunderstorms and maximum sustained winds of less than 38 miles (61 kilometers) per hour.

tropical disturbance: a cluster of thunderstorms that is beginning to demonstrate a cyclonic circulation pattern.

tropical storm: a tropical cyclone weaker than a hurricane, with organized bands of rotating thunderstorms and maximum sustained winds of 39 to 73 mph (63 to 117 kph).

tropical wave: an elongated area of low air pressure, oriented north to south, causing areas of cloudiness and thunderstorms.

tropics: the region of Earth between 23.5° north latitude and 23.5° south latitude.

tropopause: the boundary between the troposphere and the stratosphere, between 30,000 and 40,000 feet (9,000 and 12,000 meters) above ground.

troposphere: the lowest atmospheric layer, where clouds exist and virtually all weather occurs.

trough: a southward dip in the wavelike flow of upper-air westerlies, within which exists a low-pressure area. Also, the lowest point of a wave.

tsunami: a huge ocean wave that can travel at speeds up to 600 mph (965 kph) for hundreds of miles over open ocean before it hits land; caused by an earthquake, underwater volcanic eruption, or underwater landslide.

tsunami warning: an alert stating that a tsunami has been detected and is approaching the designated area. People are instructed to move to higher ground immediately.

tsunami watch: an alert stating that an earthquake has occurred with sufficient magnitude to trigger a tsunami. People are instructed to listen for further news.

typhoon: tropical cyclone that form in the China Sea or in the western North Pacific Ocean.

uncinus: "hook-shaped"; describes clouds with fibers creating the pattern called "mare's tail."

undulatus: "undulating"; describes clouds with wavelike formation within patches, layers, or sheets.

unhealthy air days: days on which surface ozone levels reach 80 parts per billion—a concentration considered unhealthy to children, people with respiratory problems, and adults who exercise or work vigorously outdoors.

unsaturated air: air that has less than 100 percent relative humidity.

updraft: a column of air blowing upward inside a vertical cloud.

upper-air westerlies: global-scale, upper-air winds that flow in waves heading west to east (but also shifting north and south) through the middle latitudes of the Northern Hemisphere.

upwelling: the rising up of cold waters from the depths of the ocean, replacing the warm surface water that has moved away horizontally.

valley breeze: an uphill wind that forms during the day as the valley air is heated and rises. Also called anabatic wind.

veering wind: a wind that shifts direction, turning clockwise as it moves higher.

vent: an opening in the surface of Earth through which molten rock, lava, ash, and gases escape.

ventifact: a rock, boulder, or canyon wall that has been sculpted by wind and wind-blown sand.

vertical cloud: a cloud that develops upward to great heights. Vertical clouds are the products of sudden, forceful uplifts of small pockets of warm air.

virga: rain that falls from clouds but evaporates in midair under conditions of very low humidity.

volcano: an opening in the surface of Earth (vent) through which molten rock, lava, ashes, and gases escape; it is also the name for the mountain or hill that is formed by the lava and other erupted material.

vortex: (plural: vortices) vertical axis of extremely low pressure around which winds rotate.

wall cloud: a roughly circular, rotating cloud that protrudes from the base of a thunderstorm cloud; it is often the beginning of a tornado.

warm front: the line behind which a warm air mass is advancing, and in front of which a cold air mass is retreating.

warm-phase ENSO (El Niño/Southern Oscillation): another name for El Niño; warmer-than-normal eastern Pacific waters.

warning: a severe weather advisory that means that a storm has been sighted and may strike a specific area.

watch: a severe weather advisory that means that while a storm does not yet exist, conditions are ripe for one to develop.

waterspout: rapidly rotating column of air that forms over a large body of water, extending from the base of a cloud to the surface of the water.

weather: the set of conditions of temperature, humidity, cloud cover, and wind speed at a given time.

weather aircraft: aircraft that carry weather instruments and collect data in the upper levels of the troposphere. They are primarily used to probe storm clouds, within which they measure temperature, air pressure, and wind speed and direction.

weather forecast: a prediction of what the weather will be like in the future, based on present and past conditions.

weather map: a map of a large geographic region, on which weather station entries are plotted. By looking at a weather map, a meteorologist can determine the locations of fronts, regions of high and low pressure, the dividing line between temperatures below freezing and above freezing, and the movement of storm systems. Also called surface analysis.

weather satellite: a satellite equipped with infrared and visible imaging equipment that provides views of storms and continuously monitors weather conditions around the planet.

westerlies: global-scale surface winds that travel from the southwest to the northeast in the Northern Hemisphere, and from the northwest to the southeast in the Southern Hemisphere, between about 30° and 60° latitude.

whiteout: a condition in which falling, drifting, and blowing snow reduces visibility to almost zero.

wildfire: a large, uncontrolled fire in grass, brush, or trees.

wind farm: a large group of interconnected wind turbines.

wind power: power, in the form of electricity, derived from the wind.

wind shear: a condition in which a vertical layer of air is sandwiched between two other vertical layers, each of which is traveling at a different speed and/or direction, causing the sandwiched air layer to roll.

wind sock: a cone-shaped cloth bag open on both ends, through which wind flows that is used to determine the direction and estimate the speed of the wind.

wind speed: the rate at which air is moving relative to the ground.

wind turbine: a windmill designed to convert the kinetic energy of wind into electrical energy.

wind wave: a wave caused by the action of wind on the water surface.

windbreak: row of trees or shrubs placed in a farm field to slow the wind and keep it from blowing away the soil.

windchill equivalent temperature: the temperature at which the body would lose an equivalent amount of heat, if there were no wind. Also called windchill index.

windchill factor: the cooling effect on the body due to a combination of wind and temperature.

windward: the direction from which the wind is blowing. Also the slope of a mountain on the side of local or prevailing winds, up which the air cools as it ascends producing moist, cloudy, or rainy conditions.

Forecasting

Weather forecasts assist people in many ways, such as helping them to decide when to plan a trip or when to plant their gardens. Predicting the weather, defined as the set of conditions of temperature, humidity, cloud cover, and wind speed at a given time, may also be a matter of life and death. Winter storms, hurricanes (the strongest form of tropical cyclones), tornadoes (violently rotating columns of air), and thunderstorms (small but intense storms) are all potential killers. A forecast can serve as a warning to those who are in the path of deadly weather.

Over the last century, meteorology and weather forecasting have made great advances. Meteorology is the scientific study of the atmosphere and atmospheric processes, especially weather and climate. Climate is the weather experienced by a given location, averaged over several decades. Meteorologists now have access to sophisticated technology and advanced methods of information gathering and analysis of atmospheric conditions, all of which make forecasting easier. The ability to make accurate forecasts is a sign that meteorology has entered the modern scientific era, not to mention every meteorologist's professional triumph.

What is a forecast?

A weather forecast is a prediction of what the weather will be like in the future, based on present and past conditions. Methods of forecasting range from very simple techniques based on wind speed and direction, temperature, cloud patterns, and experience, to very complex techniques using sophisticated computer modeling and large databases of historic information. Simple forecasting methods may be based on sayings, such as a "clear moon, frost soon"; or natural signs, such as the opening and closing of pinecones in response to humidity. Some of these sayings and so-called folk wisdom are useful, while others have no basis in fact.

On the other end of the forecasting scale are scientific methods, which involve the continuous measurement and analysis of atmospheric

WORDS TO KNOW

absolute humidity: the amount of water vapor in the air, expressed as a ratio of the amount of water per unit of air.

agricultural report: a specialized weather report tailored to the needs of farmers, which includes current temperature, precipitation, and wind speed and direction, as well as frost warnings and predictions of temperature and precipitation for the days to come.

air mass: a large quantity of air throughout which temperature and moisture content are fairly constant.

air pressure: the pressure exerted by the weight of air over a given area of Earth's surface. Also called atmospheric pressure or barometric pressure.

anemometer: an instrument used to measure wind speed. A common type is the cup anemometer.

aneroid barometer: a type of barometer that consists of a vacuum-sealed metal capsule, within which a spring expands or contracts with changing air pressure.

aviation report: a specialized weather report tailored to the needs of pilots, which provides information on the height of the clouds, visibility, and storm systems.

backing wind: a wind that shifts direction, rotating counterclockwise higher in the atmosphere.

barograph: an aneroid barometer that records changes in air pressure over time on a rotating drum.

barometer: an instrument used to measure air pressure.

blizzard: the most severe type of winter storm, characterized by winds of 35 mph (56 kph) or greater, large quantities of snow, and temperatures of 20°F (–6°C) or lower.

chaos theory: the theory that the weather, by its very nature, is unpredictable. Every time one atmospheric variable (such as heat, air pressure, or water) changes, every other variable also changes—but in ways that are out of proportion with the first variable's change.

climate: the weather experienced by a given location, averaged over several decades.

cold front: the line behind which a cold air mass is advancing, and in front of which a warm air mass is retreating.

dispersion: the selective refraction of light that results in the separation of light into the spectrum of colors.

Doppler radar: a sophisticated type of radar that relies on the Doppler effect, the change in frequency of waves emitted from a moving source, to determine wind speed and direction as well as the direction in which precipitation is moving.

drought: an extended period of abnormal dryness.

El Niño: means "the Christ child" in Spanish. A period of unusual warming of the Pacific Ocean waters off the coast of Peru and Ecuador. It usually starts around Christmas, which is how it got its name.

flash flood: a sudden, intense, localized flooding caused by persistent heavy rainfall or the failure of a levee or dam.

fog: a cloud that forms near or on the ground.

front: the dividing line between two air masses.

Pinecones react to weather changes. JLM VISUALS.

conditions. With basic weather tools, local forecasts can easily be created. With today's high-tech instruments, professional meteorologists can create global forecasts with considerable accuracy.

Skilled versus unskilled forecasts Anyone can guess at what the weather will be like tomorrow and have a fair chance of being correct. Since there is a limited range of possibilities for weather conditions at any season of the year, simple guesses will often match actual conditions. This is an example of an "unskilled" forecast. A "skilled" forecast, on the other hand, is based on observation and analysis of atmospheric conditions.

Skilled forecasting is not limited to professional meteorologists, however. Farmers and ranchers, whose livelihoods depend on the weather, can become quite skilled at predicting the weather over a twenty-four- to forty-eight-hour period, based on simple observations and experience.

When it comes to short-range weather forecasting, there are two principal types of unskilled forecasts. One is based on persistence and the other is based on long-range climatic predictions. The "persistence method" is simply predicting that tomorrow's weather will be the same as today's. If it has been hot and dry for several days, predicting another day of hot, dry weather is probably an accurate forecast. This method also works well in locations where the weather tends to be unchanging for days on end. Two examples are Los Angeles, California, where there tends to

A meteorologist studies weather patterns. ©VISUALS UNLIMITED/CORBIS.

be haze (high humidity and lots of airborne particles) in the morning and sunshine in the afternoon; and Seattle, Washington, where it is often cool and drizzling. Predicting mild and sunny weather for San Diego, California, is also a safe bet, since its weather is moderated by cold ocean currents.

Another type of unskilled forecast is created by studying weather information recorded over several decades to find the average conditions for a given location in a particular time of year. This is the kind of information often included in various almanacs. For example, the state of Michigan historically averages ten days of rain in September. Since there are thirty days in September this means that it rains, on average, on one-third of the days.

A skilled forecast, in contrast, is one that draws on global as well as local atmospheric observations. These observations include information not available to the average person, such as barometric pressure (the pressure exerted by the weight of air), winds at upper altitudes, dew point, and others. The forecasts given on television incorporate observations taken all over the world that have been processed by computers. The end result is a weather map showing temperatures, pressure highs and lows, precipitation (water falling to the ground), fronts (the dividing lines between air masses), and predictions as to how these conditions will change over the coming few days.

A skilled forecast is expected to be more accurate than an unskilled forecast. After all, wild guesses alone could produce forecasts that are accurate about half of the time. Thus the success rate of forecasting is not determined simply by how often the forecasts are correct, but by how far they exceed the success rate of unskilled forecasts.

Forecasting is a global endeavor Modern-day forecasters look at weather as a global process. The reason for this approach is that the atmosphere, where weather occurs, forms a continuous blanket around the entire planet. Therefore, weather conditions in one part of the world may eventually affect conditions in another part of the world. Although it is not necessary to have information from all around the world to produce forecasts for the short term (a few days), such information becomes necessary when making longer-term forecasts.

As a general rule, simple observation of local atmospheric conditions will be useful for predicting the weather for the following few hours. To get a picture of what the weather will be tomorrow or the next day requires regional or statewide weather data. Accurate predictions for three or more days require information from the whole continent. For still longer periods global weather, observations are necessary.

International cooperation in data collection The World Meteorological Organization (WMO) is responsible for organizing international cooperation in weather observations and reporting. This network of more than 180 national weather services, based in Geneva, Switzerland, is an agency of the United Nations. The WMO, through its World Weather Watch (WWW) program, oversees the worldwide collection and standardization of measurements of atmospheric conditions.

The WWW receives information from thousands of weather stations. About twelve thousand of these stations are on land, and another seven thousand are located at sea, on ships and oil rigs. Nearly one thousand more are radiosondes, instrument packages carried on board small weather balloons that take readings in the upper air. In addition, observations are collected from numerous aircraft, radar stations (stations that detect the location, movement and intensity of precipitation) and weather satellites, which are equipped with infrared and visible imaging equipment. Weather observers at land and sea stations are either weather professionals with government organizations or private industry, or trained nonprofessionals.

Who's Who: Hurd Willett

Hurd "Doc" Willett (1903–1992) was one of the most respected and skilled long-range forecasters of all time. Throughout his sixty-two-year career, Willett worked as a forecaster, teacher, and researcher. He authored over one hundred books and articles on meteorology and forecasting.

Willett's primary research topic was one that is still controversial within the meteorological community: the connection between sunspot cycles and long-range weather patterns. Astronomers have determined that the energy output of the sun varies somewhat with sunspot number. Willett theorized that climate change is linked to the sunspot cycles. This connection is known as the solar-climate relationship.

When Willett was nine years old he began recording winter storms and cold temperatures in a diary. Just before turning eleven, Willett knew what his future held: "In 10 years, one week, and three days, I will reach my majority," he wrote. "When I grow up, I want to be a weather man."

Hurd C. Willett. COURTESY MIT MUSEUM.

Willett began his career in weather science in 1925, when the discipline was still relatively undeveloped. He did much to advance the field. In the late 1920s and 1930s, Willett pushed for the integration of the polar front theory into U.S. meteorology. The polar front theory states that the storms of the middle latitudes are brought about by the mixing of cold, polar air from the north and warmer air from the south. The latitude at which this mixing occurs, approximately 60° north, is known as the polar front. Willett also developed some of the long-range forecasting principles that are now used in computer models.

Willett was made famous by his article, "Cold Weather Ahead," which was published in the *Saturday Evening Post.* In the article, Willett predicted that the series of devastating hurricanes

that had pounded the East Coast from 1938 to 1955 would cease by 1965. He also predicted that after 1960, the Northwest, Rocky Mountains, and the Midwest would no longer experience droughts, except for a possible period of drought from about 1975 until 1980. Willett was astonishingly accurate. New England was free of major hurricanes from 1960 until 1985. The only drought to plague the northern United States between 1960 and the early 1980s lasted from 1976 to 1978.

Willett received the first-ever Distinguished Scientific Achievement Award from the American Meteorological Society in 1951 for his contributions to meteorology and to our understanding of the large-scale circulation patterns of the atmosphere.

Processing the information Observers in the WWW network take measurements, at set time intervals, of temperature, humidity, precipitation, wind speed and direction, and air pressure. They also observe the clouds, noting their type, height, movement, and the amount of sky they cover. Observers send this information to local weather centers, where it is encoded, or translated into a type of shorthand using abbreviations and symbols. Those reports are then transferred to the three World Meteorological Centers of the WMO, located outside of Washington, D.C., in Moscow, Russia, and in Melbourne, Australia.

At the World Meteorological Centers, the reports are entered into supercomputers, which produce maps and charts representing a complete picture of the world's weather conditions. General weather forecasts are made from this information and sent out every six hours to national weather agencies. Next, these forecasts are sent to local weather agencies where they are used along with other data to create local forecasts. The local forecasts are then made available to the general public through the news media, such as newspapers, radio, television, and the Internet.

How data collection works in the United States The collection of weather information in the United States is coordinated by the National Weather Service (NWS), an agency of the National Oceanic and Atmospheric Administration (NOAA). The NWS receives information from approximately one thousand land-based weather stations across the United States, most of which are located at airports. While many of these stations are operated by NWS staff, others are run by employees of other government agencies, such as the Federal Aviation Administration, or by private citizens. Weather conditions are also recorded on more than two thousand ships and over one hundred automated stations on oil rigs, lighthouses, or buoys. These stations are located on the Great Lakes and in parts of the oceans that influence weather in the United States. Over 125 radiosondes (electronic instrument packages used in weather balloons) measure temperature, air pressure, and relative humidity as they ascend from ground level to a maximum of about 20 miles (30 kilometers) above ground.

Measurements from land and sea stations are sent to the NWS every hour. Those from radiosondes are sent twice daily. The NWS also receives information from stations around the world every three hours. In addition, about twelve thousand volunteer weather-watchers send monthly logs to the NWS. These volunteers are private citizens who take daily readings of precipitation and maximum/minimum temperatures. Some volunteers work at cooperative weather stations with equipment supplied by the NWS. Information supplied to the NWS by volunteer weather-watchers is included in studies of long-term climatic change.

Short-, medium-, and long-range forecasts A forecast is considered "short-range," "medium-range," or "long-range," depending on how far in the future its predictions extend. Short-range forecasts give detailed information about what to expect over the following twenty-four to forty-eight hours in terms of the temperature, wind speed and direction, cloud cover, and precipitation. Medium-range forecasts cover a period of two to ten days in the future. They predict the day-to-day temperature and precipitation up to five days in advance and describe likely temperature and precipitation averages for six to ten days in advance. Long-range forecasts make general weather predictions as far as three months in advance. These forecasts are limited to predicting whether rainfall and temperatures will be above or below average.

Short- and medium-range forecasts are produced by examining present atmospheric conditions. Long-range forecasts differ in that they are based on records of what the weather has been like, on average, for a particular climate at a particular time of year. Long-range forecasts are not intended to describe what the weather will be like from one day to the next, but are general guides as to what type of weather can be expected to dominate for that period, that is, warmer, colder, wetter, or drier than usual.

How accurate are forecasts? Many people recall times that forecasts have been incorrect more readily than they recall times that forecasts have been correct. This may be the case because the memory of a ruined picnic is more vivid than the memory of outdoor activities undisturbed by the weather.

The reality is that, for most parts of the world, forecasts for twelve to twenty-four hours in advance are accurate about 87 percent of the time; twenty-four hours in advance they are accurate 80 percent of the time; and three to five days in advance they are accurate 65 percent of the time.

There is every reason to believe that forecasting will continue to become more accurate in the future, and yet, the accuracy of forecasting will always have its limits. The basic problem meteorologists have to deal

Chaos theory and butterfly effect

In the early 1960s, Edward Lorenz made a discovery that has had a profound effect on weather forecasting. Lorenz's "chaos theory" explains that weather, by its very nature, is unpredictable. Lorenz used mathematical computer models to show that every time one atmospheric variable (e.g., heat, air pressure, water) changes, every other variable also changes. Furthermore, he found that even a slight change in one variable could produce significant changes in other variables. Thus, when Lorenz programmed two nearly identical sets of initial conditions into his computer model, he came up with two completely different forecasts.

Lorenz concluded that weather forecasting is chaotic because it is impossible to know, with absolute precision, every atmospheric condition at every moment. There will always be tiny discrepancies between the data used to create computerized forecasts and the actual atmospheric conditions. The effect of these discrepancies increases daily throughout a forecast so that by day ten a forecast may bear little resemblance to reality.

In theory, a small disturbance occurring in one part of the world can eventually have major implications in another part of the world. This condition is known as the butterfly effect. It gets

Edward N. Lorenz. COURTESY MIT MUSEUM.

its name from the idea that the flapping of a butterfly's wings in China, for instance, may trigger a storm system in New York.

The major conclusion of the chaos theory and the butterfly effect is that it will never be possible to predict, with complete certainty, the day-to-day weather for more than two weeks in advance.

with is the overwhelming complexity of the atmosphere. There are too many rapidly changing and erratic variables that affect weather patterns to get a complete and exact picture of the atmosphere.

Meteorologists first began to suspect that weather prediction would never be an exact science in the early 1950s. Computer modeling of weather patterns had revolutionized weather forecasting, and meteorologists believed that the new technology would rapidly and drastically improve the accuracy of forecasts. However, they were disappointed in

What can be forecast and when?

- Forecasters predict the path of a quick and violent storm, such as a tornado, from a few minutes to an hour before it strikes.
- Forecasters can warn of a large-scale storm system (such as a hurricane or heavy rain storm or snow storm) up to forty-eight hours before it arrives.
- Forecasters can alert people to an approaching cold front three to five days in advance.
- Forecasters can tell the average temperature and precipitation to expect for six to ten days into the future.

the results. While the forecasts were improving, that improvement was painfully slow. It seemed that while the technology grew by leaps and bounds, the increased accuracy of forecasts barely inched along. This led mathematician and meteorologist Edward Lorenz (1917–), a professor at the Massachusetts Institute of Technology, to investigate the slow improvement rate of forecasts.

Making your own forecast

The concepts covered in the chapter, "Weather: An Introduction" together with the information contained in this section are sufficient to allow people to make very basic forecasts. Of course, these forecasts will not be as accurate as the National Weather Service and will not include global or long-range forecasts. But it may still be instructive to create short-range, local forecasts and compare their accuracy with those broadcast on television or printed in the newspaper.

Interpreting natural signs   Throughout the ages, people have associated all sorts of natural occurrences with approaching weather. These phenomena have included animal and plant behavior as well as the appearance of the sky and shifting winds. Some of these associations have proven accurate and are scientifically sound. That is not to say that animals and plants have predictive powers. Rather, they behave as they do because they are responding to current atmospheric conditions. These conditions happen to precede certain types of weather. Other aspects of natural forecasting, particularly those based on mythology and folklore, have been shown time and again to be invalid.

While natural signs alone will not provide everything needed to prepare forecasts, they can provide important clues. Animals and plants are generally more sensitive to environmental change than are humans. Clouds and winds are also reliable indicators of certain types of weather.

All other factors being equal, the forecaster with an understanding of natural signs is likely to enjoy a higher rate of success than one without that understanding. What follows are descriptions of some of the most

Cows often lie down before it rains. ©TIM GRAHAM/ CORBIS.

common natural signs of impending weather for the middle latitudes (including the United States and Canada), where weather patterns generally move from west to east.

Animals Many animal species react to decreasing air pressure or increasing humidity, both of which are signs of rain. For instance, cows often lie down or huddle together in the grass before the rain comes. The reason for this behavior is not completely understood. One hypothesis for this behavior is that cows are preserving patches of dry grass, since they do not like to lie on wet grass. An alternate theory is that falling air pressure affects the digestive system of cows, making it more likely that they will choose to lie down rather than roam through the pasture grazing.

It is also common to see birds and bats flying at high altitudes before it rains. One proposed reason for this behavior is that they are chasing insects, which are carried upward by rising currents of warm air. This is a condition that typically precedes a thunderstorm.

A fisherman can sometimes tell that a storm is coming by the number of nibbles at his line. This pattern may be caused by fish trying to catch a meal before it is time to seek deeper, calmer waters. Rabbits, rattlesnakes, and other animal species are also known to intensify their food-gathering efforts before being driven to shelter by rain.

Other signs of rain are bees returning to their hives, gulls staying close to shore, and insects becoming more active. A whole chorus of animals seems to announce the rain: Frogs croak, geese honk, cicadas hum, and bees buzz, all more loudly than usual. Each of these types of behavior are responses to increasing humidity and/or decreasing air pressure.

One way to predict that a thunderstorm is on its way is to observe the behavior of pets. Animals are made uncomfortable by the static electricity in their fur, so a cat grooming itself constantly or a dog acting restless may indicate that a storm is approaching.

Plants   Pinecones close in response to rising humidity as do some flowers (tulips, African marigolds, scarlet pimpernels, dandelions, clover, and many others). One theory is that flowers close in response to moisture so the rain will not wash away their pollen. The leaves on trees may curl up in response to high humidity, something a person could notice as a sign of oncoming rain.

The sky   Two or three generations ago, people were much better at predicting the weather because they watched the sky much more than is common now. They especially watched cloud formations and learned how they could be used to predict weather. Cloud formations are probably the most reliable signs of an approaching storm or change in the weather. Far in advance of a warm front (the line behind which a warm air mass is moving), for example, the thin, high cirrus clouds known as "mare's tails" often appear in the sky. As the front gets closer, there may be an accumulation of high-level and or middle-level clouds as a possible indicator that a storm is brewing. The formation of low-level clouds after the middle- and high-level clouds have moved in means that rain or snow will soon follow.

An old weather proverb says: "Red sky at night, sailors' delight; red sky in morning, sailors take warning." This simple saying is often correct because weather patterns generally move from west to east. Thus, if skies are red at night, the sunlight, which is coming from the west where skies are clear, is reflecting off clouds to the east. However, if skies are red in the morning it is because the sunlight, in the east, is reflecting off clouds to the west. Clouds in the west may indicate that a storm is approaching.

Rainbows can be similarly interpreted. They are produced by the dispersion (selective bending) of sunlight through the rain. People can observe a rainbow only when the Sun is at their backs. If the rainbow is to the east, the rain has already passed. However, if a rainbow appears to the west of an observer, the rain is probably coming in her direction.

frontal system: a weather pattern that accompanies an advancing front.

frostbite: the freezing of the skin.

geostationary satellite: weather satellite that remains above a given point on Earth's equator, traveling at the same speed as Earth's rotation about 22,300 miles (35,900 kilometers) above the surface.

hair hygrometer: an instrument that measures relative humidity. It uses hairs (human or horse), which grow longer and shorter in response to changing humidity.

halo: a thin ring of light that appears around the Sun or the Moon, caused by the refraction of light by ice crystals.

haze: the uniform, milky-white appearance of the sky that results when humidity is high and there are a large number of particles in the air.

heating-degree-days: the number of degrees difference between the day's mean (average) temperature and the temperature at which most people set their thermostats. The total number of heating-degree-days in a season is an indicator of how much heating fuel has been consumed.

humiture index: an index that combines temperature and relative humidity to determine how hot it actually feels and, consequently, how stressful outdoor activity will be. Also called temperature-humidity index or heat index.

hurricane: the most intense form of tropical cyclone. A hurricane is a storm made up of a series of tightly coiled bands of thunderstorm clouds, with a well-defined pattern of rotating winds and maximum sustained winds greater than 74 mph (119 kph).

hygrometer: an instrument used to measure relative humidity. It consists of a dry-bulb thermometer and a wet-bulb thermometer. Also called psychrometer.

isobar: an imaginary line that connects areas of equal air pressure, after the air pressure measurements have been adjusted to sea level.

isotherm: an imaginary line connecting areas of similar temperature.

jet stream: the world's fastest upper-air winds. Jet streams travel in a west-to-east direction, at speeds between 80 to 190 mph (129 to 290 kph) around 30,000 feet (9,100 meters) above the ground. Jet streams occur where largest differences in air temperature and air pressure exist. (In North America, jet streams are typically found over central Canada and over the southern United States.)

latent heat: the energy that is either absorbed by or released by a substance as it undergoes a phase change.

latitude: an imaginary line encircling Earth, parallel to the equator, that tells one's position north or south on the globe.

marine forecast: a specialized weather forecast of interest to coastal residents and mariners, which gives projections of the times of high and low tide, wave height, wind speed and direction, and visibility.

meteorology: the scientific study of the atmosphere and atmospheric processes, namely weather and climate.

NEXRAD: acronym for Next Generation Weather Radar, the network of high-powered Doppler radar units that cover the continental United States, Alaska, Hawaii, Guam, and South Korea.

A key reference to: Fahrenheit and Celsius scales

Two main temperature scales are in use throughout the world: Fahrenheit and Celsius. The Fahrenheit scale was developed first, in 1714, by German-Dutch physicist Gabriel Fahrenheit (1686–1736). Fahrenheit also invented the first mercury thermometer. According to the way Fahrenheit arranged the gradations on his scale, fresh water freezes at 32°F and boils at 212°F, while saltwater freezes at approximately 0°F. The Fahrenheit scale is the one commonly used in the United States.

Anders Celsius (1701–1744), a Swedish astronomer, created his scale in 1742. Celsius felt it would be more convenient to use a system in which the freezing point of fresh water was designated as 0° and the boiling point as 100°. There was widespread agreement that these numbers were easier to work with, which prompted most of the world to adopt the Celsius scale.

A Celsius degree (°C) is larger than a Fahrenheit degree (°F). Specifically, one Celsius degree is equal to 1.8 Fahrenheit degrees. To convert from Celsius to Fahrenheit, multiply the degrees Celsius by 1.8, then add 32. To convert from Fahrenheit to Celsius, subtract 32 from the degrees Fahrenheit, then multiply by 0.56.

In other words:

$$°F = (1.8 \times °C) + 32 \text{ OR } °F = (9/5 \times °C) + 32$$

$$°C = 0.56(°F – 32) \text{ OR } °C = 5/9(°F – 32)$$

A third reliable optical sign is a halo. A halo looks like a fuzzy white (or sometimes colored) ring of light around the Sun or Moon. It is produced by the refraction (bending) of sunlight or moonlight by ice crystals that have formed at high altitudes. These ice crystals are contained within thin, upper-level clouds that may mark the beginning of an approaching storm front. In general, the larger the halo, the closer the front, and the sooner it will rain. If the halo is small, the storm is far away. There are limitations to this method of prediction, however. Whether the halo is large or small, there is no telling if it will rain or if the storm will change directions before arriving in an area.

Wind   The movement of clouds at different altitudes moving in different directions is a sign that the weather is about to change. For example, when a cold front (the line behind which cold air is moving) reaches an area, winds shift in a counterclockwise direction (as viewed from above) producing a pattern known as a backing wind. A backing wind blows low-level clouds from the north, middle-level clouds from the northwest, and high-level clouds from the west. Since winds travel counterclockwise around a low-pressure system, and low pressure is associated with rainy or stormy weather, a backing wind can often be a sign of an approaching storm.

On the other hand, winds shift clockwise after a warm front has entered a region, producing a veering wind. An example of a veering wind is one that blows low-level clouds from the north, middle-level clouds from the northeast, and high-level clouds from the east. Since winds travel clockwise around a high-pressure system, and high pressure is associated with fair weather, a veering wind may signal the approach of warm, clear skies.

Instead of clockwise and counterclockwise rules, it may be easier to remember that a veering wind is changing its direction to your right as you face it while a backing wind changes directions to your left as you face it. Remember the old sailor's rule: "A veering wind will clear the sky; a backing wind says storms are nigh."

A systematic approach to data collection   To be an amateur weather forecaster requires more than observing the clues in nature about impending weather. It also necessary to measure and record specific atmospheric conditions daily. Using this information, which can be collected in a backyard, it is possible to create short-term, local forecasts, as well as to contribute to information meteorologists rely on in their study of long-term climatic conditions.

Installing your home weather center   The first step is to set up a station at home where you can make observations. A home weather station should include a number of basic instruments, such as a thermometer to measure temperature; a psychrometer or hygrometer to measure relative humidity; a barometer to measure air pressure; a wind sock to measure wind direction; an anemometer to measure wind speed; and a rain gauge to measure rainfall. While this equipment is relatively simple compared to the satellites and supercomputers used by forecasters at the National Weather Service, it is adequate for recording local weather conditions.

Choosing the best location   In order to make daily observations, you will need to establish a permanent outdoor location for your instruments. Ideally, the site should be at least 32 feet (10 meters) from trees or buildings and large enough to accommodate an instrument shelter plus other instruments. If this arrangement is not possible, choose any outdoor site to which you have access. Just keep in mind that trees and buildings may affect readings of wind and temperature. To test the adequacy of your location, compare your air temperature readings with those announced on your local weather station. The official readings announced at this station are usually taken at the closest airport.

The instrument shelter   The instrument shelter is also called a Stevenson screen or a weather shack. It is a place to store and protect instruments outdoors. Its other purpose is to provide standard conditions under which readings are taken. The shelter is essentially a ventilated wooden box on legs, about 4 feet (1.2 meters) above ground. It protects

A weather instrument shelter.

FMA, INC.

the instruments from rain, direct sunlight, and wind, yet its slanted slats allow air to pass through the station. The roof of the shelter is double-layered, which helps prevent the sunlight from raising the temperature inside the shelter above that of the outside air. Finally, the whole shelter is painted white to reflect sunlight.

At a minimum, an instrument shelter should contain at least a thermometer, hygrometer, and barometer. It may also contain modified, automatically recording versions of these instruments as well as maximum and minimum thermometers. The other instruments—namely the wind sock, anemometer, and rain/snow gauge—should be placed near the instrument shelter, but far enough apart so that they do not interfere with each other's operation.

Where to get your instruments   Some of the instruments for your home weather center can be made, but others are more complex and should be purchased. Fortunately, all of the instruments can be purchased relatively inexpensively. Various models, however, range from the inexpensive to the very expensive. You can buy instruments at hardware stores, hobby shops, electronics stores, or catalogs. The best idea is to look into several catalogs to learn about the range of products and prices.

Measuring atmospheric conditions   Once the shelter is set up with the necessary instruments, you are ready to make measurements of weather conditions.

Temperature   Temperature is most commonly measured with a thermometer. A thermometer is a sealed narrow glass tube that has no air inside, with a bulb in the bottom containing a liquid. This liquid is usually mercury or red-dyed alcohol. When the surrounding air is warmed, the liquid expands and creeps upward through a tiny opening from the bulb into the tube. When the air is cooled, the liquid contracts and drops to a lower level in the tube. Tiny markings on the outside of the tube indicate the degree to which the liquid has risen or fallen—the temperature.

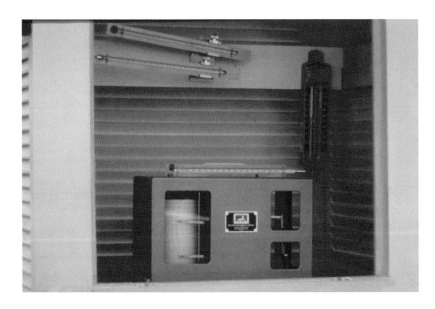

A thermograph. FMA, INC.

A type of thermometer that continually records the temperature is called a thermograph. This instrument has a needle that makes marks on a rotating drum covered with graph paper. A thermograph works by the expansion and contraction of two metal strips (usually iron and brass), welded together. When the temperature increases, each strip expands, but by different amounts. This expansion produces a slight bending of the strips, which causes a series of levers to move. The levers lead to the needle that etches on the drum.

Maximum and minimum thermometers tell the highest and lowest temperatures during an observation period (usually one day). The liquid within the tube rises in the maximum thermometer as long as the air temperature increases. The hole that connects the bulb to the tube, however, is narrower than in a regular thermometer. It is wide enough to allow the liquid to rise through it, however it prevents the liquid from passing back into the bulb. The liquid remains "stuck" at the maximum temperature.

A maximum thermometer can be reset by spinning or shaking it. In this respect, a maximum thermometer is similar to the old-fashioned, non-digital type of thermometer used to take a sick person's temperature.

A minimum thermometer usually contains alcohol, since alcohol has a much lower freezing point than mercury (–91°F [–71°C] for alcohol and –40°F [–40°C] for mercury). It looks like a regular thermometer,

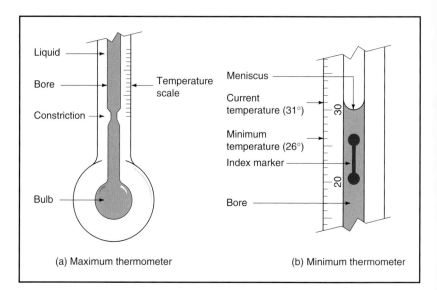

(a) Maximum thermometer

(b) Minimum thermometer

Sections of maximum and minimum thermometers.

except it is mounted horizontally. The minimum temperature is marked in this thermometer by a small dumbbell-shaped glass bar within the bore of the thermometer.

As the air temperature cools and the liquid contracts back into the bulb, surface tension drags the bar with it. However, when the temperature warms and the alcohol expands, it flows past the bar. (Surface tension causes the bar to move only when it is at the surface of the column of liquid.) The bar remains stationary, indicating the minimum temperature. This thermometer can be reset by turning it upside down, so that gravity pulls the bar to the surface of the column of alcohol.

Maximum and minimum thermometers come in other forms as well. One form is a U-shaped maximum-minimum thermometer with two temperature scales, one on each of the vertical branches. In this instrument, columns of liquid move small bars that mark the high and low temperatures. Digital thermometers with built-in memory can also serve as maximum-minimum thermometers.

Minimum temperature is the best standard by which to compare daily temperatures, since the day's low is usually reached after the sun goes down. When sunlight strikes a thermometer, the thermometer not only measures the energy of the surrounding air molecules (the true temperature), but it also measures the radiant energy from the Sun. This effect produces a higher temperature reading than the actual air temperature. Temperature readings during the day are much more

Dew-Point Temperature
Wet-bulb depression

Current Temperature	1.8°F (1.0°C)	3.6°F (2.0°C)	5.4°F (3.0°C)	7.2°F (4.0°C)	9.0°F (5.0°C)
14.0°F (−10.0°C)	5.9°F (−14.5°C)	−6.3°F (−21.3°C)	−33.3°F (−36.3°C)		
18.5°F (−7.5°C)	11.5°F (−11.4°C)	1.9°F (−16.7°C)	−13.9°F (−25.5°C)		
23.0°F (−5.0°C)	16.9°F (−8.4°C)	9.0°F (−12.8°C)	−2−2°F (−19.0°C)	−24.3°F (−31.3°C)	
27.5°F (−2.5°C)	22.1°F (−5.5°C)	15.4°F (−9.2°C)	6.6°F (−14.1°C)	−6.7°F (−21.5°C)	−42.3°F (−41.3°C)
32.0°F (0.0°C)	27.1°F (−2.7°C)	21.4°F (−5.9°C)	14.4°F (−9.8°C)	4.6°F (−15.2°C)	−11.0°F (−23.9°C)
36.5°F (2.5°C)	32.2°F (0.1°C)	27.1°F (−2.7°C)	21.0°F (−6.1°C)	13.5°F (−10.3°C)	3.0°F (3.0°C)
41.0°F (5.0°C)	37.0°F (2.8°C)	32.5°F (0.3°C)	27.3°F (−2.6°C)	21.0°F (−6.1°C)	13.3°F (−10.4°C)
45.5°F (7.5°C)	41.9°F (5.5°C)	37.8°F (3.2°C)	33.3°F (0.7°C)	27.9°F (−2.3°C)	21.6°F (−5.8°C)
50.0°F (10.0°C)	46.6°F (8.1°C)	42.8°F (6.0°C)	38.8°F (3.8°C)	34.2°F (1.2°C)	28.8°F (−1.8°C)
54.5°F (12.5°C)	51.3°F (10.7°C)	47.8°F (8.8°C)	44.1°F (6.7°C)	40.1°F (4.5°C)	35.4°F (1.9°C)
59.0°F (15.0°C)	55.9°F (13.3°C)	52.9°F (11.6°C)	49.2°F (9.6°C)	45.7°F (7.6°C)	41.5°F (5.3°C)
63.5°F (17.5°C)	60.6°F (15.9°C)	57.7°F (14.3°C)	54.5°F (12.5°C)	51.1°F (10.6°C)	47.3°F (8.5°C)
68.0°F (20.0°C)	65.3°F (18.5°C)	62.4°F (16.9°C)	59.5°F (15.3°C)	56.3°F (13.5°C)	52.9°F (11.6°C)
72.5°F (22.5°C)	70.0°F (21.1°C)	67.3°F (19.6°C)	64.4°F (18.0°C)	61.3°F (16.4°C)	58.3°F (14.6°C)
77.0°F (25.0°C)	75.7°F (24.3°C)	72.0°F (22.2°C)	69.3°F (20.7°C)	66.3°F (19.1°C)	63.5°F (17.5°C)
81.5°F (27.5°C)	79.2°F (26.2°C)	76.6°F (24.8°C)	73.9°F (23.3°C)	71.4°F (21.9°C)	68.5°F (20.3°C)
86.0°F (30.0°C)	83.7°F (28.7°C)	81.3°F (27.4°C)	78.8°F (26.0°C)	76.3°F (24.6°C)	73.6°F (23.1°C)
90.5°F (32.5°C)	88.2°F (31.2°C)	85.8°F (29.9°C)	83.5°F (28.6°C)	81.0°F (27.2°C)	78.4°F (25.8°C)
95.0°F (35.0°C)	92.8°F (33.8°C)	90.5°F (32.5°C)	88.2°F (31.2°C)	85.8°F (29.9°C)	83.3°F (28.5°C)
99.5°F (37.5°C)	97.3°F (36.3°C)	95.2°F (35.1°C)	92.8°F (33.8°C)	90.5°F (32.5°C)	88.2°F (31.2°C)
104.0°F (40.0°C)	101.8°F (38.8°C)	99.7°F (37.6°C)	97.5°F (36.4°C)	95.2°F (35.1°C)	93.0°F (33.9°C)

Relative Humidity Wet-bulb depression					
Current Temperature	2.0°F (1°C)	3.6°F (2°C)	5.4°F (3°C)	7.2°F (4°C)	9.0°F (5°C)
14.0°F (−10.0°C)	69%	39%	10%		
18.5°F (−7.5°C)	73%	48%	32%		
23.0°F (−5.0°C)	77%	54%	32%	11%	
27.5°F (−2.5°C)	80%	60%	41%	22%	3%
32.0°F (0.0°C)	82%	65%	47%	31%	15%
36.5°F (2.5°C)	84%	68%	53%	38%	24%
41.0°F (5.0°C)	86%	71%	58%	45%	32%
45.5°F (7.5°C)	87%	74%	62%	50%	38%
50.0°F (10.0°C)	88%	76%	65%	54%	44%
54.5°F (12.5°C)	89%	78%	68%	58%	48%
59.0°F (15.0°C)	90%	80%	70%	61%	52%
63.5°F (17.5°C)	90%	81%	72%	64%	55%
68.0°F (20.0°C)	91%	82%	74%	66%	58%
72.5°F (22.5°C)	92%	83%	76%	68%	61%
77.0°F (25.0°C)	92%	84%	77%	70%	63%
81.5°F (27.5°C)	92%	85%	78%	71%	65%
86.0°F (30.0°C)	93%	86%	79%	73%	67%
90.5°F (32.5°C)	93%	86%	80%	74%	68%
95.0°F (35.0°C)	93%	87%	81%	75%	69%
99.5°F (37.5°C)	94%	87%	82%	76%	70%
104.0°F (40.0°C)	94%	88%	82%	77%	72%

accurate when taken in the shade than in the sun. However, even indirect sunlight alters the actual air temperature somewhat.

Humidity The most useful measure of humidity is the relative humidity. Relative humidity is a measure of the amount of water in air compared to the total amount of water the air can hold at a given temperature. Remember that warm air can hold more water than cold air. Relative humidity is expressed as a percentage and tells how wet the air feels.

The simplest way to find the relative humidity is with a psychrometer, an instrument that consists of a dry-bulb thermometer and a wet-bulb thermometer. The dry-bulb thermometer tells the actual air temperature and the wet-bulb thermometer tells the saturated air temperature. The difference between these two temperatures is called the wet-bulb depression. Once you know the actual air temperature and the wet-bulb depression, you can refer to a standardized chart to find the relative humidity.

A dry-bulb thermometer is a regular thermometer, as described above. A wet-bulb thermometer is a thermometer with wet fabric placed around the bulb. An ideal fabric is a cotton weave called muslin, which retains moisture well. The wet cloth around the bulb provides an environment comparable to that of saturated air.

The wet-bulb thermometer almost always gives a lower temperature reading than the dry-bulb thermometer. The reason is that water from the cloth evaporates and absorbs latent heat from the bulb of the thermometer, thus cooling the thermometer. Latent heat is the heat released during the phase change, as the water turns from liquid to gas. The only exception to this is when wet-bulb and dry-bulb thermometers give equivalent readings, which occurs when water ceases to evaporate from the cloth. At this point the surrounding air is at its saturation point, meaning there is 100 percent relative humidity. The temperature at which both thermometers give the same reading is the dew point, which is the temperature at which any moisture in the air will condense and fall as snow or rain. You can determine the dew point from a standardized chart if you know the actual air temperature and the wet-bulb depression.

The greater the difference between the two temperatures (wet-bulb depression), the more water evaporates into the air, and the lower the relative humidity. A small wet-bulb depression indicates that little water is evaporating into the air, hence the relative humidity is high.

A variation on this instrument is the sling psychrometer. It consists of a dry-bulb thermometer and a wet-bulb thermometer mounted side by side on a metal strip, which rotates on a handle at one end. Operate it by holding the handle and spinning the metal strip in circles. This speeds up evaporation at the wet bulb, resulting in a quicker wet-bulb temperature reading.

Another tool for measuring humidity is the hair hygrometer. This instrument uses hairs (human or horse), which expand and contract in response to changing humidity. When there is more water in the air, the hair absorbs moisture and becomes longer. Conversely, when the air is drier, the hair loses moisture and becomes shorter. In fact, hair length changes by as much as 2.5 percent depending on the humidity. The same principle on which a hair hygrometer works can be observed in people's hair. Straight hair becomes limp in high humidity, and curly hair needs extra moisture to combat frizziness.

The hair hygrometer looks something like a thermograph in that its moving needle etches marks on a paper-covered, clock-driven, rotating drum. It works like this: Several hairs are attached to a system of levers.

Experiment: Make your own paper hygrometer

Paper can be used instead of hair to measure relative humidity, since it also absorbs water in the air. Using the following basic materials, you can create your own paper hygrometer: a piece of paper, a drinking straw, a small ball of modeling clay, a cardboard box at least one foot wide, a piece of poster board, and a toothpick.

1. To make the pointer, cut out five paper squares, each about 2 inches (5 centimeters) across. Use a hole-punch to make a hole through the center of each square. Push the straw through the holes so that the paper squares are grouped together on one end of the straw.

2. On the other end of the straw, affix a small ball of clay. Poke a toothpick into the clay, so that it extends in the line of the straw.

3. To make the pivot, cut a strip out of the poster board that is 6 inches (15 centimeters) long by 2 inches (5 centimeters) wide. Fold it twice into three squares. Unfold it to form a three-sided box and place the middle portion flat on the table, with the other two portions sticking straight up. Cut a small notch at the top-center of each of the two vertical sides.

4. To create the scale, cut an isosceles triangle (a triangle with at least two equal sides) out of the poster board that is 4 inches (10 centimeters) at the base and 6 inches (15 centimeters) tall. Fold it in half lengthwise. Draw a series of evenly spaced dashes on one side of the fold that are perpendicular to the fold.

5. Position the triangle scale at one end of the box top, so that the base is on the surface and the fold extends straight upward. The fold should point toward the opposite end of the box top. Position the pivot at the other end, across from the scale. Glue the pivot and scale into place.

6. Stick a pin through the straw, about two-thirds of the way toward the back of the straw (it should be closer to the paper than the toothpick). Balance the pointer by resting the edges of the pin in the notches of the pivot. You may have to adjust the position of the paper squares to get the pointer to balance.

When the relative humidity is high, the paper squares will absorb water and become heavier, making the pointer aim higher on the scale. When the relative humidity is low, the paper squares will be lighter and the pointer will aim lower.

When the hair length changes, it causes the levers to shift. The last lever is attached to the needle, which records the motion. The paper on the moving drum is imprinted with horizontal lines representing percentages of relative humidity. The up-and-down motion of the needle is calibrated with this scale, so the markings tell the relative humidity over time.

Air pressure   Air pressure, also called "atmospheric pressure" or "barometric pressure," is measured with a barometer. This tool was invented by Italian mathematician Evangelista Torricelli (1608–1647) in 1643. Torricelli filled a small glass tube with one sealed end with mercury. He then

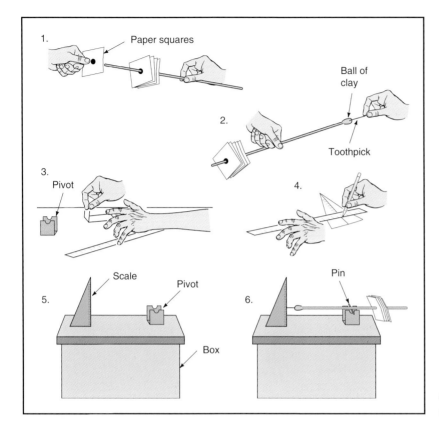

1. Paper squares

Ball of clay

2.

Toothpick

3. Pivot

4.

Scale Pivot

Pin

5.

Box

6.

Make your own paper hygrometer.

turned the tube upside down and placed the open end in a dish of mercury. The level of mercury in the tube began dropping. It stabilized when the weight of the mercury in the tube equaled the weight of the air pushing down on the surface of the mercury in the dish. The stable mercury level in the tube gave a way to describe the air pressure.

Mercury barometers still provide the most accurate method of measuring of air pressure. One drawback to using them, however, is that they must be "reduced" to sea level by calibrating the barometer so that it gives readings as if at sea level, compensating for differences caused by altitude. To calibrate a barometer to your altitude above sea level, call your local weather service office for an official reading. It is also necessary to adjust this type of barometer regularly to account for the expansion and contraction of the mercury in response to temperature change.

While the aneroid barometer is not as accurate as the mercury barometer, it needs no adjustment, making it the most convenient tool

Air pressure can be described in units of length or pressure

Units of length:

inches (in)

millimeters (mm)

(These units refer to the height of the column of mercury in a barometer)

Units of pressure:

pascals (Pa)

millibars (mb)

(These units describe air pressure specifically)

Air pressure at sea level:

between 28.64 and 30.71 in (727.45 and 780.03 mm)

between 970 and 1040 mb

Average air pressure at sea level:

29.92 in (760 mm)

1013.25 mb

for the job. In addition, aneroid barometers are smaller and easier to transport than mercury barometers. It is also possible to use an aneroid barometer in a recording device called a barograph. Aneroid barometers are the more widely used variety today.

The aneroid barometer has a vacuum-sealed capsule made of steel or beryllium alloy. The capsule contains a spring that changes in size with air pressure. When the pressure falls the capsule expands, and when the pressure rises the capsule contracts. This movement triggers a series of levers that are connected to a pointer. This pointer indicates the air pressure on a dial.

The dial of an aneroid barometer, in addition to units of atmospheric pressure, may have zones designated "rain," "change," and "fair." These terms should not be taken literally. Just because the air pressure is low does not necessarily mean it will rain. A much more useful indication of future weather is how air pressure rises or falls over time. Falling air pressure is a sign of rain and rising air pressure is a sign of clearing skies.

Mercury and aneroid barometers can be placed indoors or outdoors, since indoor air pressure adjusts very quickly to outdoor air pressure. The barometer should be mounted vertically and kept out of direct sunlight.

A variation on the aneroid barometer is the barograph. It works the same way as an aneroid barometer except in the barograph (similar to the thermograph or hair hygrometer), the levers are connected to a needle that etches its movements onto a paper-covered, rotating drum. A barograph measures changes in air pressure over time.

Wind direction Wind socks and wind vanes are both simple instruments used to determine the direction of the wind. A wind sock is a cone-shaped cloth bag, open on both ends, mounted on a pole. The wind enters through the wide end and exits through the narrow end. Thus, the wide end points to the direction from which the wind is coming. (Note: the "wind direction" in weather reports is the direction from which the wind comes, as opposed to the direction it is heading. For example, an "east wind" is one that is coming out of the east and moving to the west.)

You can buy a wind sock at a hardware store or construct your own. The sock is made by stretching a piece of weatherproof material over a series of increasingly larger metal rings, to form a cone-shape. The metal rings can be made from sturdy metal wire or cable that is cut into progressively longer pieces and twisted or clamped together at the ends. The sock is then attached to a tall, lightweight pole by a freely rotating metal ring.

Choose a place as far as possible from buildings and trees to erect the pole. The sock should be up high enough so that surface features do not interfere with the direction of the wind (10 feet or higher is ideal). Once your wind sock is up and working, you can use a compass to determine the direction the wind is blowing. When the wind is calm, it is recorded as "zero degrees." An east wind is 90 degrees, a south wind is 180 degrees, a west wind is 270 degrees, and a north wind is 360 degrees.

Another tool for measuring wind direction is a wind vane, or "weather vane." A wind vane is a free-swinging horizontal metal bar with a vertically oriented, flat metal sheet (often in the shape of a rooster or other animal) serving as a weight at one end of the bar and an arrow weighing down the other end. The arrow always points *into* the wind, toward the direction the wind is coming from.

On some weather vanes, a stationary, horizontal metal cross is positioned beneath the swinging bar, with the cardinal directions (north, south, east, and west) inscribed on the four ends. You can tell the wind direction with this type of wind vane by comparing the position of the arrow on the swinging bar with the directional cross beneath it. When there is only the swinging bar, you must use a compass to determine the direction in which the arrow is pointing. (Sometimes the wind is blowing too lightly to move a wind vane. If that is the case, use an

Evangelista Torricelli.
© BETTMANN/CORBIS.

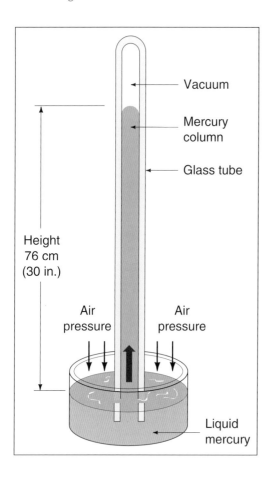

Height
76 cm
(30 in.)

Vacuum

Mercury
column

Glass tube

Air
pressure

Air
pressure

Liquid
mercury

A mercury barometer.

alternate method, such as looking at a wind sock or flag, to determine wind direction.)

Wind speed   Wind speed is measured by a tool called a cup anemometer. This device works like a speedometer. It consists of three or four cups, positioned on their sides, connected to a cap by horizontal spokes. The cap sits on top of a pole. The cap/spokes/cups unit rotates freely on the pole. The faster the wind blows, the faster the cups spin. This motion generates a weak electric current which is measured and displayed on a dial. To obtain an accurate measurement, the observer should check the wind speed several times over one minute and take the average value.

Wind speed is usually measured in units of miles per hour (mph) or kilometers per hour (kph). One kilometer is equal to 0.62 miles. The speed of wind over the water is commonly given in knots. One knot equals 1.15 mph (1.85 kph).

It is best to mount an anemometer away from buildings and trees. Place it as high as possible, but do not put it on a rooftop because winds accelerate over rooftops. If you do not have access to a suitable outdoor location, use a hand-held anemometer. This device is a small instrument you can carry into a clearing to check the wind speed.

Precipitation   The final condition to monitor in your home weather station is precipitation; that is, rainfall and snowfall. This measurement is relatively easy to make and, best of all, requires no equipment purchase. A rain gauge is simply a container that catches the rain. Any transparent container with a flat bottom and straight sides (like a drinking glass) can be used. Once or twice a day, take a ruler and measure (in inches or millimeters) the height of the water in the container. Then empty the container and set it up again.

This device will give you a rough idea of the amount of rainfall. For a more accurate and precise measure of precipitation, you can invest in the type of rain gauge used by the National Weather Service. This instrument consists of two nested cylinders (a smaller one that fits inside of a larger one), with a funnel that fits over the outer cylinder and directs water into

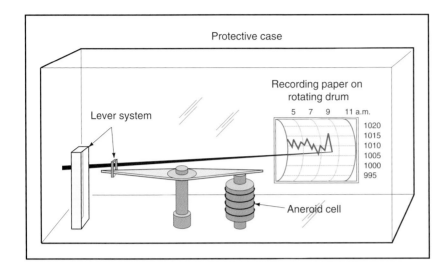

Protective case

Recording paper on
rotating drum

5   7   9   11 a.m.

1020
1015
1010
1005
1000
995

Lever system

Aneroid cell

A recording barograph.

the inner cylinder. The diameter of the mouth of the funnel will be several times wider than the diameter of the inner cylinder. If the diameter of the mouth of the funnel is ten times the diameter of the inner cylinder, than the area will be one hundred times greater. Thus, when an inch of water accumulates in the inner cylinder, it indicates that one-hundredth of an inch of rain has actually fallen.

If you want to get highly precise measurements, you can purchase a rain gauge that records patterns of precipitation over time. There are numerous varieties of this type of device, such as weighing-bucket rain gauges and tipping-bucket rain gauges. They are each driven by different mechanisms, but the outcome is the same: The rainfall is recorded on a paper-covered rotating drum.

Your rain gauge should be situated far from trees and buildings. If possible, follow this rule: Do not place the rain gauge closer to an obstacle than a distance equal to four times the height of that obstacle. For example, the rain gauge should be set up at least sixteen feet away from a four-foot-tall shrub. To prevent your rain gauge from tipping over, dig a small hole (a few inches deep) in the ground that is the width of your container and set the rain gauge in this depression.

Snow is easier to measure than rain. Just stick a ruler down through the snow until it hits the ground and take a reading. For best results, record the average of several readings taken around your weather station. If you want to find how much new snow has fallen in a given time

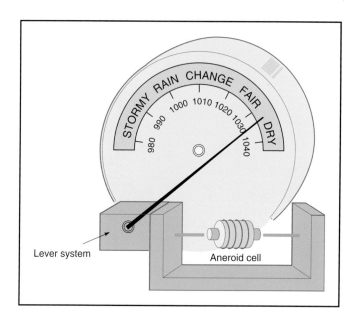

STORMY RAIN CHANGE FAIR DRY

980 990 1000 1010 1020 1030 1040

Lever system

Aneroid cell

An aneroid barometer.

period, set a board on top of the old snow and measure the snow that falls on the board.

Meteorologists are also interested in the water content of snow, called the meltwater equivalent. There are various, somewhat complicated methods of finding the meltwater equivalent. Some require the use of a modified rain gauge and antifreeze. On average, ten inches of snow equals one inch of liquid water. This value varies greatly, however, depending on how cold and dry, or warm and wet, the snow is. In fact, very dry snow can be as little as be as one-thirtieth meltwater by volume and very wet snow can be as much as one-third meltwater by volume.

Recording observations   Daily measurements that have been made over a long period are the most useful type of information about local weather conditions. Standard daily weather log sheets (such as those provided by the National Weather Service) may be quite detailed. They generally include columns for sky condition (type and amount of cloud cover); wind direction; wind speed; visibility (how far you can see due to presence or absence of haze or fog, which is just a cloud at ground level); relative humidity (recorded as wet-bulb and dry-bulb temperatures); maximum and minimum temperatures; snowfall; rainfall; soil temperatures at various depths; and hours of sunshine throughout the day. They also have

Make your own barometer
(step-by-step instructions)

You can create a barometer using the following items: a large (two-liter) plastic bottle, two rubber bands, a wooden ruler, and water.

1. Connect a ruler to a plastic bottle with two rubber bands. The ruler should be positioned vertically, with one end at the bottom of the bottle. Use one rubber band near the top of the ruler and one near the bottom.

2. Pour water into the bottle until it is about three-quarters full. Then fill a large, shallow bowl with water, nearly to the top.

3. Place your hand over the bottle top to prevent water from spilling and quickly turn it upside down into the bowl of water. When the bottle top is under water, you can remove your fingers.

4. Stand the bottle upside-down on the bottom of the bowl and steady it.

The level of water will fall until the weight of the air upon it equals the weight of the air pushing down upon the water in the bowl. To calibrate your ruler, call your local weather office or use a commercial barometer to determine the actual air pressure in inches. Then record that figure on the ruler, at the water level. You can add or subtract fractions of inches as the air pressure (and water level) changes.

Make your own barometer.

space for notes about significant weather occurrences (such as a hailstorm) and general conditions of the day.

To record your observations, fashion your own log sheet, on which you can record the conditions you are able to measure. You do not want to create an impossible task for yourself. It is better to make once- or twice-daily recordings of a limited number of conditions than to make occasional recordings of many conditions.

Try to take your readings at the same time (or times) each day, ideally each morning and afternoon. Temperature should be consistently recorded either in degrees Fahrenheit or degrees Celsius. Readings of air pressure should include the current air pressure, the change in pressure since the last reading, and whether the pressure is rising or falling (pressure tendency).

Three wind vanes and an anemometer. FMA, INC.

Wind direction, to the nearest 10 degrees, should be measured with a compass. Wind speed can be recorded in miles per hour or kilometers per hour if you have an anemometer, otherwise use the Beaufort scale.

Visibility is a measure of how far you can see. The best way to assess visibility is to determine the distance to certain landmarks, and note each day which ones you can see from your weather station. Cloud cover can be noted as one of four categories: overcast (covering more than 90 percent of the sky); mostly cloudy (covering 50–90 percent of the sky); partly cloudy (covering 10–50 percent of the sky); or clear (covering less than 10 percent of the sky).

Your notes will be briefer and more orderly if you use international weather symbols to describe wind speed, current weather conditions, and clouds. Your weather journal should have plenty of room for notes, where you can record any general or specific weather observations for the day— such as the opening or closing of pinecones, the location of a rainbow (to the east or west) in the sky, the arrival of migrating birds, or the impact of the fall's first frost on a garden. It is also helpful to supplement your written notes with drawings or photographs of clouds, frost patterns on your windshield, or icicles dripping from trees, for instance.

Making forecasts   The information you record at your home weather station will enable you to give a weather report of current conditions, but predicting the future is a more complex task. Before you try your hand at producing forecasts, it is best to just record daily observations until you have become familiar with the instruments and the methods of measuring specific conditions. It also helps to review your journal after several days or weeks, looking for any weather trends. Once you are comfortable with the whole process, you are likely to have greater success at forecasting.

A homemade forecast for one day in advance may include elements such as the expected cloud cover, precipitation, and what the minimum temperature for the night will be. While there are standard procedures for predicting these conditions, keep in mind that forecasting, as a whole, is greater than the sum of its parts. In other words, an overall description of what the next day's weather may bring takes more than plugging each measurement into some equation. It requires the ability to notice subtle changes in the natural world, as well as monitoring atmospheric conditions with your instruments.

Certain types of predictions and general assessments about the weather can be made by looking at your measurements or by taking note of general conditions. For example:

- Falling air pressure indicates that a storm may be moving in, while rising air pressure suggests skies will clear.

A rain gauge with a wind screen used to lessen the amount of catch (rain) missed due to rain streaming over the edge of the gauge. FMA, INC.

A key reference to: The Beaufort scale

In the early 1800s British Navy commander Sir Francis Beaufort developed a scale for estimating wind speed. The Beaufort Scale of Wind Force looks at the effect of the wind on water, trees, and other flexible objects on land. Beaufort's intention was to create a standard method of assessing wind speed, based on descriptions commonly used by sailors.

His scale was officially adopted by the British Navy in 1838 and became the international mariner standard in 1853. In 1926, the scale was modified so it could also be used on land. Many sailors still use the Beaufort method to measure wind speed.

The scale ranges from 0 to 12, with 0 for still conditions and 12 for hurricane-force winds. Try using the Beaufort scale provided here in various weather conditions to approximate the wind speed. Compare your results with the official wind speed reported by your local weather service.

- Feathery, high-level clouds are a sign that, while current conditions may be fair, a storm may be approaching. Thick, low-level clouds are a sign that precipitation is imminent.

- The appearance of a line of dark, middle-level clouds on the horizon indicates that precipitation is likely.

- Cloud formation is more likely when relative humidity is high than when it is low.

- Clear weather is likely forthcoming when fog burns off before noon, the percentage of cloud cover decreases, or "cracks" develop in a sheet of clouds.

- The air temperature will dip lower on a clear night than on a cloudy night, everything else being equal.

- The lowest nighttime temperatures occur when there are clear skies, light winds, and snow on the ground.

- When the dew point is below $32°F$ ($0°C$), you will get frost rather than dew.

- A veering wind (clockwise shift with height) is a sign of clearing skies and rising temperatures.

- A backing wind (counterclockwise shift with height) is a sign of stormy weather and falling temperatures.

To answer more complex questions about the weather, however, you must take into account a whole host of observations. Here are some examples of how to make general assessments and predictions about the weather by looking at several atmospheric conditions simultaneously.

Will it rain? Will it snow? A prediction of rain or snow is made by examining three specific atmospheric conditions: air pressure, sky conditions, and temperature. First, look at your last few readings of air pressure. Is it rising, falling, or staying the same? If it is rising or staying the same, precipitation is unlikely. Falling barometric pressure is often a signal of changing weather.

Wind Speed (mph)	Beaufort Number	Wind Effect on Land	Official Description
Beaufort Wind Scale			
Less than 1	0	Calm; smoke rises vertically.	CALM
1–3	1	Wind direction is seen in direction of smoke; but is not revealed by weather vane.	LIGHT AIR
4–7	2	Wind can be felt on face; leaves rustle; wind vane moves.	LIGHT BREEZE
8–12	3	Leaves and small twigs in motion; wind extends light flag.	GENTLE BREEZE
13–18	4	Wind raises dust and loose papers. Small branches move.	MODERATE BREEZE
19–24	5	Small trees with leaves begin to sway; crested wavelets appear on inland waters.	FRESH BREEZE
25–31	6	Large branches move; telegraph wires whistle; Umbrellas become difficult to control.	STRONG BREEZE
32–38	7	Whole trees sway and walking into the wind becomes difficult.	NEAR GALE
39–46	8	Twigs break off trees; cars veer on roads.	GALE
47–54	9	Slight structural damage occurs (roof slates may blow away, etc.).	STRONG GALE
55–63	10	Trees are uprooted; considerable structural damage is caused.	STORM
64–72	11	Widespread damage is caused.	VIOLENT STORM
73 or more	12	WIdespread damage is caused.	HURRICANE

The next factor to examine is sky conditions. If skies are clear, clouds are few, or only smooth, low-level clouds exist, then chances of rain are small. However, the presence of dark, low-lying clouds or development of upper-level clouds to the west, in conjunction with falling air pressure, indicates that precipitation is likely.

To determine whether that precipitation will fall to the ground as rain or snow, check the temperature. If it is above 37°F (3°C), rain is likely. However, if the temperature is 37°F or below, you can expect sleet or snow.

How cold will it get tonight? This question is one people often ask when trying to decide whether it is safe to leave their pet or plants outside for the night. By checking a minimum thermometer in the morning, you can learn the previous night's low temperature. But predicting the upcoming night's low is a more involved process that requires checking the outdoor temperature twice after the Sun goes down, and using an equation to find the answer. Bear in mind that since cloud cover and wind distort the amount of heat lost at night, this method works only under clear, calm conditions.

The first step is to find out what time the Sun will set in the evening and rise the next morning. This information is published in most local newspapers. The time of your first temperature reading depends on the month. In December or January wait one hour after sunset; in October, November, or February wait one-and-a-half hours after sunset; and in any other month wait two hours after sunset. This rule only applies to the Northern Hemisphere.

You must wait a certain length of time before taking measurements, because once the Sun sets, heat from the ground begins to radiate upward, into space. After a given period, the temperature at the surface will fall at a constant hourly rate. The length of time it takes for the temperature to begin dropping at the constant rate is shorter in the colder months and longer in the warmer months.

Assume the month is September. Two hours after sunset, go out to your instrument shelter, read the thermometer, and record the temperature. One hour later, go back and record the temperature again. The difference between the two temperatures is the "hourly drop." Next, count the hours that remain until one hour before sunrise. Multiply that number by the hourly drop. Subtract that figure from your second temperature reading and you will get the night's likely minimum temperature.

Will dew or frost form?   To answer this question you must determine the dew point and the night's predicted low temperature. The dew point depends on temperature and relative humidity. Specifically, the dew point is the temperature at which the air is saturated, resulting in the formation of dew or frost. Using wet-bulb and dry-bulb thermometers you can find the wet-bulb depression. Once you know the wet-bulb depression and the actual air temperature, you can find the dew point from the dew-point chart.

After you determine the dew point, two questions remain: Will the air become cold enough to reach the dew point and is the dew point above or below freezing? To answer the first question, use the method described above for determining minimum temperature. If the predicted minimum temperature is at or below the dew point, moisture will form on the ground. If the predicted minimum temperature is above freezing, the moisture will take the form of dew. However, if it is at or below freezing, you can expect frost.

Is the day hot or cold for the time of year?   Imagine that it is March 1 and it is very cold outside. How do you know if it just *seems* colder than normal because you are tired of the long winter or if it really *is* colder than normal? Here is a way to find out.

To determine whether the day is hot, cold, or normal for the time of year, you must look at a number of factors. These include identifying the existing air mass; comparing the day's maximum temperature with the average maximum temperature for the time of year in your locality; and recording the current wind speed and sky conditions. Then you can plot all of these variables on a chart to find out how the day compares to the norm.

The first step is to determine what type of air mass is in your area. An air mass is a large body of air that has fairly consistent temperature and moisture content. There are several clues that will help you identify whether you are within a tropical air mass or a polar air mass. The first is the season. In the United States, tropical air masses tend to dominate in the summer and polar air masses tend to dominate in the winter.

Here are other clues: polar air masses range from cool to extremely cold. One may bring bitterly cold temperatures to Montana (–10°F, or –20°C), yet on the rare occasion when it moves as far south as Florida, it may warm up to 50°F (10°C). Tropical air masses, on the other hand, range from warm to very hot. In the winter, they are generally limited to the southern states. If a tropical air mass makes it to the northern United States, it brings unseasonably mild temperatures.

The second step is to record the maximum temperature for the day. Then you must find the average maximum temperature for your location at the particular time of year. This information can be found at your local public library or weather service office. Records are generally kept for ten-year periods. One you have taken a reading of the day's maximum temperature, compare it to the average maximum temperature. Note whether it is higher or lower than the average, and by how many degrees.

The next step is to observe today's weather: Is it overcast or partly-to-mostly sunny? Are the winds calm-to-light or strong?

Putting your weather observations to use   One way to put your daily weather records to use is to become an official observer for the National Weather Service. This requires sending copies of your records to the NWS, where they will be added to the pool of data used by professional meteorologists. To learn how to do this, contact the weather service office in your area. Local radio and television stations also often receive reports from amateur observers.

State-of-the-art forecasting equipment

To complete the global atmospheric picture, a survey of the upper air is also necessary. Meteorologists rely on extremely sophisticated equipment

A radiosonde weather balloon being prepared for launch. Such balloons measure wind, temperature, and humidity to heights above 100,000 feet.
FMA, INC.

to supply information about atmospheric conditions at various levels of the troposphere (the lowest part of Earth's atmosphere). This section will describe this equipment plus the supercomputers that analyze the mountains of data and produce forecasts at incredible speeds.

Weather balloons The very first upper air measurements were obtained by standing on mountaintops or by sending up instruments attached to kites. Then came the days when scientists would ride in hot air balloons and take readings. Pioneering balloonists risked their lives, ascending thousands of feet above ground where the air is dangerously thin and cold. Modern weather balloons filled with hydrogen or helium carry electronic instrument packages called radiosondes. These unpiloted balloons can safely climb to far greater heights than their piloted predecessors.

The instruments in radiosondes measure temperature, air pressure, and relative humidity as they ascend to a maximum of 20 miles (30 kilometers) above ground. Radiosondes are equipped with radio transmitters that continuously relay measurements to stations on the ground. Rawinsondes are radiosondes that emit a signal so that their location can be tracked by radar on the ground. From the path of a rawinsonde, one can determine how wind speed and direction changes with altitude.

About 1,000 radiosonde stations have been established worldwide, approximately 125 of them in the United States. About 500 radiosondes are launched at the same time around the world twice each day. These launches take place at noon and midnight Greenwich Mean Time, which is 7:00 AM and 7:00 PM Eastern Standard Time. A balloon takes forty-five to ninety minutes to reach its maximum height. At that point the balloon bursts.

In the United States, radiosondes are equipped with parachutes so they can reach the ground intact. Each one comes with a prepaid mail bag and instructions, so the finder can return it to the National Weather

Service. About one-third of all radiosondes launched are returned in this way and reused.

A variation on the radiosonde is the dropwindsonde. This instrument package is released at high altitude by an aircraft rather than being carried aloft by a balloon. It parachutes to Earth at a speed of 11 mph (18 kph), radioing back atmospheric measurements every few seconds. Dropwindsondes are used primarily over oceans, where there are very few surface stations for launching radiosondes.

Weather aircraft   Weather aircraft also contribute to the collection of data in upper levels of the troposphere. They are used primarily to probe storm clouds, within which they measure temperature, air pressure, and wind speed, and direction. These airplanes have reinforced wings and bodies in order to withstand the hail, ice, and strong winds they encounter inside the clouds. The weather instruments are carried in pods beneath the plane's wings or attached to its nose cone. Weather aircraft are employed in small numbers by most of the world's leading meteorological agencies.

Weather aircraft have contributed greatly to our understanding of hurricanes and other tropical storms. In the fall of 1996 NOAA acquired a jet, called the Gulfstream IV-SP, specifically for studying hurricanes. The jet can cruise right through these storms at heights of up to 45,000 feet (8.5 miles or 14 kilometers). The NOAA jet contains sensors that measure air pressure, temperature, humidity, and wind speed at the edges and the core of the storm. It is just one of the eight types of research aircraft in use by NOAA.

The reason for upper-air hurricane research was explained by Commander Ron Philippsborn, one of four pilots to fly the NOAA jet, in the August/September 1996 issue of *Weatherwise* magazine: "We want to get almost to the base of the stratosphere if we can, up to the outflow

Who's who: Tom Kudloo, aerologist

Tom Kudloo operates a weather station in the Arctic, one of the thousands of weather stations across North America. He is an aerologist, someone who observes and gives reports of local atmospheric conditions. Kudloo uses weather balloons to take readings of upper-air conditions twice daily.

"I attach weather instruments and a tiny radio transmitter to the balloon," says Kudloo. "A cardboard box holds the radio transmitter and a sensor to measure air temperature, air pressure, and humidity. As the balloon rises, the sensor also measures the balloon's speed and direction. This helps me calculate the wind speed and direction. As the balloon goes up, the radio transmitter sends me information about the air masses above me."

This information is entered directly into a computer, which prints out a report. Kudloo analyzes this report and sends the results to forecast offices in several major cities.

He sends up balloons at 5:15 AM and 5:15 PM, local time, each day. These times coincide with balloon testing carried out at many other weather stations around the world. In this way, Kudloo's results can be coordinated to achieve a global picture of the atmosphere at particular times.

regions of the hurricane," said Philippsborn. "If we do that, we will finally be able to look at the entire air column throughout the environment of the hurricane, as well as the steering currents. This data will be fed into sophisticated computer models to improve forecasters' ability to figure out where these things are going to go."

The information collected by the jet is combined with readings taken at ground stations, in order to better assess where a hurricane is headed. In this way, it is possible to provide more advance warning to communities in the hurricane's path.

Other research platforms   In addition to weather aircraft, NOAA also operates several other weather data-gathering systems. The NOAA ship the *Ronald H. Brown* is a state-of-the-art oceanographic and atmospheric research platform, sailing out of Charleston, South Carolina. It was commissioned in 1997, and as of 2007, is the largest vessel in the NOAA fleet. The *Ronald H. Brown* carries a wide variety of highly advanced instruments and sensors, and can travel worldwide supporting scientific studies to increase our understanding of the world's oceans and climate. NOAA also operates nineteen other vessels based in ports around the world, from which they conduct oceanographic and atmospheric research.

A NOAA P-3 Orion research plane flies toward a hurricane, ca. 1980s. AP IMAGES.

Radar   Since its development during World
War II (1939–1945), radar has become an indis-
pensable tool for forecasting precipitation. Conventional radar (versus Doppler radar, discussed
below) detects the location, movement, and
intensity of precipitation, and gives indications
about the type of precipitation present in a
weather system. Since radar continuously scans
a large region, it can detect isolated areas of
precipitation that are often missed by instruments at widely spaced weather stations. For
this reason, radar is particularly valuable for
monitoring severe weather systems that are concentrated over small areas, such as thunderstorms. Radar is also valuable for assessing the
intensity of larger severe weather systems, such as
hurricanes.

   Radar is an abbreviation for "**Ra**dio **D**etection **a**nd **R**anging." Conventional radar operates
by emitting short-wavelength radio waves in the
microwave portion of the radio spectrum. The
microwaves are reflected by precipitation but not
by the tiny droplets of water or ice that make up

*The NOAA research ship
Ronald H. Brown. Scientists
onboard are conducting an air
pollution study in the Gulf of
Mexico, 2006.* AP IMAGES.

clouds. In this way, radar distinguishes between precipitation, which it
"sees," and clouds, which it does not "see."

   Precipitation scatters the microwaves, sending a portion of them—a
"radar echo"—back to a receiver. The radar echo shows up as pulses on a
cathode-ray monitor, which is similar to an older-style television screen.
The radar continuously rotates, scanning a complete circle with a radius
of up to 250 miles (400 kilometers) surrounding the station. It sends out
and receives hundreds of signals each second.

   Since radar waves travel at the speed of light, the distance of the
precipitation from the radar station can be determined by the length of
time between the emission and reception of a signal. The intensity of
precipitation, or "echo intensity," is determined by the strength of the
radar echo. This echo is portrayed on the monitor where intensities are
color-coded. For example, large raindrops and hailstones, which have the
greatest echo intensity, show up as red or purple, while light rain shows up
as green.

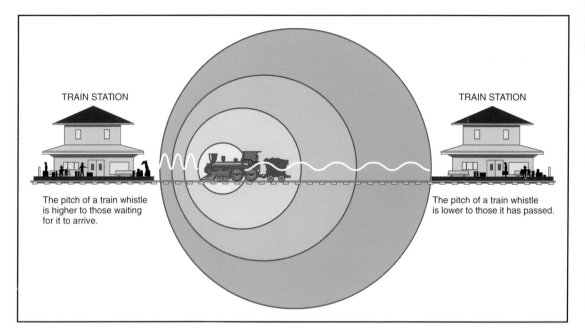

TRAIN STATION

TRAIN STATION

The pitch of a train whistle is higher to those waiting for it to arrive.

The pitch of a train whistle is lower to those it has passed.

The Doppler effect.

In the mid-1970s a new, vastly improved type of radar, called Doppler radar, was developed. Doppler radar is based on the Doppler effect, discovered in 1842 by Austrian physicist Christian Doppler (1803–1853). The Doppler effect is the change in frequency of sound waves emitted from a moving source.

Waves bunch up as they approach their target and spread out as they move away from their target. An example of this effect is that the whistle of a train moving toward an observer sounds with a higher frequency than does the whistle of a train moving away from the observer. Similarly, a storm approaching a radar station reflects radar waves with a higher frequency than a storm moving away from a radar station.

Doppler radar can perform all of the functions of conventional radar plus it can determine the direction in which precipitation is moving, as well as wind speed and direction. Doppler can even estimate rainfall rates, which is important in foretelling floods. It can also locate fronts and wind shifts even in the absence of precipitation.

Doppler radar can look within a storm system and map out the air circulation patterns. This information allows forecasters to witness the earliest stages of a thunderstorm or tornado. While conventional radar can predict a tornado only two minutes before it is fully formed, Doppler radar gives twenty minutes's advance warning. Doppler radar gives a much sharper over-all picture of precipitation and wind patterns than does conventional radar.

Aircraft pilots are particularly grateful for Doppler radar. Doppler radar can measure the velocity (speed and direction) of winds, giving advance warning of wind shear, which is a quick change in the direction or speed of the wind. A strong, downward wind that is the result of a wind shear, called a microburst, has been responsible for many plane crashes.

In the mid-1990s, the National Weather Service began replacing its conventional radars with Doppler radars. Between 1992 and 1997, 158 high-powered Doppler radars were installed. Each one can detect precipitation up to about 285 miles (460 kilometers) away and can measure winds up to about 150 miles (240

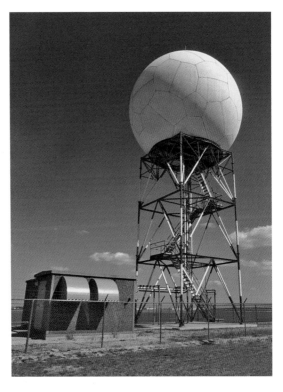

The Doppler radar tower at the National Weather Service in Wichita, Kansas. © JIM REED/ CORBIS.

kilometers) away. These radars, which cover the continental United States, Alaska, Hawaii, Guam, and Korea, make up the NEXRAD (Next Generation Weather Radar) system, a joint project of the National Weather Service, the U.S. Air Force, and the Federal Aviation Admin-istration. Additional Doppler radars known as Terminal Doppler Weather Radar (TDWR) were installed at major airports, specifically to watch for thunderstorms and microbursts.

Since Doppler radars have come into use, the success rate of identi-fying damaging thunderstorms and tornadoes has increased sharply. At the same time, the number of false alarms has been cut in half. The advance warning provided by Doppler radar has saved many lives.

Wind profilers A wind profiler is a specialized Doppler radar that probes the upper levels of the troposphere (the lowest part of Earth's atmosphere). Resembling a giant metal checkerboard, a wind profiler is a 40-foot-by-40-foot (12-meter-by-12-meter) wire mesh antenna mounted on Earth's surface. It is aimed straight up toward the sky and measures the speed and direction of winds aloft.

The technical name for a wind profiler is a "phased array antenna." It works by sending radar waves into the air. As the radio waves encounter changes in air density (caused by differences in temperature and humidity), they are reflected back to the antenna at varying intensities. A computer analyzes the data and calculates wind speeds and directions at seventy-two different levels of the atmosphere, to a maximum of 10 miles (16 kilometers) up. From that, average hourly wind speeds are calculated. This information is then sent to out to local offices of the National Weather Service and used in the creation of local forecasts.

The advantage of wind profilers over radiosondes or rawinsondes is that while rawinsondes take measurements only twice a day, wind profilers take readings every six minutes. Rawinsondes, however, measure temperature, air pressure, and humidity, as well as wind speed and direction. Wind profilers are used to complement the data collected by rawinsondes.

In 1992 the first network of twenty-nine wind profilers was erected in sixteen states throughout the Midwest. Scientists anticipated that the data they provided would assist in producing more accurate short-term weather forecasts. Up-to-the-minute information about winds aloft is particularly useful for plotting the course of a storm and for pilots who are planning flight paths. By 2004, thirty-five wind profilers had been installed in the central plains of the United States and Alaska.

Weather satellites   The weather forecaster's most valuable tool for creating long-term forecasts is the weather satellite. Weather satellites make it possible to view storms from space and to monitor weather conditions continuously around the planet. Weather satellites also provide meteorologists with pictures and other information about hurricanes and tropical storms that occur over the oceans and points on land that are beyond the range of surface weather stations.

The first weather satellite, launched in April 1960, was *TIROS 1*. TIROS stands for Television Infrared Observation Satellite. It took twenty-three thousand pictures of global cloud cover over a period of seventy-eight days, exceeding the expectations of meteorologists. In September 1961, the value of weather satellites hit home with the images sent back of Hurricane Carla. That information resulted in the first widespread evacuation in the United States. About 350,000 people along the Gulf coast were removed from the path of the killer hurricane.

Today, several nations operate weather satellites. In addition to the United States, these include member nations of the European Satellite Agency, as well as Japan, India, and Russia.

Weather satellites do more than photograph clouds For most people, the words "weather satellite" conjure up images of swirling clouds seen from space. While weather satellites do produce such photos, their function is far more extensive. Weather satellites determine the temperature at various atmospheric levels, from cloud tops down to the land and oceans. They also measure humidity and wind speeds in the upper air and even track plumes (shifting regions) of invisible water vapor. In addition, satellites relay information from one ground station to another and pick up and transmit distress signals from vessels in the air and at sea.

Imaging equipment on board satellites is capable of receiving two types of radiation from Earth: visible and several channels of infrared. Visible radiation is reflected sunlight. Sensors on board satellites take what is essentially a black-and-white photo of the visible radiation. These pictures show cloud patterns as well as surface features larger than about a half-mile (a kilometer) across that are situated under clear skies. Therefore, it is possible to distinguish storm systems, fronts, thunderstorms, hurricanes, topographical landmarks, and even snow cover on land.

One of the first TIROS weather satellite pictures broadcast back from Earth orbit in 1960. COURTESY WALTER A. LYONS.

Infrared radiation is heat that is radiated by or reflected from Earth's surface. The picture produced by infrared sensors is essentially a road map of the temperatures of the cloud tops. Temperature varies with height—generally, the higher the cloud top, the lower the temperature. An infrared image also shows the location and intensity of thunderstorms. Thunderstorms are produced by towering clouds. The higher the cloud top, the greater the intensity of the thunderstorm.

The intensity of infrared radiation is also a measure of the amount of water vapor in the air. Since rising air carries moisture aloft, areas of vertical motion can be also be assumed to have high humidity. The presence of water vapor in the air, measured on what is known as the satellite's "vapor channel," has been recognized as an important factor in the development of thunderstorms at locations far from the vapor plume itself.

The instruments on board satellites analyze the visible and infrared radiation they receive and produce soundings. Soundings are analyses of temperature and humidity at different atmospheric heights. Satellites transmit these data by radio to weather forecasting centers several times daily.

Geostationary and polar-orbiting satellites   The United States' fleet of weather satellites is operated jointly by NOAA and the National Aeronautics and Space Administration (NASA). Generally, weather satellites are either geostationary or polar-orbiting. Geostationary satellites orbit at an altitude above Earth's equator, about 22,300 miles (35,000 kilometers), that gives them the same orbital period as Earth's rotation period. Consequently, they appear to be "parked" above a given point on Earth's equator. Polar-orbiting satellites, on the other hand, travel north-south routes, crossing over both poles just 500 to 620 miles (800 to 1,000 kilometers) above Earth's surface. Together, geostationary and polar-orbiting satellites constitute a complete global weather monitoring system.

The current series of U.S. geostationary satellites is called Geostationary Operational Environmental Satellite (GOES). The first satellite in this series was launched in 1975. In late 2006, NOAA had four operational geostationary satellites. GOES-11 and GOES-12 are positioned to view the United States. Together, they provide complete scans every thirty minutes. GOES-10 has been positioned to scan much of South America. GOES-13 is operational, but has been placed in reserve (or storage) until needed.

Because of its high altitude, a geostationary satellite is able to scan nearly one-third of Earth's surface at a time, producing a picture of all of North America every thirty minutes. Most of North America is scanned by two different satellites, sometimes called GOES East and GOES West. Among other data collected by these satellites, they can detect developments in the atmosphere (which meteorologists call "triggers") that may lead to severe weather events, such as tornadoes, flash floods (sudden localized floodings), and hurricanes. Once the satellite detects a trigger, it tracks the storm's movements closely.

NOAA also operates several polar-orbiting satellites. The two oldest operational satellites are named NOAA-12 and NOAA-14. They were

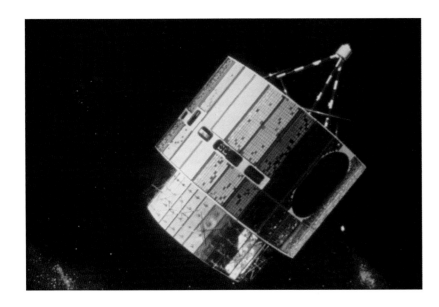

The GOES meteorological satellite—an important part of the U.S. weather satellite program. FMA, INC.

launched in May 1991 and December 1994, respectively. While still operational, they are currently considered on standby status. Launched between 1998 and 2005, NOAA-15, 16, 17, and 18 are a newer and heavier design with enhanced capabilities.

Each satellite completes just over fourteen orbits in a twenty-four-hour period. Consequently, each satellite flies over a given point on Earth's surface approximately twice each day. Between the two satellites, every place on Earth is observed four times each day, twice in the morning and twice in the afternoon. Measurements of atmospheric conditions are therefore updated every six hours for each location. A lower flying polar-orbiting satellite collects highly detailed information from 100-mile-wide (60-kilometer-wide) sections of Earth's surface at a time. The polar-orbiters, in addition to monitoring temperature, cloud cover, and humidity, are equipped with ultraviolet sensors. These sensors measure ozone levels in the atmosphere and monitor the ozone hole, where ozone gets low in the upper atmosphere, that develops over Antarctica each fall.

The most recent entry in the fleet of polar-orbiting satellites is NOAA-18, which was developed by NASA for NOAA. It collects information about Earth's atmosphere and environment to improve weather prediction and climate research across the globe. NOAA-18 has the capability to detect severe weather and report to it the National Weather

Service, which broadcasts the findings to the global community. Early warning can mitigate the effects of catastrophic weather.

NOAA-18 also has instruments to support an international search-and-rescue program. The Search and Rescue Satellite-Aided Tracking System transmits to ground stations the location of emergency beacons from ships, aircraft, and people in distress around the world. The program, in place since 1982, has saved about eighteen thousand lives. NOAA-18 is also the first in a series of polar-orbiting satellites to be part of a joint cooperation project with the European Organization for the Exploitation of Meteorological Satellites.

Oceanographic satellites   NOAA at one time also operated satellites specifically designed for surveying the oceans. The first of these, called Seasat, was launched in June 1978. After just one hundred days of operation, it ceased operation due to a power failure. While in orbit, Seasat used radar wave, visual, and infrared sensors to determine water surface temperature, wind speed, wind direction, wave height, and weather conditions on the seas.

The data collected by Seasat was used in the creation of the next oceanographic satellite, called the Ocean Topography Experiment, or TOPEX. (Topography is the shape and height of Earth's surface features.) The U.S. TOPEX, together with the French satellite Poseidon, was launched in 1992. The TOPEX/Poseidon data was used to create near-perfect maps of ocean topography, complete with ice floes (chunks of floating ice), wind, and waves.

In December of 2001, TOPEX/Poseidon was operationally replaced by Jason-1, a joint program of NASA and the French Centre National d'Etudes Spatiales. Jason-1 has vastly improved understanding of ocean circulation and its effect on global climate. This new system completed its fifth year in orbit on December 7, 2006. From its vantage point 860 miles (1,330 kilometers) above Earth, Jason-1 has provided measurements of the surface height of the world's oceans to an accuracy of 1.3 inches (3.3 centimeters).

Computer forecasting models   Due to the complex and partly chaotic nature of weather forecasting, the National Weather Service has come to depend on computers to store and analyze the vast quantities of data received from surface weather stations, weather balloons, aircraft, radar, wind profilers, and satellites.

This visualization of Hurricane Rita shows the sea surface temperature from September 17–21, 2005. Temperatures in the Gulf of Mexico remained one to two degrees warmer (areas in yellow, orange, and red) than the 82 degree minimum needed to sustain a hurricane. ©NASA/CORBIS.

Before the use of computers in forecasting, which began in the mid-1950s, day-to-day forecasts could be made only thirty-six hours in advance. Now that computers have been developed to perform numerical forecasting, daily forecasts can be made for six to ten days in advance. Numerical forecasting is the use of mathematical equations and computer models to predict the weather.

The National Weather Service has contracted with IBM to provide supercomputer facilities to aid in hurricane forecasting through 2012. The computer system is a cluster of forty-four IBM eServer p690 servers located in Gaithersburg, Maryland. All together the system is capable of 7.3 trillion calculations per second. This improved forecasting was put to a severe test during the 2005 hurricane season, but it aided the NWS in making accurate landfall predictions for hurricanes Katrina and Rita. It also revealed gaps in our basic understanding of the forces controlling hurricanes.

NOAA and the NWS continue to upgrade and develop computer systems to improve the range and accuracy of forecasts. A wide variety of computer systems are used to run a variety of different numerical and dynamical models to provide local, aviation (for pilots), marine (for sailors), and other forecasts.

WORDS TO KNOW

occluded front: a front formed by the interaction of three air masses: one cold, one cool, and one warm. The result is a multi-tiered air system, with cold air wedged on the bottom, cool air resting partially on top of the cold air, and warm air on the very top.

ozone hole: the region above Antarctica where the ozone concentration in the upper atmosphere gets very low at the end of each winter.

ozone layer: the layer of Earth's atmosphere, between 25 and 40 miles (40 and 65 kilometers) above ground, that filters out the Sun's harmful rays. It contains a higher concentration of ozone, which is a form of oxygen that has three atoms per molecule.

polar front: the region or boundary separating air masses of polar origin from those of tropical or subtropical origin.

polar orbiting satellite: a weather satellite that travels in a north-south path, crossing over both poles just 500 to 625 miles (800 to 1,000 kilometers) above Earth's surface.

precipitation: water particles that originate in the atmosphere (usually referring to water particles that form in clouds) and fall to the ground.

psychrometer: an instrument used to measure relative humidity. It consists of a dry-bulb thermometer and a wet-bulb thermometer. Also called hygrometer.

radar: an instrument that detects the location, movement, and intensity of precipitation, and gives indications about the type of precipitation. It operates by emitting microwaves, which are reflected by precipitation. It is an abbreviation for **Ra**dio **D**etection **a**nd **R**anging. Radar may be called conventional radar to distinguish it from Doppler radar.

radiosonde: an instrument package carried aloft on a small helium- or hydrogen-filled balloon. It measures temperature, air pressure, and relative humidity from the ground to a maximum height of 19 miles (30 kilometers).

rain gauge: a container that catches rain and measures the amount of rainfall.

rainbow: an arc of light, separated into its constituent colors, that stretches across the sky.

refraction: the bending of light as it is transmitted between two transparent media of different densities.

relative humidity: a measure of humidity as a percentage of the total moisture that a given volume of air, at a particular temperature, can hold.

shower: a brief spell of localized rainfall, possibly heavy, that only occurs in warm weather.

sling psychrometer: an instrument that measures relative humidity. It consists of a dry-bulb thermometer and a wet-bulb thermometer mounted side by side on a metal strip, which rotates on a handle at one end.

In addition, NOAA is developing an extensive system for storing and analyzing data. Two NOAA sites began using the system, called the Comprehensive Large Array-data Stewardship System (CLASS), in

2004. It provides researchers and policy-makers access to NOAA environmental data and products, obtained either from spacecraft or ground-based observations.

These national and global forecasts and maps are then handed down to local weather agencies and private meteorologists in the media and at airlines. Local weather forecast offices use this information, in combination with other data, to produce basic public forecasts (including warnings of hazardous weather such as floods, thunderstorms, thick fog, or high winds) and aviation reports. Weather offices on the coasts also provide marine forecasts.

Understanding forecasts

The final product of the measurement is a weather forecast. The basic elements of a professional, local forecast are presented in a straightforward way that can easily be understood. Rather than page after page of data, daily forecasts use a type of shorthand consisting of internationally recognized weather symbols and weather maps. Learning this weather "language" makes it possible to understand professional forecasts, and will also be a handy tool to use in a weather journal.

What a forecast says   A typical local forecast found in a newspaper, on the radio, television, or on the Internet will include information on at least the following conditions: temperature, humidity, air pressure, winds, sky conditions, and precipitation. On particular days, or in certain locations, forecasts may include additional information, such as storm warnings, marine advisories, aviation forecasts, and air quality reports. Forecasts may also give the times of sunrise and sunset and tell the phase (how much of the Moon is visible from Earth; how "full" it is) of the Moon.

Who's who: Lewis Fry Richardson, forecaster by the numbers

British mathematician Lewis Fry Richardson (1881–1953) introduced the use of mathematical equations in forecasting with his 1922 report "Weather Prediction by Numerical Process." It took Richardson many months to devise a set of calculations that could represent the behavior of the various atmospheric processes necessary to create a sample twenty-four hour forecast. Although his calculations were far from perfect and his results quite inaccurate, he had set the stage for the development of the computer models which generate our forecasts today.

Richardson demonstrated that an enormous number of calculations would have to be made very quickly to produce accurate numerical predictions. In fact, he estimated that the creation of forecasts by his numerical process would require the efforts of sixty-four thousand mathematicians with calculators working around the clock every day of the year. Only with the advent of microcomputers did numerical prediction become feasible. With today's sophisticated equations that more closely model the behavior of the atmosphere, numerical prediction using computer models continues to produce increasingly reliable forecasts.

Temperature   In addition to giving the current temperature, most weather forecasts include the high and low temperatures for the preceding twenty-four hours. By way of comparison, they also include the normal high and low temperatures, as well as the record high and low temperatures, for that location on that date.

In winter or in cold climates, where the danger of frostbite (freezing skin) exists, weather forecasters include an index called the windchill equivalent temperature (WET), or windchill index, or just windchill. It is a measure of how cold the air feels, due to the interaction of wind and temperature. The WET is the temperature at which the body would lose an equivalent amount of heat if there were no wind. For instance, if it were 30°F (–1°C) with winds blowing at 15 mph (24 kph), the WET would be 9°F (–13°C).

During winter, or in any place where it is cold enough to require home heating, local weather forecasts may include a measurement called heating-degree-days. A degree-day is the number of degrees' difference between the day's mean (average) temperature and a temperature selected to represent the temperature at which most people set their thermostats. By tallying the total number of degree-days throughout a season officials can get a good idea of how cold the period has been and, consequently, how much heating fuel has been consumed.

To calculate the mean temperature, add together the day's high and low temperatures and divide by two. For example, say the high temperature for the day is 50°F (10°C) and the low is 20°F (6°C). The mean temperature is 35°F (50°F + 20°F, divided by 2). Now assume that in an average home the thermostat is set at 65°F (18°C). For this particular day, subtract the mean temperature, 35°F, from 65°F and come up with 30 degree-days. The colder the climate and the more severe the winter, the greater the number of heating-degree-days for the season.

Humidity   What is referred to as "humidity" in forecasts is actually the relative humidity. It is expressed as a percentage of the amount of moisture in the air compared to the total moisture the air is capable of holding at that temperature. This measurement will not necessarily tell how wet or muggy the air will feel, since that is greatly dependent on temperature. For instance, 85 percent relative humidity will feel much more uncomfortable when it is 90°F (32°C) than when it is 50°F (10°C).

One way to determine "mugginess" is to look at the wet-bulb temperature. A wet-bulb thermometer will always give a reading that is lower than the actual air temperature except when the outside air has 100 percent relative humidity. When it is hot out, the lower the wet-bulb reading, the faster sweat evaporates, and the less muggy it feels. As the wet-bulb temperature approaches the air temperature, the slower sweat evaporates and the muggier it feels.

The temperature at which the wet-bulb temperature equals the actual air temperature is the dew point. The dew point, the temperature at which moisture condenses out of the air (because the air is saturated), can be used as a measure of mugginess or comfort. In general, if the dew point is below 40°F (4°C), the air feels dry. If it is between 40°F and 59°F (15°C), the air feels comfortable. If the dew point is higher than 59°F, the air feels muggy.

Air pressure   Measurements of air pressure always include the pressure itself (which may be given in a variety of different units) and whether the pressure is rising or falling. The latter piece of information is more significant than the former, since it is the change in air pressure that gives clues about weather patterns. Recall that rising pressure generally means fair weather and falling pressure means changing weather.

There are no set values defining "high pressure" and "low pressure," since these are meaningful only when two pressures are compared to one another. That is, air pressure is "high" only if it is higher than an adjacent system or "low" if it is lower than an adjacent system.

At sea level, the average air pressure is 29.92 inches (1013 millibars). While it is tempting to categorize anything above that as "high" and anything below that as "low," consider this: The air pressure at one location may be 30.12 inches (1020 millibars) adjusted to sea level, considerably higher than average. Yet that location may be situated within a high-pressure belt where the average pressure is 30.25 inches (1024 millibars). In light of this information, is that air pressure "high" or "low"?

Winds   Most weather forecasts provide two pieces of data about the wind: speed and direction. The speed describes current conditions, while the direction is most valuable as an indicator of what is to come.

Here is a general guideline for categorizing how windy a day is: From 0 to 10 mph (0 to 16 kph) the wind is somewhere between still and gentle; from 10 to 20 mph (16 to 32 kph) the wind is moderate or "breezy"; from 20 to 30 mph (32 to 48 kph) the wind is strong; and anything above 30 mph (48 kph) is a gale-force wind.

The humiture index.

Air temperature (°F)	Relative humidity (%)									
	10	20	30	40	50	60	70	80	90	100
104 (Uncomfortably warm)	90	98	106	112	120					
102	87	95	102	108	115	123				
100 (Pleasant)	85	92	99	105	111	118				
98	82	90	96	101	107	114				
96	79	87	93	98	103	110	116			
94	77	84	90	95	100	105	111			
92	75	82	87	91	96	101	106	112		
90	73	79	84	88	93	97	102	108		
88	70	76	81	85	89	93	98	102	108	
86	68	73	78	82	86	90	94	98	103	
84	66	71	76	79	83	86	90	94	98	103
82	63	68	73	76	80	83	86	90	93	97
80	62	66	70	73	77	80	83	86	90	93
78		63	67	70	74	76	79	82	85	89
76 (Crisp)		60	63	67	70	73	76	79	82	85

(Upper right region labeled "Unbearably hot")

Wind direction often provides a clue as to what type of weather is coming, although the specifics vary from location to location. See if you can draw a connection between wind direction and weather patterns in your area by examining trends in your weather journal.

Sky conditions   This section of the forecast includes information on the amount and type of cloud cover, as well as fog and haze, when relevant. It also includes changes in conditions, such as "increasing cloudiness," "decreasing cloudiness," "clearing," or "fog lifting before noon." In general, increasing cloudiness indicates a greater chance of precipitation while decreasing cloudiness and lifting fog indicate that fair weather is in store.

Precipitation   This category contains information on the amount of rain or snow that has fallen within the previous twenty-four hours and amount predicted to fall during the coming twenty-four hours. In the United States, rainfall and snowfall are generally measured in inches. Any rainfall over one-half inch (about one centimeter) in one day is considered heavy. It takes about five or six inches (about fifteen centimeters) of snow to be considered a heavy snowfall. Snow occupies roughly ten times the volume of its meltwater equivalent although this varies with temperature. The warmer and wetter the snow, the higher the meltwater equivalent, and the colder and drier the snow, the lower the meltwater equivalent.

Most forecasts state that there is a certain percent chance that rain or snow will fall during the coming twenty-four hours. Alternatively, the probability of precipitation may be characterized by terms such as "chance of rain" or "slight chance of snow."

The percentages are determined by examining ten days in the past which had weather conditions comparable to the present day. The first step is to tally up how many of those ten days had at least 0.01 inch of rainfall or the meltwater equivalent of snowfall. Then that number is divided by ten and multiplied by 100 percent. Thus, if precipitation occurred on four out of ten similar days, there is a 40 percent chance of precipitation for the present day.

Many forecasters prefer to use phrases to describe the chance of rain or snow. Here is a key to understanding those phrases, as well as some other forecasting language relating to precipitation:

- slight chance of precipitation—10 or 20 percent chance
- chance of precipitation—30 to 50 percent chance
- occasional precipitation—over 50 percent chance (but will last less than half of the forecast period)
- showers—localized, brief rainfall ("snow showers" refers to snowfall)

A key reference to: The humiture index

The humiture index, also known as the "temperature-humidity index," is another way to measure how hot and muggy it feels and consequently how stressful outdoor activity will be. The index is based on the same principle as the wet-bulb temperature, namely that the faster water (or sweat) evaporates, the less muggy it is (and the cooler people feel), and vice versa.

The humiture index is most useful during the hottest part of the day. The value for any given set of conditions can be determined by solving a rather complex equation for given values of temperature and relative humidity. Fortunately, there is a chart that serves the same purpose. The lower the humiture index, the more comfortable the air feels. Any value over 89 on the chart is in the "uncomfortably hot and muggy" range.

Most television and newspaper weather forecasts include some form of humiture index when conditions are so hot and muggy that people are in danger of suffering heat stroke. This index may be listed as a "heat-stress index" or "apparent temperature." It generally includes one of the following four danger categories: caution, extreme caution, danger, or extreme danger.

- rain—steady rainfall covering a wider area
- isolated showers—showers that fall on less than 10 percent of the forecast area
- scattered showers—showers that fall on 10 to 50 percent of the forecast area
- numerous showers—showers that fall on the majority of the forecast area
- periods of rain (or snow)—on-and-off rain (or snow) throughout the whole area, for the duration the forecast period
- snow squall—very heavy, brief snowfall
- snow flurries—very light snowfall that results in little or no accumulation
- heavy snow—snow that is accumulating at a rate of at least 1 inch per hour, with visibility less than 5/16 of a mile

International weather symbols   The set of weather symbols in use today was developed as a way to standardize the data collected by the thousands of weather stations around the globe. Using this universal shorthand, a weather station can describe many conditions—winds, temperature, visibility, present weather conditions, dew point, cloud cover, precipitation, and air pressure—for each time period (usually every three hours) in a space the size of a postage stamp. Forecasters also use symbols for fronts, pressure highs and lows, and regions of equal pressure, in the creation of weather maps. A weather station entry, sometimes called a station circle, is the form in which information is summarized by each individual weather station and sent to regional offices. A forecaster, by glancing at a station circle, can quickly discern the overall conditions at a given station.

Weather maps   A weather map, also called a surface analysis, is created by national or regional weather agencies and is intended for use by forecasters. Weather maps generally encompass an entire nation or group of nations. In North America, the basic map before weather patterns are added shows state/provincial borders, large cities, major rivers, and other important topographical features.

Station circles are plotted on the map at their appropriate locations. The collection of local data is then examined for patterns of air pressure and temperature. From this, meteorologists can determine the locations of fronts, regions of high and low pressure, the dividing line between

EXPLANATION OF WEATHER STATION MODEL AND SYMBOLS

At Weather Bureau offices, maps showing conditions at the earth's surface are drawn 4 times daily or oftener. The location of the reporting station is printed on the map as a small circle. A definite arrangement of the data around the station circle, called the station model, is used. The station model is based on international agreements. Thru such standardized use of numerals and symbols, a meteorologist of one country can use the weather maps of another country even though he does not understand the language. An abridged description of the symbols is presented below.

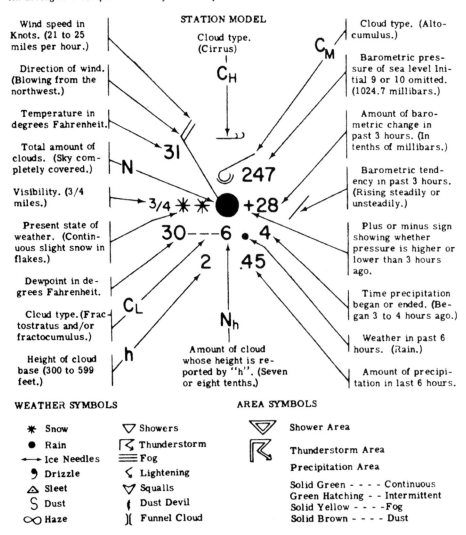

STATION MODEL

Wind speed in Knots. (21 to 25 miles per hour.)

Direction of wind. (Blowing from the northwest.)

Temperature in degrees Fahrenheit.

Total amount of clouds. (Sky completely covered.)

Visibility. (3/4 miles.)

Present state of weather. (Continuous slight snow in flakes.)

Dewpoint in degrees Fahrenheit.

Cloud type. (Fractostratus and/or fractocumulus.)

Height of cloud base (300 to 599 feet.)

Cloud type. (Cirrus)

Amount of cloud whose height is reported by "h". (Seven or eight tenths.)

Cloud type. (Altocumulus.)

Barometric pressure of sea level Initial 9 or 10 omitted. (1024.7 millibars.)

Amount of barometric change in past 3 hours. (In tenths of millibars.)

Barometric tendency in past 3 hours. (Rising steadily or unsteadily.)

Plus or minus sign showing whether pressure is higher or lower than 3 hours ago.

Time precipitation began or ended. (Began 3 to 4 hours ago.)

Weather in past 6 hours. (Rain.)

Amount of precipitation in last 6 hours.

WEATHER SYMBOLS

- ✳ Snow
- ● Rain
- ⟶ Ice Needles
- 𝟫 Drizzle
- △ Sleet
- S Dust
- ∞ Haze
- ▽ Showers
- ⟨ Thunderstorm
- ☰ Fog
- ⟨ Lightening
- ▽ Squalls
- ⦙ Dust Devil
-)(Funnel Cloud

AREA SYMBOLS

- ▽ Shower Area
- ⟨ Thunderstorm Area
- Precipitation Area

Solid Green - - - - Continuous
Green Hatching - - Intermittent
Solid Yellow - - - - Fog
Solid Brown - - - - Dust

A weather station journal entry.

temperatures below freezing and above freezing, and the movement of storm systems. Each of these patterns is labeled on the map using symbols. The weather maps on television or in the newspaper are greatly simplified versions of the type used by forecasters.

A set of features found on many weather maps is a series of lines known as isobars. Isobars are lines that connect points of equal air pressure. On some maps, an air pressure value is tagged on each isobar. Closed isobar curves represent centers of high and low pressure. These areas are usually marked on a map with a capital "H" or "L." The isobars in the figure form concentric circles of increasingly high pressure. Between the high pressure areas are isobars of low pressure, where the lowest pressure is along the circle at the center.

Isobars are also guides to wind speed and direction. First, the closer the isobars are to one another, the steeper the pressure gradient and hence, the stronger the winds. Second, remember that winds do not flow into the center of high- and low-pressure areas, but around them. In the Northern Hemisphere, winds flow counterclockwise around the lows and clockwise around the highs. Isobars are generally closer together as they approach low-pressure areas, where winds also tend to be strong. Conversely, isobars are generally farther apart as they approach high-pressure areas, where winds are relatively calm.

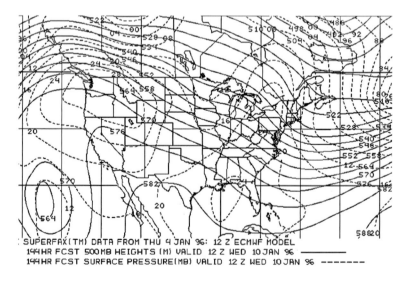

An atmospheric weather map.
COURTESY WEATHER SERVICE
INTERNATIONAL
CORPORATION.

SUPERFAX(TM) DATA FROM THU 4 JAN 96: 12 Z ECMWF MODEL
144 HR FCST 500 MB HEIGHTS (M) VALID 12 Z WED 10 JAN 96 ————
144 HR FCST SURFACE PRESSURE(MB) VALID 12 Z WED 10 JAN 96 - - - - - - -

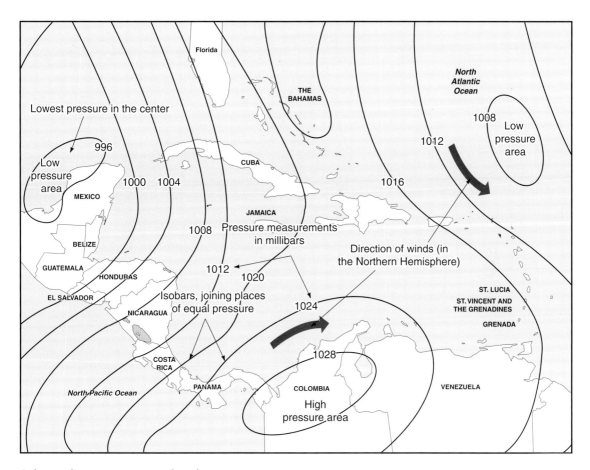

Florida

THE BAHAMAS

North Atlantic Ocean

Lowest pressure in the center

996

Low pressure area

MEXICO

CUBA

1008 Low pressure area

1012

1000   1004

1016

JAMAICA

1008   Pressure measurements in millibars

BELIZE

GUATEMALA

HONDURAS

EL SALVADOR

NICARAGUA

COSTA RICA

North Pacific Ocean

PANAMA

1012

1020

Isobars, joining places of equal pressure

1024

Direction of winds (in the Northern Hemisphere)

ST. LUCIA
ST. VINCENT AND THE GRENADINES
GRENADA

1028

COLOMBIA

High pressure area

VENEZUELA

Isobars are lines connecting areas of equal pressure.

Fronts, the boundaries between relatively warm and cold air masses, are also labeled on a weather map. The locations of fronts are determined by using both surface data and satellite images. Clues to the position of a front are found in surface readings for wind direction, dew point, sky conditions, and precipitation. The locations of temperature differentials on satellite images also help identify where air masses begin and end.

As illustrated in the national weather map, a line with triangles represents a cold front and line with half-circles represents a warm front. The triangles and half-circles point in the direction the air mass is heading. A line with triangles on one side and half-circles on the other represents a stationary front (the line between a cold and a warm air mass,

National weather
The **Wunderground.com** forecast for noon, Wednesday, Sept. 27

Lines separate high temperature zones for the day.

© 2006 Wunderground.com

FRONTS:
COLD   WARM   STATIONARY

High   Low   Showers   Rain   T-storms   Flurries   Snow   Ice   Sunny   Pt. Cloudy   Cloudy

Via Associated Press

System Drops into Central U.S., Storms Persist in Fla.
A strong system is expected to drop southward into the Central U.S. on Wednesday, bringing an expansive area of precipitation from the Northern Plains eastward into the Great Lakes and Ohio Valley. A cold front will keep scattered showers and storms going over Florida.

A U.S. weather map showing many of the international weather symbols. AP IMAGES.

neither of which is moving) and a line with triangles and half-circles both on the same side represents an occluded front (a front formed by three air masses).

Satellite and radar images also indicate where precipitation is falling. These areas are marked on weather maps with certain colors or gray shading, or are superimposed with diagonal lines. The maps also indicate temperature by applying different shades of gray or colors to areas that fall within given temperature ranges.

Weather maps are also created for the upper levels of the atmosphere, using information provided by radar, weather aircraft, weather satellites, and radiosondes. These maps differ from surface maps in that they are constructed along an imaginary surface of equal pressure (i.e., 500 millibars, where the atmosphere is at half its sea-level pressure). Air pressure varies with altitude, primarily due to temperature differences. Air pressure drops with altitude at a faster rate in cold air masses than it does in warm air masses.

People can also discern the pattern of upper-air winds from upper-air maps. This information is valuable because the motion of winds aloft is a key component in the development of weather patterns at the surface.

Forecasting in the media

What most people know about the weather is based solely on reports they see on television, read in the newspaper, hear on the radio, or find on the Internet. These reports include general information about the nation's weather as well as more detailed analyses and predictions for the local area.

Television weathercasts   Television is the medium from which most people today get their weather information. Weather is an element of practically every local and national television news show, and the true weather fanatic with cable television can tune in to it twenty-four hours a day.

In addition to providing the basic information that helps people decide how to dress in the morning, TV weather can be quite educational. Television weathercasts have featured lessons on the dynamics of frontal systems, jet streams (the fastest upper-air winds), El Niño (strong episodes of Pacific warming), highs and lows, hurricanes, tornadoes, and other phenomena.

Weather reports first appeared on television in the early 1940s. The original broadcasts were extremely primitive, even laughable by today's standards. To assure some measure of professionalism in TV forecasts, the American Meteorological Society began issuing its Seal of Approval in 1959 to those weather shows it deemed trustworthy. A similar system of offering credentials was adopted by the National Weather Association in 1982.

In the early years, television weathercasters drew fronts, highs and lows, and other information by hand, or placed stick-on symbols onto large maps, as they gave their reports. In the early 1980s these methods were replaced by computer-generated color graphics. Coupled with images provided by geostationary satellites, which first began appearing on TV screens in the mid-1970s, television weathercasts became an impressive visual presentation.

The five-minute weather presentation seen during a TV news show may appear simple, but producing the segment is actually quite a laborious task. It begins about five hours before the broadcast, when the weather reporter pores through the stacks of computer-generated forecasts

A meteorologist explains weather patterns. ©SW PRODUCTIONS/ BRAND X/CORBIS.

provided by the National Weather Service, as well as radar and satellite images. It is the weather reporter's task to make sense of it all, condense it into a short report, and choose satellite images to go along with it.

Next comes the creation of weather graphics, including maps, forecasts, and animated satellite images. These animated images are actually a string of satellite pictures shown in quick succession, so it looks as if they are moving. While many television stations rely on private weather graphics firms to design the visuals for their weather shows, some stations, including The Weather Channel, design their own computerized graphics.

Then, just before the show, the weather reporter must get all the information in order, check for any last-minute changes in conditions, and rehearse the report. Finally, it's show time—five minutes later, it is over.

Newspaper weathercasts   There is no such thing as a standard newspaper weather report. Newspaper weather pages are often colorful, with easy-to-understand symbols (such as pictures of sun and clouds), and they contain a great variety of information presented in many different ways. For instance, newspapers may feature a large weather map of the entire nation, a local map, or both.

Regardless of the differences, some basic ingredients show up in one form or another in weather pages of most newspapers, particularly large ones. These include a weather map, a local report, national and local forecasts, a list of high and low temperatures for select cities in the North America, and, in some cases, around the world. Most weather maps include fronts and pressure systems. While many weather maps display isobars, an even greater number display isotherms, which are bands representing areas of similar temperature.

Most weather pages contain information that goes beyond the basic report. The specifics of those supplements generally depend on the economic, geographic, and recreational interests of the inhabitants of the locality. For instance, a weather page may contain a ski report, a marine forecast, a farm and garden report, or an air quality index. Some weather pages also contain sections for children, including pictures, activities, or "fun facts." Others may contain satellite photos, an analysis of the jet stream, or a tally of heating-degree-days.

> ## Weather report: Wooly Lamb— the first weather reporter
>
> The very first televised weather report was shown on October 14, 1941, on WNBT (later WNBC) in New York City. The report was presented by a cartoon character named "Wooly Lamb." The little lamb began each report by first looking at the sky through a telescope, then facing the camera and singing this song: "It' hot, it's cold. It's rain, it's fair. It's all mixed up together. But I, as Botany's Wooly Lamb, predict tomorrow's weather." ("Botany" referred to the show's sponsor, Botany's Wrinkle-Proof ties.) A written forecast for the next day's weather then appeared on the screen. Even more amazing than the notion of a cartoon lamb presenting the weather, is the fact that Wooly Lamb kept its job for seven years!

Radio weathercasts   Without the aid of weather maps and other visuals, weather reporting is quite challenging. Thus, most commercial and public radio stations present only general current weather information and what listeners may expect over the next twenty-four hours. Other information, such as shipping reports or agricultural reports (generated especially for farmers), are broadcast in locations where they are relevant.

One source of extensive, local weather information on the radio, available all across the United States, is provided by the National Oceanic and Atmospheric Administration. NOAA Weather Radio is transmitted on seven different high-band FM frequencies, ranging from 162.400 to 162.550 megahertz. To hear this transmission, listeners may need a special receiver called a "weather radio." In some places, NOAA Weather Radio comes in on special radio bands such as the weather band, citizens' band, and some automobile, aircraft, and marine bands. In a few areas the transmission can be picked up on standard AM/FM radios.

NOAA Weather Radio continuously broadcasts the latest weather information, twenty-four hours a day. Reports are usually four to six

A key reference to: The marvelous chroma key

Television weather reporters do not see what viewers see. The colorful weather map so familiar to TV audiences, to which the reporter appears to point as he or she describes the weather, does not show up in the studio. Instead, the background seen by the reporter is a single color, typically green or blue. The reporter relies on monitors on either side of the screen to determine the position his or her hands or body relative to the map.

The color images viewers see on a TV weathercast are produced by a process called "chroma key," or "color-separation overlay." A computer in the station's control booth electronically superimposes single-color portions of a graphic on top of one another, producing a full-color image. When the forecaster gives a verbal cue or when the color of the screen behind the reporter (the "chroma key") changes, a new graphic is appears.

minutes long and are updated about every one to three hours. Reports are changed more frequently during rapidly changing or severe weather.

In response to hazardous weather, NOAA Weather Radio will sound an alarm that alerts listeners to turn up the radio and stay tuned. Some receivers are programmed to turn on whenever a hazardous-weather alarm is activated. NOAA Weather Radio also broadcasts reports from local weather service offices that are relevant to the region. For instance, one may offer marine reports while another offers agricultural reports and climatological forecasts.

NOAA Weather Radio broadcasts are prepared by local offices of the National Weather Service (NWS) and sent out from four hundred transmitters throughout the United States, Puerto Rico, Guam, and Saipan. Each station transmits to a radius of only 40 miles (64 kilometers), an area covered by the report. Presently, NOAA Weather Radio can be received by 80 to 95 percent of the U.S. population, provided they have a radio.

Weather on the Internet   The Internet serves as a link between the general public and just about every type of weather information imaginable. It is a valuable resource for professional meteorologists, the media, and weather enthusiasts alike. On the Internet, users can find satellite and radar images, photos of storms and storm-related damage, the predicted courses of hurricanes and inland storms, detailed forecasts for particular regions, reports tailored to specific interest groups (e.g., mountain climbers, boaters, and skiers), and much more.

National Oceanic and Atmospheric Administration   The most extensive and most reliable source of weather information on the Internet is from the National Oceanic and Atmospheric Administration. Much more than weather information is available: NOAA also covers fisheries, navigation, and other topics related to the oceans. It does, however, give

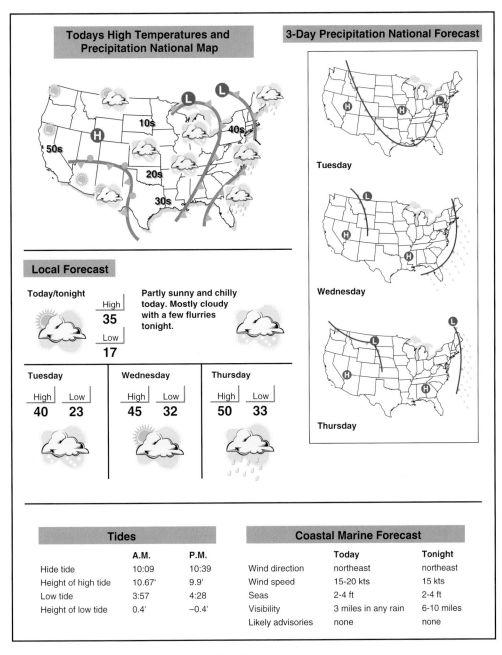

Todays High Temperatures and Precipitation National Map

3-Day Precipitation National Forecast

Tuesday

Wednesday

Thursday

Local Forecast

Today/tonight

High
35

Low
17

Partly sunny and chilly today. Mostly cloudy with a few flurries tonight.

Tuesday		Wednesday		Thursday	
High	Low	High	Low	High	Low
40	23	45	32	50	33

Tides	A.M.	P.M.
Hide tide	10:09	10:39
Height of high tide	10.67'	9.9'
Low tide	3:57	4:28
Height of low tide	0.4'	−0.4'

Coastal Marine Forecast	Today	Tonight
Wind direction	northeast	northeast
Wind speed	15-20 kts	15 kts
Seas	2-4 ft	2-4 ft
Visibility	3 miles in any rain	6-10 miles
Likely advisories	none	none

Newspaper weather maps including national and local forecasts and marine forecast.

WORDS TO KNOW

stationary front: the dividing line between two stationary air masses. It occurs when a cold air mass comes in contact with a warm air mass, with neither air mass moving.

sunspot: an area of magnetic disturbance on the surface of the Sun, sometimes referred to as a sun storm.

thermograph: an instrument consisting of a thermometer and a needle that etches on a rotating drum, continually recording the temperature.

thermometer: an instrument used to measure temperature. It consists of a vacuum-sealed narrow glass tube with a bulb in the bottom containing mercury or red-dyed alcohol. Also called dry-bulb thermometer.

thunderstorm: a relatively small but intense storm system, that produces moderate-to-strong winds, heavy rain, and lightning, sometimes with hail and tornadoes.

topography: the shape and height of Earth's surface features.

tornado: a rapidly spinning column of air that extends from a thunderstorm cloud to the ground. Also called a twister.

veering wind: a wind that shifts direction, turning clockwise as it moves higher.

warm front: the line behind which a warm air mass is advancing, and in front of which a cold air mass is retreating.

warning: a severe weather advisory that means that a storm has been sighted and may strike a specific area.

watch: a severe weather advisory that means that while a storm does not yet exist, conditions are ripe for one to develop.

weather: the set of conditions of temperature, humidity, cloud cover, and wind speed at a given time.

weather aircraft: aircraft that carry weather instruments and collect data in the upper levels of the troposphere. They are primarily used to probe storm clouds, within which they measure temperature, air pressure, and wind speed and direction.

weather forecast: a prediction of what the weather will be like in the future, based on present and past conditions.

weather map: a map of a large geographic region, on which weather station entries are plotted. By looking at a weather map, a meteorologist can determine the locations of fronts, regions of high and low pressure, the dividing line between temperatures below freezing and above freezing, and the movement of storm systems. Also called surface analysis.

weather satellite: a satellite equipped with infrared and visible imaging equipment that provides views of storms and continuously monitors weather conditions around the planet.

wind sock: a cone-shaped cloth bag open on both ends, through which wind flows that is used to determine the direction and estimate the speed of the wind.

wind speed: the rate at which air is moving relative to the ground.

windchill equivalent temperature: the temperature at which the body would lose an equivalent amount of heat, if there were no wind. Also called windchill index.

in-depth information on satellites (weather and others) and provide a link to the National Weather Service, which is a branch of NOAA.

Using forecasts

Most people listen to or read a forecast to decide how to dress the next day or whether to set up their party indoors or outdoors. But forecasts take on much greater significance when the weather is severe. Warnings of an approaching storm are intended to give local inhabitants time to take safety precautions and, if possible, secure their property. Forecasts take on economic significance for people who make their living outdoors or at sea.

Improving on forecasts   Understanding the basics of weather enables one to make greater use of forecasts. With knowledge of how the landscape (mountains, valleys, lakes, buildings, trees, etc.) affects weather conditions surrounding a locality, a local forecast can be customized to fit. For instance, in a city, the temperature, on average, may be a few degrees warmer than at the airport weather station. Large buildings block the wind, making it slower than what is reported.

Knowing how weather works, ordinary people can check the accuracy of a forecast. Remember that weather reports sent out through the media are generally based on information that is at least two hours old, and the weather is notorious for its quick changes. A cold front, for example, may advance more rapidly or more slowly than predicted, or a completely new weather system may develop quickly.

Severe weather warnings   One of weather forecasters' most important duties is to alert the public to approaching severe weather. In recent years, the amount of time between the warning of a potential disaster and its actual occurrence has greatly increased. This improvement is due primarily to better computer forecasting models. In fact, major storms such as hurricanes, blizzards (the most severe type of winter storm), and heavy rains can now be predicted by computer even before the weather conditions they produce are detected by weather stations.

Tools such as computer modeling, Doppler radar, and weather satellites have significantly improved the accuracy with which the course of severe storms can be predicted. This process is important because forecasters do not want to initiate evacuations of people who are not really in a storm's path. Evacuations, which are often carried out in advance of a hurricane, are very expensive. People spend money boarding up their houses and purchasing supplies. Businesses lose money when they are forced to close. More importantly, when people are evacuated without reason, they tend to lose faith in weather warnings. The next time a warning is issued, they may decide there is no reason to leave, even though that time they may really be in harm's way.

Far more challenging than predicting when a major storm will strike is predicting the approximately ten thousand violent thunderstorms and one thousand tornadoes that occur in the United States each year. In recent years, only modest gains have been made in this area. One reason why it is much more difficult to forecast small-scale storms than it is to forecast large-scale storms is that small, localized patterns are usually not predicted by computer models. The warning signs of tornadoes and thunderstorms must be picked up at weather stations before any type of advisory can be issued—and then there is usually not much time before the storm strikes.

Thanks to Doppler radar, recent improvements have been made in determining when thunderstorms become severe, as well as assessing the course of tornadoes. This technology, which gathers information from the heart of the storm, is responsible for increasing the warning times for violent thunderstorms, as well as halving the number of false alarms.

Meteorologists make use of two main categories of severe weather advisories: watches and warnings. A "watch" means that while a storm does not yet exist, conditions are ripe for one to develop. A "warning" is more serious. This message indicates that a storm has been sighted and may strike a given area. While numerous subsets of these categories are issued for each type of storm, these two words alone provide important clues about the status of a storm and how to respond appropriately. It is important to stay tuned to forecasts and heed all warnings. While some storms are merely exciting spectacles that cause little damage, others may create life-threatening conditions.

Specialized forecasts   Specialized forecasts are generated for particular geographic areas and are tailored to the interests of specific groups of people, such as pilots, boaters, travelers, and farmers.

Aviation reports provide information on the height of clouds, visibility, and storm systems. In response to reports of storms or poor visibility, a pilot may change his or her course and fly around a storm. Reports of poor conditions at an airport may force a pilot to delay landing or to proceed to a different airport. The National Weather Service operates a toll-free telephone information line to help keep pilots informed.

Marine forecasts are issued for areas along the coastlines of North America. Such forecasts are of interest to the nearly two-thirds of the population who live within 50 miles (80 kilometers) of a coast. These forecasts give projections of the times of high and low tides, wave heights, wind speed and direction, and visibility. When rough weather is brewing over the water, the NWS issues small-craft advisories and other warnings that may affect fishermen and other boaters, as well as workers on oil rigs.

Agricultural reports include current temperature, precipitation, and wind speed and direction, as well as predictions of temperature and precipitation for the days to come. One example of how farmers use this information is in deciding when to apply pesticides. The temperature projections help a farmer determine which insects will likely pose a threat to which crops. If a pesticide is deemed necessary but rain is predicted, a farmer will delay applying chemicals since rain will wash the chemicals off before they take effect. The farmer also takes into account the current wind information, as a safety measure, before spraying.

Another element of an agricultural forecast is a frost warning, which is issued to warn farmers of the danger to their crops. Decisions about when to irrigate, obviously, are also dependent on predicted rainfall. So is cutting hay, since fresh hay needs at least two days to dry once it has been cut.

Travelers' reports tell what the weather is like at a traveler's destination. Some TV or newspaper weather sources regularly include forecasts for popular vacation spots, while others list temperature highs and lows and general conditions for major cities around the world. Some travelers' reports indicate whether or not airlines are operating on schedule at airports in major travel destinations.

Ski reports, which describe conditions of interest to skiers, generally list forecasts for popular ski destinations.

The future of forecasting

In the early 1960s Edward Lorenz demonstrated that it may never be possible to predict the weather with perfect accuracy; just how close to perfection forecasting can come is still not known. However, the meteorological community is determined to push the success rate of forecasting to the theoretical limit, whatever that may be. With that goal in mind,

Weather report: Marine forecast

The following is an example of a marine forecast taken from NOAA on March 7, 2007: "Point Arena, California: Tonight: west winds 5 to 10 knots switching northwest late. Wind waves 1 to 2 feet with swell 4 to 6 feet at 11 seconds. Thursday: northwest winds 10 knots. Wind waves 1 to 2 feet with swell 5 to 7 ft at 10 seconds." A marine forecast for Plymouth, Massachusetts, on the same day reads follows: "SMALL CRAFT ADVISORY IN EFFECT FROM THURSDAY MORNING THROUGH THURSDAY EVENING. Tonight: west winds 15 to 20 knots. Seas 2 to 4 feet. A slight chance of snow showers after midnight. Light freezing spray after midnight with visibility 1 to 3 nautical miles. Thursday: west winds 20 to 25 knots, becoming northwest 25 to 30 knots. Seas 4 to 6 feet. Light freezing spray. A chance of snow showers in the morning. Visibility 1 to 3 nautical miles."

meteorologists are pursuing various strategies, including achieving a greater understanding of the forces at work in creating weather, obtaining higher quality observational data, and improving computer capabilities.

Toward a greater atmospheric understanding

During the World War I era (1914–1918), the discovery of fronts, air masses, and upper-air patterns revolutionized how we look at weather. It sparked the rapid development that the field of meteorology continues to enjoy to this day. Along with increased knowledge of how weather works, however, has come the realization that there is still much to learn.

New facets of atmospheric science are continually being discovered and probed. Some topics currently under study include interaction between the ocean currents and temperatures and atmospheric circulation; the role of the stratosphere (the layer of Earth's atmosphere above the troposphere); the effect of plumes of water vapor in the air; the effect of ice particles in thunderstorm clouds, and lightning above the clouds, on the global electrical circuit; and the interaction of winds and clouds in the formation of storms.

As meteorologists learn how these factors fit with other pieces of the atmospheric puzzle, they can incorporate them into computer forecasting models. While technological advances in recent years have greatly improved the abilities of computers to process information, in the end, a computer merely does what it is programmed to do. The quality of the results depends on the sophistication of the program. The sophistication of the program, in turn, is a reflection of the programmer's understanding of atmospheric processes.

More and better observations   Another way that meteorologists are working to improve the accuracy of weather forecasts is by collecting more detailed data, with greater frequency. If they start out with incorrect, incomplete, or out-of-date data, it does not matter how good their computer model is—the results will be skewed. When more precise and current data are entered in a computer model, more accurate forecasts are produced.

One problem that forecasters are working to overcome is that in some parts of the world, such as sparsely populated lands and the oceans, observations are scant. An increase in the number of automated weather stations and weather satellites, anticipated to become operational over the next several years, will help remedy this shortfall.

The quality of observational instruments is also being improved. Older equipment is undergoing modernization and greater numbers of newer, high-tech instruments (particularly Doppler radar, wind profilers, and satellites) are being deployed.

Improving computer capabilities Along with improvements in data collection, the future will also see more effective computers. The National Weather Service's supercomputers will certainly be replaced with newer, faster, and more powerful models that are capable of processing an increased volume of data. They will be programmed with more complex and sophisticated models and will produce forecasts with greater range and accuracy.

Another important criterion in a computer's performance is resolution. Resolution refers to the number of squares that make up the computer's grid system. The entire area under study, such as the continental United States, is divided into squares. The computer produces one forecast for each square in the grid by averaging conditions at all points throughout that square.

The number of squares in a grid is inversely proportional to the size of each square. The greater the number of squares, the smaller each square is. Likewise, as the square size decreases, the resolution increases and the more precise the forecast becomes.

Consider a low-resolution grid in which each square is 100 miles (161 km) across. Conditions can vary greatly over this 100-square-mile (260-square-kilometer) area. For example, temperatures may differ by $15°F$ ($8°C$)or more. Thus, a forecast based on average conditions will not be relevant for many points within the square.

Meteorologists have a goal to increase resolution so that each square within a grid is as small as 4 square miles (10 square kilometers). In that way, the variation of conditions within a square will be much lower and forecasts will become more accurate for every point within the square.

Ensemble forecasting Meteorologists are currently experimenting with a new method of forecasting called ensemble forecasting. This method takes into account the predictability of the behavior of the atmosphere at the time a forecast is made. If the atmosphere shows signs of stability, the forecast is more likely to be correct than when atmospheric conditions are showing signs of rapid and erratic change.

The predictability of the atmosphere can be determined by running a series of computer simulations, starting with slightly different atmospheric variables each time. If the forecasts generated for ten days in advance in each simulation are similar to one another, then the atmosphere is in a predictable phase. However, if the forecasts start to differ from one another by day three, then the atmosphere is unpredictable.

The predictability of the atmosphere influences how accurate a forecast will be beyond a few days. Thus, using the ensemble method, a forecaster can determine the probability that his or her forecast will be correct. When the atmosphere is unpredictable, a forecaster may decide to limit a forecast to three days ahead. However, when the atmosphere is predictable, a ten-day forecast could be made with confidence.

[*See Also* **Climate; Clouds; Human Influences on Weather and Climate; Hurricane; Precipitation; Weather: An Introduction**]

For More Information

BOOKS

Aguado, Edward, and James Burt. *Understanding Weather and Climate.* 4th ed. Englewood Cliffs, NJ: Prentice Hall, 2006.

Ahrens, C. Donald. *Meteorology Today: An Introduction to Weather, Climate, and the Environment.* 7th ed. Belmont, CA: Thomson Brooks/Cole, 2006.

Hodgson, Michael. *Basic Essentials. Weather Forecasting.* 3rd ed. Guilford, CT: Globe Pequot Press, 2007.

Kahl, Jonathan D. W. *Weather Watch: Forecasting the Weather.* Toronto, Ontario, Canada: Monarch Books of Canada Limited, 2002.

Vasquez, Tim. *Weather Forecasting Handbook.* 5th ed. Garland, TX: Weather Graphics Technologies, 2002.

WEB SITES

"Do-It-Yourself Weather Forecasting." *Weather Michigan.* <http://www.weathermichigan.com/u_do_it.htm> (accessed March 25, 2007).

"Official Weather Forecasts and Warnings." *The World Meteorological Organization.* <http://www.wmo.int/> (accessed March 25, 2007).

"Weather." *National Oceanic and Atmospheric Administration.* <http://www.noaa.gov/wx.html> (accessed March 24, 2007).

"Weather Office." *Environment Canada.* <http://weatheroffice.ec.gc.ca/canada_e.html> (accessed March 25, 2007).

"Welcome to the Weather Underground," *Weather Underground* <http://www.wunderground.com/> (accessed March 25, 2007).

Climate Change and Global Warming

Climate is the weather experienced by a given location, averaged over several decades. A region's climate tells how hot or cold, wet or dry, windy or still, and cloudy or sunny it generally is. Climate is determined not only by average weather conditions, but also by seasonal changes in those conditions and weather extremes. Thus, for example, a climate can be described as hot and wet year-round, frigid and dry year-round, or warm and rainy in the summer and cold and dry in the winter.

Climate has been an important factor in determining where groups of people choose to settle. While humans are resourceful enough to survive almost anywhere on the planet, most population centers are in areas where temperature and rainfall are adequate to sustain some form of agriculture. There are fewer settlements in regions of extreme dryness or cold, such as deserts or the arctic. Climate also influences how people live. It largely defines choices of architecture, clothes, food, occupation, and recreation.

The climates of the world are distinguished by several factors, including latitude (distance north or south of the equator), temperature (the degree of hotness or coldness of an environment), topography (the shape and height of land features), and distribution of land and sea.

Climate is not a fixed property. The global climate has changed continuously and dramatically over the 4.6 billion years since the Earth was formed. It continues to change today, and it will in the future. Understanding climate change and its causes will help us to anticipate future climates.

Elements of Climate

The two factors that are most significant in defining climate type are temperature and precipitation. These criteria, in turn, are influenced by a number of atmospheric, oceanographic, and topographic factors.

WORDS TO KNOW

air pollutant: any harmful substance that exists in the atmosphere at concentrations great enough to endanger the health of living organisms.

Cenozoic era: the historical period from sixty-five million years ago to the present.

deforestation: the removal of all or most of the trees from an area.

desert climate: the world's driest climate type, with less than 10 inches (25 centimeters) of rainfall annually.

desertification: the process by which semiarid lands turn to desert (also called land degradation). It is caused by prolonged drought, during which time the top layers of soil dry out and blow away.

drought: an extended period during which the amount of rain or snow that falls on an area is much lower than usual.

eccentricity: a measure of how much an orbit deviates from a circle. A circular orbit has zero eccentricity. An ellipse has eccentricity between zero and one.

ecosystem: a community of plants and animals, including humans, and their physical surroundings.

El Niño: means "the Christ child" in Spanish. A period of unusual warming of the Pacific Ocean waters off the coast of Peru and Ecuador. It usually starts around Christmas, which is how it got its name.

equinoxes: the days on which the Sun appears to cross Earth's equator in its yearly motion.

flood: the inundation of normally dry land with water.

food chain: the transfer of food energy from one organism to another. It begins with a plant species, which is eaten by an animal species; it continues with a second animal species, which eats the first, and so on.

fossil fuels: coal, oil, and natural gas—materials composed of the remains of plants or animals that covered Earth millions of years ago and are today burned for fuel.

global warming: the observed global increase in atmospheric temperature. Also called global climate change.

Temperature Climate is affected by annual mean (average) temperature and annual temperature range. High mountain deserts such as in central Asia and the high mountain plateaus of South America may experience extreme temperature variation, with daytime temperatures exceeding 100°F (38°C) and nighttime temperatures plunging below freezing. At the opposite extreme, regions in the tropics may have little daily or yearly variation in temperature.

The annual temperature range is found by subtracting the year's lowest average monthly temperature from the year's highest average

greenhouse effect: the warming of Earth due to the presence of greenhouse gases, which trap upwardly radiating heat and return it to Earth's surface.

greenhouse gases: gases that trap heat in the atmosphere. The most abundant greenhouse gases are water vapor and carbon dioxide. Others include methane, nitrous oxide, and chlorofluorocarbons.

heat wave: an extended period of high heat and humidity.

Holocene: the most recent part of the Cenozoic era, from ten thousand years ago to the present.

ice age: a period during which significant portions of Earth's surface are covered with ice.

interglacial period: a relatively warm period that exists between two ice ages.

Maunder minimum: a period of time from 1645 to 1715, during which sunspot activity was almost nonexistent.

Mesozoic era: the historical period from 225 million years ago to 65 million years ago, best known as the age of the dinosaurs.

Milankovitch theory: the theory stating that the three types of variation in Earth's orbit, taken together, can be linked with warm and cold periods throughout history. These variations include: the shape of Earth's orbit, the direction of tilt of its axis, and the degree of tilt of its axis.

obliquity: the angle of the tilt of Earth's axis in relation to the plane of its orbit.

ocean current: the major routes through which ocean water is circulated around the globe.

paleoclimatologist: a scientist who studies climates of the past.

Paleozoic era: the historical period from 570 million years ago to 225 million years ago.

precession of the equinoxes: the reversal of the seasons every thirteen thousand years. This occurs because Earth spins about its axis like a top in slow motion and wobbles its way through one complete revolution every twenty-six thousand years.

season: a period of the year characterized by certain weather conditions, such as temperature and precipitation, as well as the number of hours of sunlight each day.

---

monthly temperature. The annual temperature range reveals whether or not a location experiences different seasons, which is just as important as the annual average temperature in identifying climate type.

Average annual sea-level temperatures plotted on a map roughly correspond to latitude. That is, temperatures are highest at the equator, decline with increasing latitudes, and are lowest at the poles. This is due to the uneven heating of Earth by the Sun due to the varying angle of the Sun's rays.

An imaginary line connecting locations with the same temperature is called an "isotherm." Because water takes longer to heat up and retains

Comet Ikeya-Zhang, 2002. AP IMAGES.

heat longer than does land, isotherms veer where landmasses meet the sea. Ocean currents, which are the major routes that carry warm water toward the poles and cold water toward the equator, also cause the bending of isotherms along the coasts.

Precipitation   In addition to temperature, precipitation (water in any form falling out of the air) is the other factor determining climate. Both the total precipitation and the distribution of precipitation throughout the year have an impact. For example, a city that receives all of its precipitation during a few torrential rainfalls during the hottest summer months might have an arid climate, while a city that receives the same amount of precipitation distributed evenly through the year might have a climate able to support trees and grasses.

Wet and dry regions are scattered across the globe. However, there are some general trends corresponding to global air circulation patterns. Around the equator, where the trade winds (dominant surface winds that blow from east to west) converge and air rises, precipitation is relatively high. Precipitation is also high around 60° latitude, in the middle latitudes, where the warm westerly air currents rise as they meet the cold polar easterlies.

In the subtropical regions, around 30° latitude, conditions are much drier. It is there that most of the world's deserts exist. The polar regions are also characterized by dryness. However, these latitudes are not fixed. As Earth makes its yearly revolution around the Sun the amount of sunlight received at each latitude changes, causing northward and southward shifts in "wet" and "dry" latitudes.

History of Climate Change

Throughout Earth's 4.6-billion-year existence, the global climate has changed continuously. Most of what scientists know of the history of climate change is based on the most recent 10 percent of Earth's history—the last 500 million years or so. There are fewer clues about the climate in the more distant past. However, by using the clues that do exist plus drawing conclusions from more recent data, scientists have been able to construct a climatic picture spanning the entire existence of Earth.

There have been times when Earth has been alternately warmer or colder than it is today. There have also been several periods during which significant portions of the planet's surface have been covered with ice. These are popularly known as ice ages. Each ice age has brought about the extinction of numerous species of plants and animals as well as dramatic shifts in the distribution of plant and animal species, which means that the process by which plants and animals have evolved has not been a smooth one. Rather, it has been halted many times and begun anew with each new warm period.

The geologic history of Earth is conventionally divided into six main eras: Hadean, Archaean, Proterozoic, Paleozoic, Mesozoic, and Cenozoic.

Comets

Another theory of the origin of Earth's atmosphere suggests that the atmospheric gases were deposited at least in part by comets colliding with Earth. Debris from comets is known to have carbon dioxide and nitrogen in roughly the same proportion as found in the early atmosphere. There are numerous impact craters on Earth from past collisions with asteroids, comets, and other objects from space. The role of comets in the formation of Earth's early atmosphere and life remains an area of vigorous scientific debate.

Precambrian era (Hadean, Archaean, Proterozoic)   The Precambrian period begins with the formation of Earth around 4.6 billion years ago, along with the rest of our solar system, and ends 570 million years ago. Earth began its existence as a ball of molten liquid rock. Within about 900 million years, its surface cooled and solidified. Earth's atmosphere was first produced from gases of volcanoes and possibly with additional gases from comets, which are chunks of rock and ice that orbit the Sun. These gases included nitrogen compounds, water vapor, carbon dioxide, sulfur dioxide, and argon.

At first, the atmosphere contained a lot of water vapor. The water vapor condensed into rain, which fell to the surface forming vast oceans. The rain washed most of the carbon dioxide and sulfur dioxide out of the atmosphere. The carbon dioxide and sulfur dioxide eventually formed into limestone rocks. This left primitive Earth with an atmosphere composed of nitrogen, argon, water vapor, and a small amount of carbon dioxide. The small amount of carbon dioxide and other gases produced a modest greenhouse effect, which is the warming of Earth due to the presence of gases that trap heat, making the planet capable of supporting life. However, there was no free oxygen in Earth's early atmosphere. Since there was no free oxygen, there was also no ozone in Earth's upper atmosphere.

Soon after the formation of the early atmosphere, the first forms of life appeared. Geologists mark this as the beginning of the Archaean era. Since there was no free oxygen in Earth's atmosphere at this time, the organisms were probably some form of anaerobic bacteria known as Archaeans. (Anaerobic means capable of living without oxygen.) Archaeans of today are known to thrive in extremely harsh conditions—they were first discovered in the hot springs of Yellowstone National Park—so they were likely to be capable of thriving in the high temperatures and methane-rich environment of early Earth.

About 3.5 billion years ago, the first photosynthesizing organisms appeared. Photosynthesis is the process in which an organism combines water and carbon dioxide to form a simple sugar, driven by the heat of the Sun. Oxygen is given off as a byproduct.

Over time, oxygen accumulated in the atmosphere. By 2 billion years ago, it accounted for 1 percent of its present concentration; by 700 million years ago, it accounted for 10 percent; and by 350 million years ago, the concentration of oxygen in the atmosphere reached its present value of 21 percent. Oxygen molecules (O_2) then combined with free oxygen atoms, which were formed when oxygen molecules broken apart by sunlight, to form ozone (O_3). The ozone formed a separate atmospheric layer, 25 to 40 miles above ground, that filters out the harmful ultraviolet rays. Together with the protection provided by the ozone layer, the oxygen in the atmosphere encouraged the burst of biological diversity that marked the end of the Precambrian era.

Paleozoic era   The Paleozoic era, lasting from 570 to 225 million years ago, began with a dramatic increase in the number of marine animal species. The Paleozoic era saw dramatic temperature changes. Much of the time it was significantly warmer than the Precambrian era, but there were two glacial periods. The first was relatively short and began around 430 million years ago. At the end of this cold period, around 400 million years ago, plants began to take hold on land.

The first land plants were little more than rigid stems. They reproduced by releasing spores, the same reproduction mechanism used today by ferns and mushrooms. Within fifty million years, however, plants had begun producing seeds, which are capable of being dispersed over far greater distances than spores.

The spread of plants across the land had a significant impact on climate. Primarily, it reduced the albedo (reflectivity) of Earth's surface by 10 to 15 percent. As a result, more sunlight was absorbed, which raised the planet's surface temperature. The second cold period occurred during the last portion of the Paleozoic era, from 330 to 225 million years ago.

Around 250 million years ago, Earth's two supercontinents, called Laurussia (containing Greenland, North America, Scandinavia, and most of Russia) and Gondwana (containing most of the rest of the landmass), joined together. The newly formed supercontinent, Pangaea, extended from the North Pole almost all the way to the South Pole.

Mesozoic era   The Mesozoic era, which is often known as the age of the dinosaurs, lasted from 225 to 65 million years ago. In the latter half of this era, Pangaea split into two continents, Laurasia and Gondwana. Laurasia included North America, Europe, and Asia. Gondwana included most of the southern continents. About 100 million years ago, these land masses further subdivided, roughly into the present continents. However, the landmasses were still situated very close together.

Throughout the Mesozoic era, temperatures everywhere on Earth were, on average, 11 to 18°F (6 to 10°C) warmer than they are today. They were also relatively uniform across the planet. This was most likely due to the efficient distribution of heat from the equator to the poles by ocean currents and global winds. Land masses, even by the end of the Mesozoic era, were not as widely dispersed across the globe as they are today. Thus, ocean currents (the major routes through which ocean water is circulated around the globe) and winds had a relatively clear path between the equator and poles.

The Mesozoic era experienced a number of temperature swings, culminating in a sudden, brief ice age. This coincided with the extinction of about 70 percent of Earth's life forms, including dinosaurs. One theory is that the ice age was brought about by the collision of an asteroid with Earth that created a dust cloud that blocked out the Sun's rays.

Cenozoic era   The Cenozoic era began sixty-five million years ago and continues to the present. Throughout this era, the continents have continued to drift apart, moving to their present configuration. The process of supercontinent formation and breakup will likely repeat several

The Muir Glacier at Glacier Bay National Park in Alaska is retreating. © TOM BEAN/ CORBIS.

more times as the continental plates continue to move. This era is also characterized by the emergence of mammals, including humans, as the dominant animal group.

The early part of the Cenozoic era was warmer than it is today, and there were no polar ice caps. Beginning around fifty-five million years ago, a long cooling trend began. This cooling occurred both gradually over time, and through a series of extremely cold periods. One of these cold spells took place about fifty million years ago, and another about thirty-eight million years ago. The most recent was about fifteen million years ago, the results of which can still be seen in the polar ice caps and the glaciers nestled in protected areas of tall mountains.

Over the last 2.4 million years there have been two dozen ice ages (periods during which the global temperature plummeted). At seven different times over the last 1.6 million years, up to 32 percent of Earth's surface has been covered with ice. Scientists estimate that throughout the Cenozoic era, new ice ages have occurred about every one hundred thousand years and have been interspersed with warmer, interglacial periods, each lasting at least ten thousand years.

The most recent ice age peaked about twenty thousand years ago, when there were glaciers up to 10,000 feet (3,000 meters) thick over most of North America, northern Europe, and northern Asia, as well as the southern portions of South America, Australia, and Africa. The sea level fell, exposing large areas of land that are currently submerged, such as the Bering land bridge, which connected the eastern tip of Siberia with the western tip of Alaska.

This era was followed by a warm period, beginning around fourteen thousand years ago. By eight thousand years ago, most of the ice had melted, and between seven and five thousand years ago, the world was about 5°F (3°C) warmer than it is today. The sea level rose and the current shape of continents emerged.

Holocene epoch   The most recent division of the Cenozoic is called the Holocene epoch. It began approximately ten thousand years ago and continues to today. Extensive climatic data exist for this time period. The history of modern civilization begins during this postglacial period, about six thousand years ago.

About five thousand years ago, when Earth was slightly warmer and wetter than it is today, agriculture was developed, and the earliest cities were established in Egypt and Mesopotamia, which is part of modern Iraq. There was a relatively cool period that began around 900 BCE and lasted until about 500 BCE, which resulted in crop failures. There are also indications that, beginning around 800 CE, there was a prolonged drought, or period of extreme dryness, which may have contributed to the decline of the great Mayan civilizations in Mexico and Central America.

In the Middle Ages (500 to 1500 CE), the global climate was similar to today. During that time, the civilizations of Europe flourished and the Vikings colonized Iceland and Greenland. However, the end of the thirteenth century saw the beginning of a cold spell. Summer after summer was cold and wet, which caused famine throughout Europe.

Conditions were more moderate during the fifteenth century and then became colder again between about 1500 and 1850, a period referred to as the "Little Ice Age." Rather than being continuously cold, the Little Ice Age consisted of a series of cold spells, each up to thirty years long, separated by warmer years. For the most part, this period was characterized by bitterly cold winters and cold, wet summers. The canals of Holland, as well as the Baltic Sea and the River Thames in England, were often covered with layers of ice several inches thick. Food became scarce throughout Europe, the mountain glaciers grew, and the colonists in Greenland and Iceland perished.

After the Little Ice Age, temperatures warmed. In the years since 1850, however, significant fluctuations have occurred in global temperatures. About a dozen cool periods have alternated with warmer periods. From 1900 to the present, there has been a 1°F (0.5°C) increase in global temperature. Scientists now think that this increase is not merely a natural part of Earth's continually changing climate, but rather constitutes part of a trend of human-influenced global warming, or temperature increase.

There are various ways of looking at the Holocene epoch. Some consider it a "warm period," since ice exists only at the polar regions, covering 10 percent of the planet. Others believe the world is still in the

This Dutch painting from the 1700s illustrates how during the "Little Ice Age" rivers in Europe that were usually ice-free froze over. THE ART ARCHIVE / GALLERIA SABAUDA TURIN / DAGLI ORTI (A).

final stages of the most recent ice age. What many scientists do agree on, however, is that another ice age is in store for the future.

Reasons for Climate Change

In an attempt to find some order in the series of climatic shifts that describes the history of Earth, scientists have sought to define a pattern of warm-cool cycles that repeat after a given period of time. However, they have been largely unsuccessful. The proposed cycles either do not apply to all times in the past or do not hold true for all parts of the world.

One problem in determining patterns of climatic change is that many factors are involved. Some of those factors affect Earth's climate for millennia while others affect it only for decades. In addition, some factors, such as Earth's shifting orbit around the Sun, are predictable and regular, while others, such as collisions with large objects in space, are not.

Human activity constitutes a whole category of factors affecting climate change in the very recent past, present, and future. Among the possible agents of climate change are deforestation, which is the removal of trees; the burning of fossil fuels, such as coal, oil, and natural gas; acid precipitation, which is rain and snow that are made more acidic when carbon, sulfur, and nitrogen oxides in the air dissolve in the water; and smog, a layer of hazy, brown air pollution at Earth's surface caused by industrial emissions. Though the impact of human activity on climate change has be the subject of much debate in recent years, a February 2007 report by the United Nations' Intergovernmental Panel on Climate Change made one of the strongest arguments yet that recent sharp rises in global temperature, also known as global warming, are a direct result of human actions. The Intergovernmental Panel on Climate Change was established in 1988 to study the global climate. Its 2007 report stated that "most of the observed increase in globally averaged temperatures since the mid-twentieth century is very likely due to the observed increase in anthropogenic (human-generated) greenhouse gas concentrations."

There are a handful of forces that have affected Earth's climate throughout its history: continental drift, shifts in Earth's orbit, volcanoes, asteroids and comets, and solar variability. Another phenomena that is currently being studied as a possible factor in long-term climate change is El Niño /Southern Oscillation (ENSO).

Continental drift   The theory of continental drift was first suggested by German meteorologist Alfred Wegener (1880–1930) in 1915. That theory states that 200 to 250 million years ago, all land on Earth was

Growth of traffic congestion and the popularity of automobile transportation in developing nations such as China, the world's second-largest vehicle market, may hinder efforts to reduce greenhouse gas emissions.
© CLARO CORTES IV/ CORBIS.

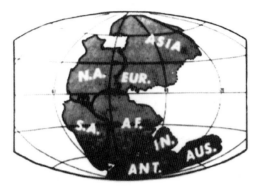

PERMIAN - 225 million years ago

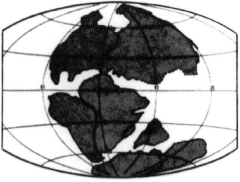

TRIASSIC - 200 million years ago

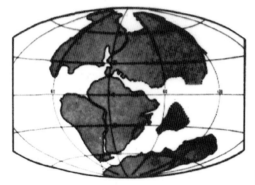

JURASSIC - 135 million years ago

CRETACEOUS - 65 million years ago

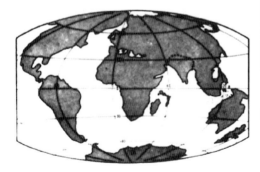

CENOZOIC - Present

Global maps showing continental drift. AP IMAGES.

joined together in one supercontinent that Wegener named Pangaea. Then, over the years, the supercontinent broke up and the pieces drifted to where they are today. Although there was substantial evidence supporting the theory of continental drift, Wegener could not suggest a mechanism causing the breakup and drift of the continents. The theory was not considered for decades. Then, in the late 1950s and early 1960s, a new theory incorporating the ideas of continental drift was developed. This new theory, plate tectonics, explained the motion of the plates as being due to convection currents (the transfer of heat by the mass movement of heated particles into an area of cooler fluid) in Earth's upper mantle, the layer beneath the crust, which is the planet's thin outer-most layer.

Evidence of continental drift can be found in the fossils of dinosaurs and other mammals that migrated across once-connected land masses, and in the fossilized remains of tropical plants beneath polar ice sheets. Another piece of evidence that land masses were once connected is that shapes of the continents fit together like pieces of a jigsaw puzzle. The Atlantic coastlines of Africa and South America are the most striking examples of this phenomenon. In addition, satellites today are able to record the subtle, extremely slow movements of the continents.

Continental drift is believed to affect both the climates of individual continents and the climate of the entire planet. The climates of the individual continents have been altered by their gradual, but radical, change in position around Earth. For instance, parts of Europe and Asia that once sat on the equator are now at high latitudes in the Northern Hemisphere. India moved to its current low-latitude Northern Hemisphere position from deep in the Southern Hemisphere. Glaciers once covered parts of Africa, and Antarctica gradually slid from warmer latitudes to the South Pole.

On a global level, the position of land masses affects how the heat from the Sun is distributed around Earth. When the continents were joined together, ocean currents and global winds produced a different pattern of global heat distribution than they do at present. Global climatic conditions 200 to 250 million years ago were more uniform than they are today. As the continents separated and moved out around the globe, greater extremes in climatic conditions began to appear around the world.

Another consequence of continental drift has been the formation of mountain ranges. When land masses come together, the land is forced upward. Examples of mountain ranges formed in this way are the Rocky Mountains, the Andes, the Himalayas, and the Kunlun and Qilan

A cape of clouds forms as warm, moist air rises up the windward slope of a mountain in New Zealand. ©JASON HOSKING/ ZEFA/CORBIS.

mountain ranges bordering the Tibetan Plateau. Mountain ranges affect temperatures, winds, and rainfall over limited areas. Very tall ranges, particularly those with north-south configurations, can influence air circulation patterns over very large areas.

The Tibetan Plateau is a prime example of this phenomenon. Called "the roof of the world," it was formed fifty million years ago by the collision of the Indian and Asian continents and is one of the world's tallest and widest plateaus. It affects wind patterns across the entire Northern Hemisphere. Fossil records show that almost immediately following the formation of the Tibetan Plateau, the climate of the Northern Hemisphere cooled and large glaciers formed. The presence of glaciers led to further cooling. Snow accumulates on the ice, which reflects sunlight rather than absorbing it.

Another aspect of continental drift that affects global climate is the distribution of land masses at various latitudes. For instance, as land moved away from the tropics and toward the poles, tropical oceans replaced the land. These bodies of water absorbed huge amounts of incoming heat, which led to global cooling. Also, the movement of continents into polar regions provided a surface on which ice layers could accumulate.

Earth's orbit   In the 1930s, the Yugoslavian astronomer Milutin Milankovitch (1879–1958) proposed another theory to explain changes in

Earth's climate. He listed three factors that could affect the planet's climate: the shape of Earth's orbit and the angle and direction of Earth's axis.

The shape of Earth's orbit around the Sun changes over long periods of time. At times, the orbit is almost circular. At other times, it has a more elliptical shape. The eccentricity of Earth's orbit changes in a regular cycle—from circular to elliptical to circular again—that takes about one hundred thousand years.

When the orbit is circular, there is less variation in the levels of solar energy received by Earth throughout the year than when it is elliptical. At present, the orbit is in a stage of low eccentricity, meaning that it is nearly circular. Earth receives only 7 percent more solar energy in January, when Earth is closest to the Sun, than July, when it is farthest from the Sun. In contrast, when the orbit is highly eccentric, the solar energy received at points closest to and farthest from the Sun differ by up to 20 percent. In addition, a more elliptical orbit means the relative lengths of the seasons are different. Springs and falls are shorter, while a particular hemisphere might have a long summer and short winter, or vice versa.

The second orbital factor that affects climate is the wobble in Earth's axis of rotation. This effect is what causes the Northern and Southern Hemispheres to receive different amounts of sunlight throughout the year.

Earth spins like a top in slow motion, so that its axis follows a cone-shaped path. It wobbles its way through one complete revolution every twenty-six thousand years, a phenomenon called the precession of the equinoxes. Equinoxes are the days on which the Sun appears to cross Earth's equator in its yearly motion, and "precession" refers to the motion of Earth's axis of rotation. The precession of the equinoxes means that every thirteen thousand years the seasons gradually reverse. Eventually, unless the calendars are adjusted to compensate, the Northern Hemisphere will experience winter in July and the Southern Hemisphere, in January. Precession also influences Earth's distance from the Sun at different seasons. When it is winter in the Northern Hemisphere in July, Earth will also be at its closest point to the Sun in that month.

The third variable affecting Earth's climate is the angle of the tilt of Earth's axis compared to the plane of its orbit. This angle is called obliquity. Over the course of forty-one thousand years, this angle fluctuates between 21.5 degrees and 24.5 degrees. It is currently 23.5 degrees. When the angle is smaller, sunlight strikes various points on Earth more evenly and the seasonal differences are smaller, bringing milder winters and cooler summers. Yet when the angle is larger, there is a greater variation in the level of solar radiation received across Earth and seasons are more pronounced.

The smaller angle of tilt tends to favor the formation of glaciers in polar regions. The reason for this effect is that when winters are warmer, the air holds more water and snowfall is heavier. That snow then has a greater probability of remaining on the ground during the cool summer.

Evidence has been found in deep ocean sediments that strongly support Milankovitch's theory. By analyzing the chemical composition of these sediments, scientists have deduced that glaciers have advanced and retreated in roughly one-hundred-thousand-year cycles over the last eight hundred thousand years. Within those cycles, glacier formation occurs in secondary cycles, reaching peaks every twenty-six thousand and forty-one thousand years. These time intervals correspond to the cycles of the three types of orbital variation described here. However, there are many difficulties in correlating climatic change to the Milankovitch cycles, which remains an active field of scientific inquiry.

Volcanoes   In the early stages of Earth's history, thousands of volcanoes dotted the surface. These volcanoes underwent frequent, large eruptions, which had a significant impact on the climate. In addition to releasing gases that rose up and formed Earth's atmosphere, these eruptions sometimes spewed out ash and dust so thick that they nearly blocked out the Sun. Volcanic eruptions have probably been the catalysts for some periods of glaciation.

While volcanic eruptions still occur today, they are far less frequent and intense than they once were. A very large volcanic eruption today affects global climate only for a few years. For example, in 1815 the Indonesian volcano Mount Tambora erupted. Dust from the eruption was carried around the world by upper-air winds. In conjunction with smaller eruptions of other volcanoes over the preceding four years, the Tambora event led to a decrease in global temperature. A severe cold spell in 1816 earned that year the nickname "the year without a summer."

The eruptions with the gravest climatic consequences are those rich in sulfur gases. Even after the ash and dust clears from the atmosphere, sulfur oxides continue to react with water vapor to produce sulfuric acid particles. These particles collect and form a heavy layer of haze. This layer can persist in the upper atmosphere for years, reflecting away a portion of the incoming solar radiation. The result is a global decrease in temperature.

Mount St. Helens in Washington erupts in March, 2005. AP IMAGES.

Asteroids Throughout Earth's history, there have been at least five abrupt, dramatic changes in global climate, occurring 500 million years ago, 430 million years ago, 225 million years ago, 190 million years ago, and 65 million years ago. One possible explanation for these changes is that a large body from space, such as an asteroid or a comet, crashed into Earth. Many scientists think that the extinction of the dinosaurs, which occurred around 65 million years ago, was caused by a collision with an asteroid.

The impact of an asteroid at least 6 miles (10 kilometers) across, traveling at a speed of at least 12 miles (20 kilometers) per second, would produce a crater about 95 miles (150 kilometers) in diameter. It would release energy equivalent to that of four billion atomic bombs such as those dropped on Hiroshima, Japan, during World War II, heating the atmosphere near the impact to temperatures of 3,600 to 5,400°F (about 2,000 to 3,000°C). Another result of this energy release would be the production of huge concentrations of nitric and nitrous acids. These acids would react with and destroy the ozone layer. They would fall to the ground as highly acidic rain, destroying plants and animals.

If the asteroid were to fall on land, a thick dust cloud would rise and could block out all sunlight for several months. Following an early wave of wildfires caused by the high temperatures, any surviving plants and animals would die during a long, dark winter.

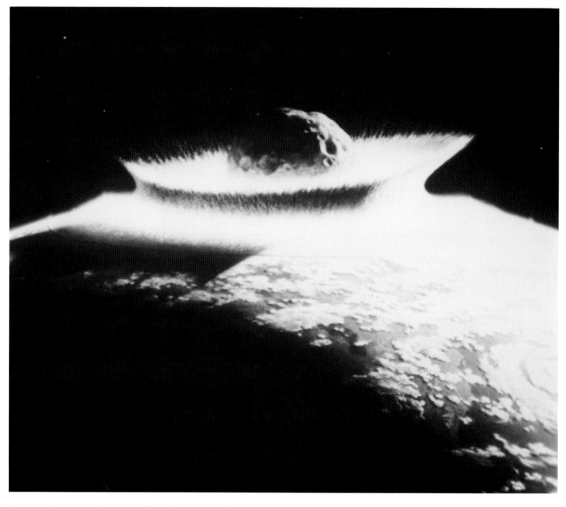

An artist's creation of an asteroid crashing into Earth. An impact of a large asteroid or comet could cause catastrophic climate changes. © PREMIUM STOCK/CORBIS.

It is more likely that an object from space would fall into the ocean, since oceans cover almost three-quarters of Earth's surface. In this case, the impact would stir up carbonate-rich sediments and produce vast quantities of carbon dioxide. Increase of carbon dioxide in the air traps reradiated infrared radiation from Earth's surface, leading to an increased greenhouse effect.

The possibility of such an asteroid impact happening within our lifetimes is remote. However, it has become more of a concern following the July 1994 crash of fragments of Comet Shoemaker-Levy into Jupiter.

These collisions, which occurred over several days, caused disturbances on an Earth-sized area of the giant gaseous planet's atmosphere. Had the same impact occurred on Earth, the results would probably have been disastrous.

Solar variability It has long been understood that the amount of energy emitted by the Sun varies slightly over the years. In recent years, scientists have made correlations between changes in cycles of solar output and particular weather patterns. While there have been several theories linking solar variation to long-term climate change, many more years of data collection will be necessary before such links can be proven. However, the evidence collected thus far presents a compelling case for the link between solar variability and climate change—at least climate change on the scale of decades.

The variation in solar output is primarily based on cycles of sunspot activity. Sunspots are dark areas of magnetic disturbance on the Sun's surface. When the number and size of sunspots is at a maximum, which occurs roughly every eleven years, the Sun's energy output is highest. This heightened solar output is due to an increase in bright areas, called faculae, which form around the sunspots.

Astronomer Keith Pierce measures sunspots at the McMath-Pierce Solar Telescope in Arizona, 1990. © ROGER RESSMEYER/ CORBIS.

Measurements taken by special instruments called radiometers on board satellites have shown that 0.1 percent, and possibly up to 0.4 percent, more solar energy reaches Earth during a sunspot maximum than during a sunspot minimum. The length of sunspot cycles varies over time, from seven to seventeen years. There is a growing body of evidence supporting a link between the length of sunspot cycles and temperature patterns around the world. It has been shown that over the last century, global temperatures, in general, are higher during shorter sunspot cycles than during longer sunspot cycles. In addition, a reduction in the amount of sea ice around Iceland, another sign of warming, has been noted during shorter sunspot cycles.

Another piece of evidence linking sunspots and global temperatures is that the period of lowest sunspot activity in several centuries coincided with the coolest period in several centuries. Between 1645 and 1715, the stretch of years known as the Maunder minimum (named for the British solar astronomer E. W. Maunder who discovered it in the late 1880s), sunspot activity was at a very low level. It is even possible there were no sunspots at all during this period. The period also coincides with the coldest part of the Little Ice Age.

Ways to Measure Climate Change

A paleoclimatologist, a scientist who studies climates of the past, uses many methods. The first step in learning about climates of the past is to discover objects that were formed long ago and to determine an accurate date for those objects. Then the problem is to extract information from the objects that describe the climate at that time.

There are many types of materials, both on Earth's surface and embedded far underground, that have been preserved over thousands and millions of years that provide clues about Earth's past. Paleoclimatologists use these materials in a variety of ways.

Rocks and rock formations   The oldest exposed rocks on Earth are found in northwestern Canada near Great Slave Lake. They are about 4.0 billion years old. These rocks are the only objects that still exist from the earliest period in Earth's history, the Precambrian era. Thus, scientists must rely entirely on rocks to learn about the climate of that time.

To determine the age of rocks, paleoclimatologists use a technique called radiometric dating, which was developed in the late 1800s. This can be used for rocks that contain radioactive elements, such as uranium, radium, and potassium. Radioactive nuclei exist in an unstable configuration and emit high-energy particles (alpha particles or positrons) over time, to achieve greater stability. When the parent nuclei shed alpha particles, or "decay," they transform into daughter nuclei (in the case of a uranium parent, the daughter is lead).

The age of a sample is determined by comparing the percentage of parent nuclei to daughter nuclei. Since scientists know the rate at which radioactive elements decay, they can determine how long ago the sample was entirely made of parent atoms; in other words, when the sample was formed.

Once scientists have established the age of a sample, they can study it for clues about the climate at that time. First, the shape of a rock tells them about the medium in which it once existed. For example, rocks with rounded surfaces probably once existed in a body of water, and rocks with eroded (worn-away) surfaces were probably once covered by glaciers.

To take this a step further, if rounded rocks from the same time period are found all over Earth, it can be assumed that the average temperature at that time was above freezing. The presence of surface water also indicates the existence of some form of atmosphere, without which water would quickly evaporate. By the same token, if eroded rocks of the same age are found at far-flung locations, this signals that an ice age was in progress.

Evidence of primitive organisms begins showing up in rocks dated about 4.0 billion years ago. Studying fossils provides information not only about the progression of life forms at different time periods, but also about the climate. For instance, rocks formed during cooler times, such as ice ages, have little or no fossils embedded within them. In contrast, rocks that were formed during warmer times contain fossils in far greater numbers.

A particularly valuable source of evidence of climate change is rock formations made from layers of particles, deposited incrementally and hardened over time. An analysis of samples of each layer of a rock formation provides information about Earth's climate at that time. Of particular interest are the fossils within each layer, which make up a timeline of the emergence of various species.

The presence of marine animals in a given layer indicates that the region was once covered with water. By studying the chemical composition of fossilized shells, which are primarily composed of calcium carbonate, it is even possible to determine the relative warmth of the water. Oxygen in calcium carbonate exists in two forms: oxygen-16, which is by far the most plentiful, and oxygen-18 (the number refers to how many neutrons the atom possesses). It has been found that during periods of glaciation, the concentration of oxygen-18 increases in the oceans. Thus, the ratio of oxygen-18 to oxygen-16 in fossilized shells can be used to estimate water temperature.

Ice cores Ice cores drilled into the 2-mile-thick (3-km-thick) polar ice caps provide unique insights into climates of the past. The ice has been accumulating in layers, one year at a time, for thousands of years. Though individual layers of ice can be counted for the last 50,000 years in Greenland, patterns can be discerned from this ice that yield information as far back as 250,000 years. In Antarctica precipitation is so meager that annual layers of ice cannot be distinguished from one

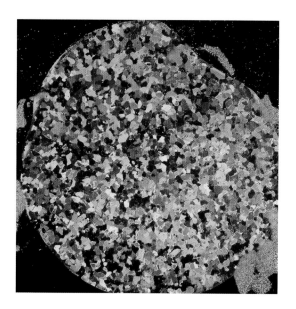

A round sample of an ice core taken from the Greenland ice sheet, shown under polarized light. ©ROGER RESSMEYER/ CORBIS.

another. However, information contained in the thick layer describes conditions from as far back as 500,000 years ago.

The layers of ice contain many types of climatic evidence, all perfectly preserved. For instance, the thickness of a layer tells how much precipitation fell during a given year. That, in turn, yields information about temperature, since greater levels of precipitation fall during warmer times.

Chemicals detected within the ice are also clues as to the air temperature at the time the precipitation fell. The approximate temperature during a particular period can be determined by comparing ratios of oxygen-16 and oxygen-18 present in a given medium.

By determining the nature of the dust contained within ice cores from the North Pole, it is possible to determine the origin of that dust. That, in turn, provides information about the wind patterns at that time. This type of evidence is not useful in South Pole ice cores, since Antarctica is surrounded by oceans, and is a great distance from all other land masses.

In addition, air bubbles in ice can be analyzed for the composition of the atmosphere. In addition, the timing of volcanic eruptions can be guessed at based on the presence of high levels of acidity in the ice. When volcanoes erupt, they emit dust and gases that are highly acidic.

Ocean and lake sediments   The sediments collected from the bottoms of oceans and lakes contain information about the global climate dating back millions of years. The sediment accumulates in layers, much the same as rock formations and ice. The age of sediment layers is determined using chemical analysis.

The fossils of tiny marine organisms that have evolved and become extinct over time are embedded within the layers of sediment. Each species was adapted only to a narrow range of water temperatures. Therefore, the presence of a species in a given layer of sediment reveals the ocean temperature at that time.

Pollen has also settled in layers on ocean and lake floors. Pollen provides clues to past conditions because every plant species requires a particular set of conditions for survival. The first step in pollen analysis is to identify the pollen species. The next step is to determine its age by finding the age of the surrounding sediment. Studying the times in which particular plant species inhabited a given location teaches scientists about that location's climatic history.

For example, a study of a bog in northern Minnesota identified pollen of fourteen plant types dating back eleven thousand years. In the oldest layer, the greatest pollen concentration was spruce. Since spruce trees inhabit cold climates, it could be inferred that at that time conditions were cold. The next layer yielded primarily pine pollen. Since pine trees grow in warmer regions than do spruce, conditions must have been warmer then. In the next layer, dated eighty-five hundred years ago, oak pollen was widespread. Oak grows in drier conditions than does either spruce or pine, which means that conditions must have been drier at that time. By examining the pollen within each layer, it was possible to construct a climatological history of the bog.

Tree rings   Dendrochronology, the study of the annual growth of rings of trees, is another important component of paleoclimatology. Trees are the oldest living entities on Earth. Some bristlecone pines that are still alive today are more than 4,700 years old.

A core sample of sediment taken from Chesapeake Bay, 1979. ©LOWELL GEORGIA/ CORBIS.

A cross-section of a cedar tree stump shows growth rings.
FIELD MARK PUBLICATIONS.

As trees grow, they add new cells to the center of their trunk each year. These cells force the previous years' growth outward, forming concentric rings with the oldest ring on the outer edge. A tree's woody material acts like a library of climatic data, creating a record for each year of its lifetime. This information can be found in living trees, dead (but not rotten) trees, and tree stumps.

Dendrochronologists measure the width of a given year's growth ring in order to assess the overall conditions of that year. In warm, wet years, trees grow more (and therefore have wider growth rings) than in cool, dry years. Therefore, the difference in the width of growth rings is an indicator of climate.

In order to separate the effect of temperature from that of precipitation, it is necessary to examine trees growing at the edge of their temperature or rainfall range. An example of this is the fir trees growing at the edge of the subpolar zone in Canada. Since temperatures are quite cold every year, an increase in growth from one year to the next would be due almost entirely to precipitation. To study temperature, consider the case of Joshua trees in the heart of a North American desert. There, rainfall is continuously very light, so variations in the width of tree rings would be caused by temperature changes.

Global warming

Global warming is the name given to the recently observed phenomenon of rising global temperatures believed to be caused by human, not natural, activities. A better name is "global climate change," because some places on Earth may actually experience lower temperatures during a period of global warming. According to many atmospheric and planetary scientists, the rapid rise in global temperatures is primarily due to the corresponding rapid increase of gases in Earth's atmosphere called "greenhouse gases." The most important greenhouse gases in Earth's atmosphere are water vapor, carbon dioxide, and methane. Nitrous oxide and chlorofluorocarbons are also greenhouse gases but they contribute an insignificant amount to the global greenhouse effect.

The rapid increase of carbon dioxide in the atmosphere during the nineteenth and twentieth centuries is thought to be the main reason for global warming. Although this remains an area of vigorous scientific debate, the February 2007 report "Climate Change 2007" issued by the United Nations Intergovernmental Panel on Climate Change, which incorporates the input of hundreds of scientists from around the world, offered strong evidence that human-generated pollution is indeed the primary cause of global warming. Carbon dioxide is produced by burning fossil fuels, such as coal, fuel oil, gasoline, and natural gas, and is emitted into the air from homes, factories, and motor vehicles. During the last century, the amount of carbon dioxide in the atmosphere increased by 30 percent. During that same period, the planet has become, on average, slightly more than 1.0°F (0.5°C) warmer.

Watch this: *An Inconvenient Truth*

Former vice president Al Gore's 2006 film *An Inconvenient Truth* explores the political and environmental consequences of unchecked global warming, and calls on viewers to take immediate action to learn how they can help reverse destructive climate trends. The film won an Academy Award for best documentary feature.

Since 1880, when accurate temperatures were first recorded around the world, the years 1998 and 2005 were on record as the world's warmest years, and every other year from 1995 to 2005 were among the warmest years on record. In fact, tree rings and sea coral growth indicate that the 1990s was the hottest decade in the last one thousand years and the twenty-first century looks to be even warmer. (Trees and sea corals grow outward from the center, depositing concentric rings every year; each ring yields information about rainfall and temperature for that year.)

In the November 6, 2000, issue of *U.S. News & World Report*, David Rind, a researcher with National Aeronautics and Space Administration's Goddard Institute for Space Studies, commented that warming in the twentieth century was "a magnitude of change that has not been seen for thousands of years." According to a February 2007 United Nations report, if present trends continue, we can expect an average global temperature increase, heat waves and droughts to become more persistent and severe, and tropical cyclones (hurricanes and typhoons) to become more intense and destructive. Some scientists studying global warming using sophisticated computer programs predict that Earth's climate will undergo as great a change in the next century as it has in the last ten thousand years.

Global warming is a significant concern because it has the potential to disrupt ecosystems—entire communities of plants and animals,—and contribute to the extinction of numerous species. Many scientists blame global warming for the increasing number of severe storms. It may also be

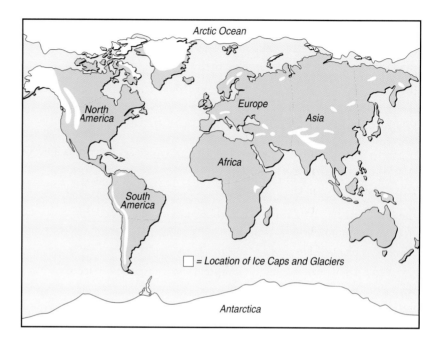

Map showing the location of ice caps and glaciers around the globe.

a contributing factor to global extremes of droughts and floods. Rising sea levels, another consequence of global warming, threaten to put island nations and coastal cities underwater.

Rising sea levels   Because of global warming, ocean levels have increased 4 to 10 inches (10 to 25 centimeters) since 1900. The rate at which the sea level is rising is expected to increase in the coming century. Current projections have ocean levels climbing as much as 2.5 feet (0.8 meter) by the year 2100. Such an increase would put many coastal areas underwater.

The primary reason for rising water levels is that ocean water becomes less dense and expands as its temperature increases. Water from melting glaciers in Greenland, Alaska, and Antarctica, as well as in the Rockies, Urals, Alps, and Andes mountain ranges, also contributes to rising sea levels.

"The melting of glaciers is emerging as one of the least ambiguous signs of climate change," wrote science writer Fred Pearce in the March 31, 2000, *Independent* of London. "Amid arcane arguments about the meaning of yearly fluctuations in the weather, it is hard to argue with the wholesale melting of some of the largest glaciers in the world. Mankind, it seems, has hit the defrost button."

Melting in Antarctica   The melting of the West Antarctic ice sheet, which is an enormous glacier in Antarctica, poses the greatest threat to coastal cities and island nations. At its thickest point, the ice sheet is 9.75 miles (15.7 kilometers) deep—ten times the height of the tallest skyscraper in the United States. Since the ice sheet sits on land below sea level, ocean waters lap at its edges and make it vulnerable to melting.

If the West Antarctic ice sheet were to collapse and pour into the sea, it would raise global sea levels by 13 to 20 feet (4 to 6 meters). A sea-level rise of that size would flood coastal regions, including much of Florida and New York City. Global warming experts, however, believe that it would take five hundred to seven hundred years for the West Antarctic ice sheet to collapse if global warming continues at its present rate.

Melting in Greenland   The melting of Greenland's ice sheet, the world's second largest expanse of ice after all of Antarctica's ice, is also a grave concern. The Greenland ice is 2 miles (3.2 kilometers) thick on average and covers 708,000 square miles (1.84 million square kilometers)—almost all of Greenland.

Studies conducted by the National Aeronautics and Space Administration (NASA) between 1993 and 1999 show that Greenland's ice is thinning on about 70 percent of its margins—in some places by 3 feet (1 meter) per year. In total, more than 2 cubic miles (8.2 cubic kilometers) of Greenland's ice melts each year. That amount of melting accounts for about 7 percent of the yearly rise in sea levels. If Greenland's entire ice sheet were to melt, ocean levels would rise by about 25 feet (7.6 meters), and there would be massive flooding in many parts of the world.

Melting in the Himalayas   The Himalayan Mountains, one-sixth of which are covered with glaciers, contain more snow and ice than any other place in the world except for the polar regions. (The Himalayas cover 1,500 miles [2,340 kilometers] across northern India, Nepal, and Tibet.) In the summer of 1999, researchers from Jawaharlal Nehru University in Delhi, India, announced their findings that the Himalayan glaciers are melting faster than anywhere else in the world. Their study showed that the Gangotri glacier, situated at the head of the Ganges River—a 1,550-mile-long (2,418-kilometers-long) river flowing southeast from the Himalayas into the Bay of Bengal—is shrinking at a rate of approximately 90 feet

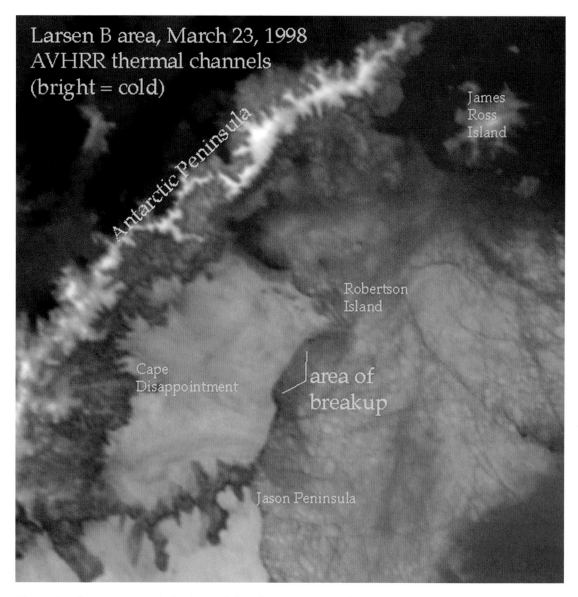

Larsen B area, March 23, 1998
AVHRR thermal channels
(bright = cold)

Antarctic Peninsula

James
Ross
Island

Robertson
Island

Cape
Disappointment

area of
breakup

Jason Peninsula

This satellite photo shows a 75-mile chunk of ice shelf on the Antarctic Peninsula that snapped off in 1998. © AP PHOTOS/
NATIONAL SNOW AND ICE DATA.

(27 meters) per year. If melting in the Himalayas continues at present levels, those glaciers could disappear by the year 2035.

The meltwater from the Himalayan glaciers has formed dozens of lakes, many of which are in danger of bursting through their natural dams.

These dams consist of walls of debris that were deposited by retreating glaciers over the last three hundred years. As the water level in these lakes continues to rise, it puts pressure on the natural dams. Eventually, the force of the water will grow too great, and the dams will give way, causing walls of water to surge down the mountainsides. Such catastrophes used to occur about once every ten years, but for the last decade they have been occurring once every three years. Geologists anticipate that by 2101, lake-bursts in the Himalayas will be annual events.

The worst lake-burst in recent history took place in 1985 in the Khumbal Himal region of Nepal. A wall of water 50 feet (15 meters) high swept downstream, killing villagers and destroying a hydroelectric plant. In 1994 a lake-burst in northern Bhutan killed twenty-seven people and ruined buildings and farmland. Tsho Rolpa, a lake at the edge of the Trakarding glacier, northeast of Katmandu, is also in danger of bursting. Engineers for the Tsho Rolpa Hazard Mitigation Project have installed a hazard warning siren on the lake that can be heard far down the valley and is linked to satellite communications. In addition, engineers cut a slot in the natural dam and installed a sluice gate to allow controlled discharge of the meltwater. However, there are many other glacial lakes in India, Nepal, Pakistan, and Tibet that are in imminent danger of collapse that feature no such warning systems.

The increased melting of the Himalayan glaciers also threatens to disrupt the region's supply of water for drinking and crop irrigation.

Snow-covered Himalayan peak, India. ©RIC ERGEN-BRIGHT/CORBIS.

Glacial meltwaters supply two-thirds of the flow of the Ganges River and other nearby waterways. If the glaciers melt entirely, those rivers will shrink and cease to supply the region. If that happens, almost five hundred million people in India would be at risk of starvation.

Island nations in trouble   The effects of the swollen seas are already being felt by small island nations. On the South Pacific islands of Kiribati and Tuvalu, for example, rising waters have destroyed roads and bridges and washed out traditional burial grounds. Many residents of those islands have had to move to higher ground. In Barbados, rising ocean levels have caused salt water to contaminate fresh-water wells near the coasts. The salination (process of making salty) of drinking water is a grave concern in Barbados, where drinking water is already in short supply.

At the global warming summit held in The Hague, the Netherlands, in November 2000, representatives of thirty-nine small island nations expressed their frustration at rising sea levels. They described the threat that rising waters pose to tourism and agriculture, which are concentrated on the coasts and are primary sources of income for island nations. "These are serious issues of economics and livelihood—issues that can disrupt the social fabric of countries," stated Leonard Nurse, a representative from Barbados in a news report of November 17, 2000.

Nurse and other delegates from island nations responded angrily to suggestions made that they should cope with rising sea levels by building surge barriers and storm drains. They blamed industrialized nations, foremost among them the United States, for emitting large amounts of carbon dioxide into the air and accelerating global warming. Those sentiments were underscored by Yumie Crisostomo of the Marshall Islands, who stated to the press: "Whoever caused the problem has to clear up the problem."

What causes global warming?   It is likely that global warming is partially the result of natural processes. For example, Earth could be still recovering from the most recent ice age. However, the rate of global warming is higher now than at any time in Earth's geologic history. This suggests some abnormal cause, such as the recent rapid increase of greenhouse gases in the atmosphere.

While the term "greenhouse effect" has a negative popular connotation because of its association with pollution and global warming, Earth's natural greenhouse effect keeps Earth at a suitable temperature for life on Earth. Without a modest greenhouse effect, the planet's average surface temperature would be about $0°F$ $(-18°C)$.

How the greenhouse effect works   The greenhouse effect is so-named because of the resemblance of the heat-trapping function of Earth's atmosphere to that of a greenhouse. However, the similarity is

Rising sea levels due to global warming may cause the island chain of Tuvalu in the South Pacific to disappear.
©MATTHIEU PALEY/
CORBIS.

Why melting icebergs don't contribute to rising sea levels

Many people are under the false impression that melting of icebergs and the floating ice cap that covers the waters around the North Pole are contributing to the rise in sea level. In fact, the melting of floating ice has no effect on the sea level. Ice, with its crystalline configuration of molecules, takes up more space than liquid water. Ice floats because it displaces a weight of water equal to the weight of the ice. When the ice melts, it becomes water with the same weight and volume as the water it was displacing. Consequently, there is no change in water level. The following experiment demonstrates this principle.

1. Take a large clear bowl and fill it half way with water.
2. Empty a tray of ice cubes into the water and measure the height of the water.
3. Wait for the ice to melt, and then measure the height of the water again.

So why do scientists say melting ice caps will cause a rise in sea level? If ice sheets melt, ice and snow covering the polar regions will no longer have anything holding them in place. If Antarctic ice, for example, slides into the ocean and melts, then the sea level will rise.

only superficial. In a greenhouse, the glass panels allow solar radiation to pass through. The plants and other objects in the greenhouse absorb the radiation and heat the surrounding air. Since the warm air cannot escape, the air in the greenhouse can become quite warm when the Sun is shining. This is the same phenomenon that can cause the interior of an automobile to become blistering hot in the summertime.

Earth's greenhouse effect is a different process. Solar radiation is primarily visible light. This shorter-wavelength radiation passes through Earth's atmosphere and reaches the surface. Some is reflected back to space by clouds and by Earth's surface itself. The rest is absorbed by the surface and by plants. As the surface warms, it begins to emit infrared radiation. Infrared is longer wavelength than visible light, and Earth's atmosphere does not allow infrared to pass. Consequently, much of this outward-bound radiation is either absorbed by the atmosphere or reflected back to the surface, raising the temperature even further. Eventually, Earth achieves heat balance, with as much energy radiated by the surface as is absorbed, but the presence of greenhouse gases in the atmosphere means heat balance is achieved at a higher temperature.

The most plentiful, and most effective, greenhouse gas is water vapor. Nighttime temperatures in winter often do not drop as low when there is a cloud cover. All other things being equal, the surface temperature remains higher on cloudy nights than it does on clear nights. On clear, dry nights, most of the reradiated heat can escape and the surface temperature can drop to low temperatures. This happens in the high deserts of Asia and South America, where daytime temperatures can soar to over 100°F (40°C) during the day and plummet below freezing at night. Since clouds block incoming solar radiation, they have a cooling effect on the surface during the day.

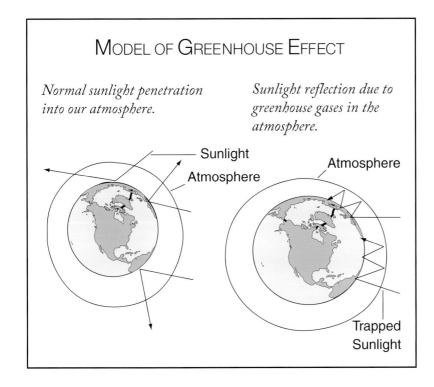

MODEL OF GREENHOUSE EFFECT

Normal sunlight penetration into our atmosphere.

Sunlight reflection due to greenhouse gases in the atmosphere.

Sunlight

Atmosphere

Atmosphere

Trapped Sunlight

An atmosphere with natural levels of greenhouse gases (left) compared to an atmosphere of increased greenhouse effect (right).

Why has the greenhouse effect has been getting so much negative publicity in recent years, when it is necessary to sustain life? The answer is that too much of a good thing, in this case the warming of Earth, can be harmful. The natural systems on Earth exist in a delicate balance and require a specific temperature range. If the heat is turned up, the balance is disrupted. The concentration of some greenhouse gases has increased rapidly in recent years, meaning that more heat is being trapped and returned to Earth. This condition is technically called enhanced greenhouse effect, but is commonly known as global warming.

Carbon dioxide and global warming A majority of planetary and atmospheric scientists now agree that an increase in the amount of carbon dioxide in the atmosphere is almost certainly the primary reason for the enhanced greenhouse effect and the resulting global warming. Carbon dioxide is an industrial byproduct that has been accumulating in the atmosphere since the start of the Industrial Revolution (around 1760–1830). Carbon dioxide is produced by the burning of coal, oil, gas, and wood, and is emitted by factory smokestacks and motor vehicles.

Levels of carbon dioxide, measured at the Mauna Loa Weather Observatory in Hawaii, rose from about 315 parts per million (ppm) in 1960 to about 350 ppm in 1990. During the twentieth century, the level of carbon dioxide in the air rose by 25 percent. In 2001, the rate of increase of carbon dioxide in the atmosphere was about 0.5 percent. Since then, the rate of increase has steadily grown. Atmospheric carbon dioxide levels were 381 ppm in March 2006. Measurements show that 2005 saw one of the largest increases on record, 2.6 ppm, which is a rate of 0.75 percent per year.

Another reason why levels of carbon dioxide are increasing is deforestation, which is the removal of the forests. Deforestation affects the atmosphere in two ways. First, trees naturally absorb carbon dioxide by converting it to oxygen through the process of photosynthesis. With fewer trees, less carbon dioxide is absorbed. Second, in clearing forests to allow for other land use (such as farming), many trees are burned; this places large amounts of carbon dioxide into the atmosphere.

Other greenhouse gases   Carbon dioxide is not the only pollutant responsible for enhancing the greenhouse effect. Concentrations of other greenhouse gases, such as chlorofluorocarbons (CFCs), nitrous oxides, and methane, are also on the rise. While the concentrations of each of these other gases is substantially smaller than the concentration of carbon dioxide, these gases are much more efficient than carbon dioxide at absorbing infrared radiation.

Chlorofluorocarbons are similar to hydrocarbons, except that some or all of the hydrogen atoms have been replaced by chlorine or fluorine atoms. CFCs can be liquids or gases. They are used in refrigerators and air conditioners; as propellants in aerosol spray cans (such as deodorants, spray paints, and hairsprays) and foam-blowing canisters; and in some cleaning solvents.

Nitrous oxides, like carbon dioxide, are emitted from industrial smokestacks and car exhaust systems. They are also components of some fertilizers sprayed on agricultural fields.

Methane is a product of anaerobic (in the absence of oxygen) decay of organic matter. Some sources of methane are swamps, rice paddies, garbage dumps, and livestock operations. Approximately 60 percent of atmospheric methane is the result of human activity. Of that portion, most is due to livestock. By growing rice for millions of people, dumping refuse in landfills, and raising livestock, humans contribute to a rising concentration of methane in the atmosphere. Since methane only survives fifteen to twenty years in the atmosphere, and is twenty times more potent than carbon dioxide as a greenhouse gas, reducing methane emissions could be an effective means of reducing climate warming in a relatively short time.

Consequences of global warming   Recent findings by scientists on the Intergovernmental Panel on Climate Change (IPCC) and others about the trend in global warming maintain that within the next century the world may reach its warmest point in the history of civilization. The effects, according many scientists, could be far-reaching. One consequence of global warming, as discussed above, is an increase in ocean levels around the world. The warmer weather is also expected to alter rainfall patterns, increase the severity of storms, and have negative effects on human health. By many accounts, global warming has already harmed certain animal species. A review of 866 scientific studies in the journal *Annual Review of Ecology, Evolution and Systematics* finds that many species of frogs are becoming extinct, and cold-dependent animal species such as penguins and polar bears are also threatened.

Drought, floods, and storms   Global warming is expected to increase the amount of rainfall in the tropics and produce drought throughout temperate regions (for example, the northern three-quarters of the United States, southern Canada, and much of Europe). In places suffering from a lack of rainfall, crop yields would be lower, and natural vegetation would suffer. Grazing animals would either have to migrate to find food and water or would die off.

Climatologists (scientists who study climate) point to the occurrence, over the last two decades, of two of the most extreme El Niños on record as further evidence of global warming. El Niño is the extraordinarily strong episode of the annual warming of the Pacific waters off the coast of Peru.

Some scientists also assert that global warming has been responsible for recent, unusually severe, weather such as strong blizzards, hurricanes, tornadoes, heat waves (extended periods of high heat and humidity), and wildfires. They warn that these weather disasters will intensify as global warming increases. Other scientists dispute the effect of global warming on the weather, pointing out that there has been no increase in the number of major hurricanes in recent decades.

Risks to human health   By many accounts, global warming is bad for human health. A group of researchers in the United States warns that

The retreating Arctic ice pack is affecting wildlife in the region. Scientists have documented multiple deaths of polar bears off Alaska, where they likely drowned after swimming long distances in the ocean. ©GREENPEACE/HANDOUT/EPA/CORBIS.

the number of U.S. residents dying of heat stress may double by the year 2075 (presently two thousand to three thousand people per year die from heat stress). Sustained rains, predicted for warm regions, may produce flooding that causes drinking water to be contaminated with sewage; people drinking the contaminated water would become sick. Warmer air also increases ground-level ozone pollution (smog), which aggravates symptoms of asthma and other respiratory ailments.

Disruptions to animal life   Many scientists are also concerned about the harm global warming causes to wildlife. "Global climate change has the potential to wipe out more species, faster, than any other single factor," stated Patty Glick, coordinator of the Climate Change and Wildlife Program at the National Wildlife Federation, in a November/December 2000 *International Wildlife* interview. The World Wildlife Fund estimates that 20 percent of species in northern regions, from New England to the North Pole, could die out by the year 2100 because of the loss of habitat brought about by global warming.

As reported by the World Wildlife Federation in June 1999, tropical fish have been forced to migrate to colder waters in search of food. Animals that depend on fish for sustenance, such as sharks, sea lions, and marine birds, have also been forced to migrate or face starvation.

The reason for the migration is that the warming of ocean waters in recent years has led to a reduction of the fishes' food source, ocean

Antarctic penguin species declining

An animal species suffering from higher temperatures in recent years is the Adelie penguin. The Adelies live on the Antarctic continent and on the great sheets of off-shore pack ice. They survive on krill, tiny shrimplike animals that live in the icy waters. The krill, in turn, feed on the algae that bloom within the layers of sea ice and are released into the water as the ice melts.

The Adelies' reproductive cycle is tied to the changing of the seasons. They give birth just at the start of the Antarctic summer, when algae fill the water and krill are plentiful. If the temperature is too high and the thawing begins too early, however, the algae are scattered far and wide (as are the krill) at the time the chicks are born. In that case, the Adelie parents are forced to travel great distances to gather food for their young, all the while leaving their young unattended. A study found that Adelies were spending sixteen hours a day to gather food, up from previous years' average of six hours a day. As a consequence, the young may not get enough food or may fall prey to predatory birds.

Over the last twenty-five years, Adelie penguin populations in areas under study by American researchers have declined dramatically. Numbers of breeding pairs in five large colonies dropped from 15,200 to 9,200, and several small colonies were entirely wiped out. In the last two years alone, the Adelie population in the study area dropped by 10 percent. The decline in Adelies corresponds to an increase in temperature over the last fifty years, during which time Antarctica has become warmer by 3 to 5°F (1.7 to 2.8°C) in the summer and 10°F (5.6°C) in the winter. Seals, whales, and other species of penguins are also threatened by dwindling krill supplies near Antarctica. For example, an average blue whale eats 4 to 6 tons (3.6 to 5.4 metric tons) of krill each day.

plankton, in waters where plankton have traditionally thrived. Plankton are microscopic plants (phytoplankton) and animals (zooplankton) that occupy the bottom rung of the food chain, in which food energy is transferred from one organism to another one as each feeds on another species. Plankton are the beginning of the chain. Off the west coast of North America, plankton populations have decreased by 70 percent since 1977. As a result of that change, there has been a 90 percent decline in seabird populations since 1987.

Effects on arctic wildlife   The effects of global warming on wildlife are seen most vividly in the arctic. In parts of that far northern region, temperatures increased 7 to 10°F (4 to 5.6°C) in the thirty-five-year span from 1965 to 2000. During the 1990s the number of salmon in Alaska's rivers decreased dramatically, as did the numbers of Stellar sea lions and harbor seals in the Bering Sea and Gulf of Alaska. More than one million

The habitat of king penguins, who live in the subantarctic regions, is quickly changing as glaciers in the area are melting. ©MOMATIUK-EASTCOTT/ CORBIS.

seabirds starved to death in the Bering Sea in the years 1997 and 1998 alone, because of dwindling food supplies in the warmer waters.

The warmer weather also triggered much heavier snowfalls in Alaska. For some animals, such as the Peary caribou, the large quantities of snow make it difficult to get to buried food. This factor has led to a reduction in the numbers of this species of small caribou from 24,500 in 1961 to only about 1,000 in the year 2000.

The human factor   Since global warming was identified as a problem in the 1970s, there has been vigorous debate over what role, if any, human activity plays in the trend. Since 1995, however, many global climate scientists agree that increased carbon dioxide levels and other forms of atmospheric pollution are a major factor in contributing to global warming, and that immediate action is necessary. Scientists from a variety of public and private agencies recommend that governments regulate greenhouse gas emissions now, instead of waiting until the problem is worse and the remedy more costly. They warn that even if the emission of pollutants were curbed today, it would take many years for the global warming trend to stop (primarily because heat, stored in the oceans, would continue to be slowly released). There is also debate over the projections of how fast climate changes will occur in the future and the effects of those changes.

Is global warming a natural phenomenon?
Some scientists and others remain skeptical that humans are the primary cause of global warming. They point out that annual average temperatures in the continental United States have varied from decade to decade, with no significant upward or downward trend throughout the century. It was relatively cool from the beginning of the century until 1920; warmed up in the 1920s through the 1950s; cooled down in the 1960s and 1970s; and began warming again in the 1980s. One theory suggested to explain the warm 1990s is that the heat given off by the Sun has increased. In recent years, however, a growing number of corporations have abandoned the position that global warming is not a social problem.

Earth Summit addresses global warming
The debate over the role of human activity in global warming has been carried out all over the world. The first international meeting to address the problem of global warming was held in June 1992 in Rio de Janeiro, Brazil. Formally called the United Nations (U.N.) Conference on Environment and Development, but better known as the Earth Summit, the 1992 meeting was attended by representatives of 178 nations, including 117 heads of state.

One outcome of the Earth Summit was the drafting of a document called the Declaration on Environment and Development, also known as the Rio Declaration. The document spelled out twenty-seven guiding principles of environmentally friendly economic development. Conference attendees came to an informal agreement on the need to change energy policies in order to halt global warming.

The Kyoto conference In December 1997, representatives of 166 nations gathered in Kyoto, Japan, for the U.N. Framework Convention

Global warming and the United States

In June 2000, a report commissioned by the U.S. Congress painted a grim picture of the effect of global warming on the United States. The national assessment report, compiled by scientists from both within and outside of the government, gave a detailed summary of what will likely occur if average temperatures rise 5 to 10°F (2.8 to 5.6°C) over the next century. While recognizing the "significant uncertainties in the science underlying climate-change impacts," the study concluded that "based on the best available information, most Americans will experience significant impacts" from global warming.

The report predicts that as temperatures rise, entire ecosystems will move northward. For instance, as New England warms, that region's sugar maple forests will die off, to be replaced by forests in Canada. Salmon currently inhabiting the Columbia River (in the Pacific Northwest) will be unable to survive in the warmer water, while other warmer-water fish species will move in. The report also warned that rising sea levels may cause coastal marshes and wetlands to spread inland, completely submerging the barrier islands off the coast of the Carolinas.

Among the report's other projections were sweltering heat waves in urban areas, frequent droughts in the Midwest, the conversion of forests in the Southeast into grasslands, the reduction of water levels in the Great Lakes (because of increased evaporation), and damage to roads and buildings in Alaska due to the thawing of the ground.

on Climate Change. The conference focused on the growing problem of global warming and ways to reduce greenhouse emissions.

Delegates to the meeting produced the Kyoto Protocol, a document that called upon industrialized nations (relatively wealthy nations, such as those in North America and western Europe) to take the lead in reducing emissions of greenhouse gases. The protocol specifically directed thirty-six industrialized nations to reduce greenhouse-gas emissions between the years 2008 and 2012 to 5.2 percent below 1990 levels. These nations are the largest producers of greenhouse gases. The United States, for instance, is responsible for 25 percent of global carbon dioxide emissions—more than any other nation. Poorer, developing nations (in Africa, Latin America, parts of Asia, and the Middle East) were spared the treaty's requirements. Conference participants agreed that it would pose too great an economic burden on developing nations to greatly reduce greenhouse emissions.

In November 1998 the administration of President Bill Clinton endorsed the Kyoto Protocol. The signing of the document, however, was largely symbolic since the Senate did not give its approval. (The U.S. Constitution states that all treaties are subject to ratification by two-thirds of the Senate.) Given the treaty's certain defeat in the Senate, President Clinton chose not to put it to a vote.

Senate leaders made their concerns about the Kyoto Protocol clear in a 1997 resolution, passed by a vote of 95–0 shortly after the convention. Senators vowed to oppose the agreement unless it required developing countries to reduce greenhouse emissions during the same time period as mandated for industrialized nations. They pointed out that developing nations, especially India and China, are rapidly increasing their use of fossil fuels.

Despite the United States' refusal to participate in the Kyoto Protocol, it has been signed by 169 countries and other governmental entities and became part of the United Nations Framework Convention on Climate Change on February 16, 2005.

Talks in The Hague end in stalemate   In November 2000, delegates from more than 180 countries met in The Hague, the Netherlands, with the goal of implementing the Kyoto accord. They sought to develop a method for monitoring greenhouse gas emissions and to devise penalties for countries that did not reduce their emissions.

The two-week-long meeting, however, ended without an agreement. The talks broke down over a demand by the United States and some other

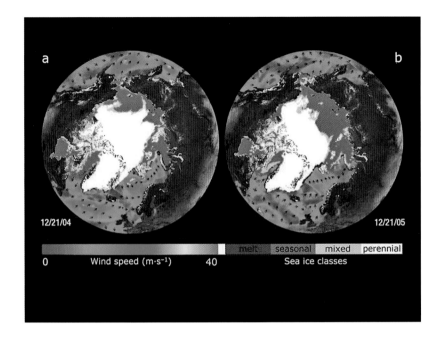

| | | melt | seasonal | mixed | perennial |

0   Wind speed (m·s⁻¹)   40   Sea ice classes

The area of sea ice over the Arctic has shrunk dramatically in the last few years. AP IMAGES.

industrialized nations to receive credit for carbon dioxide "sinks," which are areas covered with vegetation that naturally absorb carbon dioxide, such as forested land and farmland. The credits would have partially offset the amount by which those nations were required to cut their emissions.

The future of global warming

If global warming continues at the current rate, dramatic changes in the global climate are likely. Forests in the U.S. Southeast could be converted to grasslands. Deserts might spread around the globe at middle latitudes. The tropics might become virtually uninhabitable. Paradoxically, some areas might become cooler. For example, if the Gulf Stream (a warm water circulation pattern in the North Atlantic) is diverted to the south by meltwater from the Arctic ice, the British Isles could experience much colder weather.

At the same time, much of the frozen north would thaw and become habitable. The great coniferous forests of Asia, Europe, and North America could be converted to agriculture. The polar regions themselves might be habitable. This would lead to much conflict in areas such as Antarctica, where land would be at a premium. Whatever the ultimate consequences, it is clear that unchecked global climate change will have a profound effect on Earth.

[*See Also* **Climate; El Niño; Flood; Forecasting; Human Influences on Weather and Climate; La Niña; Weather: An Introduction**]

For More Information

BOOKS

Flannery, Tim. *The Weather Makers: How Man Is Changing the Climate and What It Means for Life on Earth.* New York: Atlantic Monthly Press, 2006.

Gore, Al. *An Inconvenient Truth* 2nd ed. New York: Rodale Books, 2006.

Kolber, Elizabeth. *Field Notes from a Catastrophe: Man, Nature, and Climate Change.* New York: Bloomsbury USA, 2006.

Linden, Eugene. *The Winds of Change: Climate, Weather, and the Destruction of Civilizations.* New York: Simon & Schuster, 2006.

Pearce, Fred. *When the Rivers Run Dry: Water—The Defining Crisis of the Twenty-First Century.* Boston, MA: Beacon Press, 2006.

PERIODICALS

Appenzeller, Tim, and Dennis R. Dimick. "Signs from Earth." *National Geographic* (September, 2004): pp. 2–12.

Hayden, Thomas. "Super Storms: No End in Sight." *National Geographic* (August, 2006): pp. 66–77.

Parmesan, Camille. "Ecological and Evolutionary Responses to Recent Climate Change." *Annual Review of Ecology, Evolution, and Systematics*, vol. 37 (December, 2006): pp. 637–669.

Trenberth, Kevin. "Uncertainty in Hurricanes and Global Warming." *Science* (June 17, 2005): pp. 1753–1754.

Zwingle, Erla. "Meltdown: The Alps under Pressure." *National Geographic* (February, 2006): pp. 96–115.

WEB SITES

"Climate Change." *United States Environmental Protection Agency.* <http://www.epa.gov/climatechange/> (accessed March 24, 2007).

"Climate Change Impacts: Feeling the Heat." *Nature Conservancy.* <http://www.nature.org/initiatives/climatechange/issues> (accessed March 24, 2007).

"Climate Change." *World Wildlife Fund.* <http://www.panda.org/about_wwf/what_we_do/climate_change/index.cfm> (accessed March 24, 2007).

"Climate Change." *New Scientist: Environment.* <http://environment.newscientist.com/channel/earth/climate-change> (accessed March 25, 2007).

De Roy, Tui. "Caught In a Melting World: Adelie Penguins May Be the Canaries in the Coal Mines of Global Warming." *International Wildlife*

(November-December, 2000). <http://findarticles.com/p/articles/mi_m1170/is_2000_Nov-Dec/ai_66309910/pg_1> (accessed April 25, 2007.)

Intergovernmental Panel of Climate Change. <http://www.ipcc.ch/> (accessed April 25, 2007).

"Working Together." *The Pew Center on Global Climate Change.* <http://www.pewclimate.org> (accessed March 25, 2007).

Human Influences on Weather and Climate

Human activity affects weather, climate, and the environment. Some human activity is harmless, but much human activity degrades the environment. While the environment can absorb some abuse without long-term effects, much harmful human activity exceeds the environment's ability to recover. The most significant way that humans damage the environment is by emitting harmful chemicals into the air and water. This activity has wide-ranging results, such as increasing the temperature of the planet, lowering the quality of the air we breathe, and killing forests and aquatic animals. (Global warming, the worldwide increase in atmospheric temperature, is discussed in detail in "Climate Change and Global Warming".) Other environmental consequences include air pollution and smog, acid rain, and ozone depletion. Each of these have multiple effects and there is mounting evidence that they result in increased impact on the environment over the last few years. The search for solutions to these environmental problems has yielded some results, including promising research on alternative energy sources.

Air pollution

Air pollution is the presence of high concentrations of undesirable gases and particles in the air. Although some air pollution is caused by natural processes, such as volcanic eruptions and wildfires, much is the result of human activity and is emitted by smokestacks and car exhaust systems. According to the U.S. Centers for Disease Control, air pollution contributes to between 50,000 and 120,000 deaths in the United States (primarily due to asthma, heart disease, and bronchitis) each year. Estimated yearly costs of treating illnesses in the United States triggered by air pollution are between $40 and $50 billion. In addition to posing a hazard to the health of humans and all other living things, air pollution creates unpleasant odors and diminishes the planet's natural beauty.

WORDS TO KNOW

acid precipitation: rain and snow that are made more acidic when carbon, sulfur, and/or nitrogen oxides in the air dissolve into water. Also known as acid rain.

active solar collector: system for gathering and storing the Sun's heat that uses pumps and motors. Is often used for heating water.

air pollutant: any harmful substance that exists in the atmosphere at concentrations great enough to endanger the health of living organisms.

Air Quality Index (AQI): measurement of air quality, based on concentrations of surface ozone averaged over an eight-hour period for specific locations.

chlorofluorocarbons (CFCs): compounds similar to hydrocarbons in which one or more of the hydrogen atoms are replaced by fluorine or chlorine.

Clean Air Act: set of environmental regulations limiting pollutants emitted by cars, factories, and other sources. First enacted by the U.S. Congress in 1970 and updated several times since then.

Environmental Protection Agency (EPA): government agency charged with implementing the provisions of the Clean Air Act.

fossil fuels: coal, oil, and natural gas—materials composed of the remains of plants or animals that lived on Earth millions of years ago and are today burned for fuel.

fuel cell: device that generates electricity by combining hydrogen and oxygen; it emits water vapor as a by-product.

global warming: the observed global increase in atmospheric temperature. Also called global climate change.

greenhouse effect: the warming of Earth due to the presence of greenhouse gases, which trap upwardly radiating heat and return it to Earth's surface.

While air quality has improved in the last three decades, half of all U.S. citizens live in counties where air pollution exceeds national health standards. Every large city in the world currently experiences some degree of air pollution. In a report released in 2004, the American Lung Association reported that particulate matter (fine particles suspended in the air) is an especially difficult problem. According to the report:

- 81 million Americans live in areas with unhealthy short-term levels of particulates
- 66 million Americans live in areas with unhealthy year-round levels of particle pollution
- 136 million Americans live in counties with unhealthy levels of ozone

greenhouse gases: gases that trap heat in the atmosphere. The most abundant greenhouse gases are water vapor and carbon dioxide. Others include methane, nitrous oxide, and chlorofluorocarbons.

ozone days: days on which the smog threshold is surpassed.

particulates: small particles suspended in the air and responsible for most atmospheric haze. Particulates can irritate the lungs and cause lung disease with long exposure.

passive solar collector: system for collecting and storing the Sun's heat that has no moving parts and is generally used for home heating.

photochemical smog: a hazy layer containing ozone and other gases that sometimes appears brown. It is produced when pollutants that are released by car exhaust fumes react with strong sunlight.

photovoltaic cell: light-sensitive device containing semiconductor crystals (materials that conduct an electric current under certain conditions) that convert sunlight to electricity. Also called solar cells.

phytoplankton: tiny marine plants that occupy the lowest level of the food chain.

skin cancer: a disease of the skin caused primarily by exposure to the ultraviolet rays in sunlight.

smog: common name for photochemical smog—a layer of hazy, brown air pollution at Earth's surface comprised of ozone and other chemicals.

smog threshold: the level of smog allowed by law and set by the Environmental Protection Agency at 80 parts per billion (ppb) of surface ozone.

unhealthy air days: days on which surface ozone levels reach 80 parts per billion—a concentration considered unhealthy to children, people with respiratory problems, and adults who exercise or work vigorously outdoors.

wind farm: a large group of interconnected wind turbines.

wind power: power, in the form of electricity, derived from the wind.

wind turbine: a windmill designed to convert the kinetic energy of wind into electrical energy.

- 159 million Americans live in counties with one of the three conditions: unhealthy levels of ozone, unhealthy short-term levels of particulates, or unhealthy year-round levels of particulates
- 46 million Americans live in counties where all three levels are unhealthy

In a report published in 2001, the World Health Organization estimates that 1.5 billion city dwellers face levels of outdoor air pollution that are above the maximum recommended levels. According to the report, about half a million deaths each year can be attributed just to particulate matter and to sulfur dioxide in outdoor air. While air pollution is usually considered a problem of developed countries, as a result of their high level of industrial activity and vehicle use, more than 70 percent

A factory emitting chemical pollutants into the atmosphere. ©GEORGE LEPP/CORBIS.

of deaths from outdoor air pollution occur in the developing world. In developing nations, populations tend to be larger and pollution standards often are less strict than in the more developed nations.

Air pollution in history   Air pollution by humans is as old as the discovery of how to make fire. Air pollution first emerged as a public concern around the twelfth century, when legislation was passed in England restricting coal burning. By the mid-1600s, coal burning had noticeably worsened the quality of the air, particularly in London. By the mid-1800s, London's air was so thick with soot and smoke it was described as "pea soup."

London's air pollution was not only unsightly, it was deadly. In two incidents, one in 1873 and the other in 1911, the "pea-soup fog," sometimes called smog (combining the words "smoke" and "fog"), claimed nearly two thousand lives. It was not until a five-day bout of smog killed nearly four thousand Londoners in 1952 that legislation was passed to curb the pollution. The Clean Air Act of 1956 was an act of the Parliament of the United Kingdom in response to the Great Smog of 1952. The act banned the burning of peat and soft coal, which are relatively cheap and easy to obtain, but produce excessive amounts of soot and smoke. Instead, households were encouraged to burn gas, oil, or hard coal (anthracite), or convert to electrical heat.

Air pollution is not limited to Britain. The problem exists worldwide, especially where industrialization is coupled with lax, unenforced, or ineffective environmental regulations.

The United States has had a problem with air pollution for the last century or more. The soot from burning coal blanketed St. Louis, Missouri, and Pittsburgh, Pennsylvania, in the first half of the twentieth century. This type of pollution has given way in many large cities to photochemical smog, which is formed by the interaction of sunlight with unburned hydrocarbons from industrial process, gas stations, petroleum processing, and automobile exhaust. The problem is not limited to urban areas; polluted air blankets many beautiful natural areas as well. Big Bend National Park in far west Texas is plagued each summer by haze that may come from as far away as the petroleum processing facilities along the Texas Gulf Coast.

Air pollution   An air pollutant is any harmful substance that exists in the atmosphere at concentrations great enough to endanger the health of

Smog hangs over farmland outside of Beijing, China, 2006. AP IMAGES.

living organisms. An air pollutant may take the form of a gas, a liquid, or a solid (such as particulates). When a pollutant is emitted directly into the air, it is called a primary air pollutant. A primary air pollutant may undergo chemical reactions with water, sunlight, or other pollutants, and produce additional pollutants, called secondary air pollutants.

Some substances that exist naturally in the air in small concentrations, such as carbon monoxide and sulfur dioxide, are considered pollutants at higher concentrations. Other substances that do not occur naturally, such as benzene, can cause damage to organisms even at very low concentrations.

Pollutants make their way into the air either through natural processes or by human activities. Examples of natural processes that put pollutants in the air include forest fires, dispersed pollen, wind-blown soil, volcanic eruptions, and organic decay.

The primary human-related cause of air pollution is motor vehicle emissions. Other examples of human-created pollution include: the combustion of fuel for generating heat and electricity in "stationary" sources such as houses, power plants, and office buildings; industrial processes such as paper mills, oil refineries, chemical production plants, and ore smelting; the breakdown of organic waste at landfills; and crop dusting with pesticides or insecticides.

The amount of air pollution produced in the United States is difficult to calculate accurately. The best estimates are that in 2001, somewhere

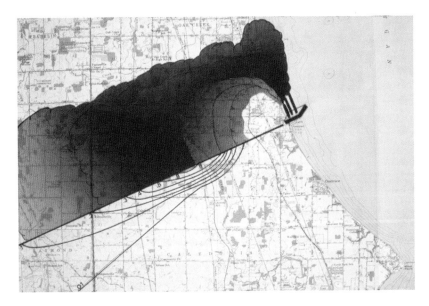

A computer model of power plant pollution. FMA, INC.

between 150 million and 300 million tons (130 to 270 million metric tons) of air pollutants were produced, an average of around 0.5 to 1.0 tons (0.45 to 0.89 metric tons) per year for every man, woman, and child living in the United States. About 63 million tons (56 metric tons) of pollutants were produced by motor vehicles alone. Due in part to federal and state regulations designed to reduce air pollution, total emissions of select air pollutants in the United States decreased by 25 percent between 1970 and 2001.

Categories of major air pollutants and their effects   There are several different categories of air pollutants. One major category includes particulate matter, which are solid or liquid particles that are tiny enough to be suspended in the air. Air pollution created by particulate matter is the most visible type of air pollution. Some forms of particulate matter, such as dust, smoke, and pollen, are irritating to humans, but not toxic. Other types of particulate matter, such as asbestos fibers, arsenic, sulfuric acids, and a number of pesticides, are toxic. Long-term exposure to toxic particulate matter causes a variety of recurring health problems.

Certain types of heavy metal particulate matter, namely iron, copper, nickel, and lead, cause respiratory illnesses. Lead particles

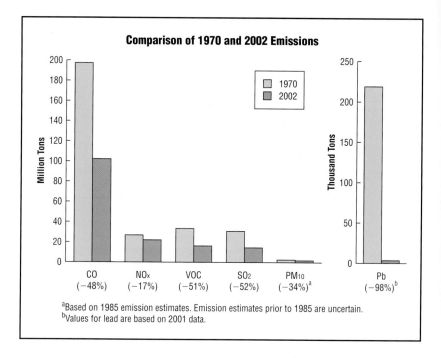

Emissions have decreased since 1970.

accumulate in body tissues and can damage the central nervous system. At high enough concentrations, lead is fatal. Levels of lead in the air have been greatly reduced in recent years because of laws requiring the use of lead-free gasoline.

One of the most widespread gaseous air pollutants is carbon monoxide (CO). Carbon monoxide is produced by the combustion of carbon-containing fuels. It is emitted by car exhaust, home heating systems, and industrial smokestacks. Carbon monoxide is colorless, odorless, and poisonous. Due to recently adopted air-quality standards, CO levels in the United States have been reduced by about 40 percent since the early 1970s. When it collects in enclosed places, CO can cause unconsciousness, and even death.

A colorless, but not odorless, polluting gas is sulfur dioxide (SO_2). Sulfur dioxide is produced during the burning of coal and oil, primarily in power plants, petroleum refineries, ore smelting plants, and paper mills. The gas causes a host of respiratory problems in humans and has been shown to reduce the yield of certain crops, such as lettuce and spinach. After clean air standards were enacted, SO_2 concentrations in the United States declined by 48 percent between 1980 and 2005.

Methane is another gaseous air pollutant. It is also a greenhouse gas, which means it traps heat in the atmosphere and therefore contributes to the greenhouse effect, which warms Earth. Methane belongs to a class of organic compounds called hydrocarbons whose molecules are formed from chains of one or more carbon atoms with hydrogen atoms attached to the chain. Hydrocarbons that evaporate into the air easily are in a class called volatile organic compounds (VOCs). There are thousands of VOCs, which may be in solid, liquid, or gaseous states at room temperature. Some, such as methane, are naturally occurring and pose little danger to human health at low concentrations other than as a greenhouse gas. Other VOCs, such as formaldehyde and chlorofluorocarbons, are dangerous. Some VOCs, such as benzene and benzopyrene, are carcinogens (cancer-causing substances). The primary sources of VOCs that pose a threat to human health are emissions by motor vehicles and industrial processes.

Nitrogen oxides are also a major air pollutant. The oxides of nitrogen include nitrogen dioxide (NO_2) and nitrogen oxide (NO). These gases can be produced naturally, by the action of bacteria, but they are also produced during fuel combustion, through the combination of nitrogen and oxygen. Due to fuel combustion (which occurs in motor vehicles and industrial processes), nitrogen oxide levels are up to one hundred times greater in cities than they are outside of urban areas. While nitrogen oxides are usually colorless, at high enough concentrations (such as those that exist over Los Angeles), nitrogen dioxide takes on a reddish-brown color.

High levels of nitrogen oxides may cause a higher incidence of some types of cancer in humans and may make the body more susceptible to heart and lung disease. Nitrogen oxides also undergo reactions with other chemicals in the air that result in increased levels of photochemical smog.

Photochemical smog   In the United States, photochemical smog is commonly referred to simply as "smog." It is different from the pea-soup smog of London, which is a combination of sulfurous smoke and fog. Photochemical smog is a layer of air pollution near Earth's surface. This is the type of smog familiar to residents of Los Angeles and other large cities. The main component of smog is ozone, an odorless, colorless gas composed of three atoms of oxygen. Near-surface ozone is formed when nitrogen oxides and hydrocarbons (chemicals emitted by car

Smog covers the Los Angeles basin, California. FMA, INC.

exhaust systems, coal-burning power plants, chemical plants, oil refineries, aircraft, and other sources) react with strong sunlight.

Surface ozone is characterized by the Environmental Protection Agency (EPA), the U.S. government agency that deals with air pollution, as "the most widespread and persistent urban pollution problem." Surface ozone differs from "good" ozone in Earth's upper atmosphere. Upper atmosphere ozone shields us from the Sun's harmful ultraviolet rays.

Photochemical smog is difficult to see at ground level. When looking down at it from above, however, it appears as a brown haze. Photochemical smog is irritating to the eyes and throat.

The continuing saga of smog   Smog in the United States, while down from its peak in 1988, is a continuing problem. In the 1980s, the federal government imposed a series of laws mandating cleaner exhaust from cars, smokestacks, and other sources of pollution. Those measures are credited for keeping the smog problem in check. At the same time that emission systems have become cleaner, however, there has also been a rise in the consumption of fossil fuels, like coal, oil, and natural gas. The increasing number of motorists, using greater amounts of gasoline, as well as the burning of increasing quantities of coal by utility companies, at least partially offsets any gains made in air quality.

The persistence of pollution by near-surface ozone (a primary component of photochemical smog) is particularly puzzling because emissions of the two ozone precursors, oxides of nitrogen and volatile organic compounds, have been declining in the United States and are tightly regulated by federal and state governments. Levels of other air pollutants regulated by the EPA, such as particulates, lead, sulfur dioxide, nitrogen dioxide, and carbon monoxide, have fallen by half or more since 1970.

In 2005, the EPA completed phasing in new standards for ozone, the so-called "smog threshold." The old standard allowed 120 parts per billion (ppb) of ozone averaged over a one-hour period. The new standard sets a limit of 80 ppb, averaged over a longer eight-hour period. (The old standard remains in effect for a region until that region meets or exceeds the old standard for three years in a row.) The U.S. government imposes penalties, such as withholding highway funds, on states that frequently surpass the threshold. Days on which the threshold is surpassed are called "ozone days."

Ozone concentrations of 80 ppb or higher are considered unhealthy to children, people with respiratory problems (such as asthma or emphysema), and adults who exercise or work vigorously outdoors. The EPA considers those categories of people "sensitive groups." Days on which ozone levels reach 80 ppb are considered "unhealthy air days." Ozone concentrations of 105 ppb or higher pose a health risk to the general population.

When the ozone concentration reaches 105 ppb, the government issues health advisories, cautioning people to remain indoors as much as possible and to avoid exertion outdoors. Such days are known as "shut-in days." The year 1988 logged the greatest number of ozone days for many eastern cities since smog record-keeping began in 1974. New York City, for example, had forty-three ozone days in 1988. Since 1998, the number of ozone days has generally declined. This is probably due to a reduction of smokestack emissions and different weather conditions in smog-prone areas.

The Air Quality Index   To simplify air quality reporting, the EPA has developed the Air Quality Index (AQI) for specific locations. The index is based on concentrations of each of four major air pollutants regulated by the Clean Air Act, passed by Congress in 1970 and updated several times since then: ground-level ozone, particle pollution (also known as particulate matter), carbon monoxide, and sulfur dioxide. Each is each averaged over

Brush fires send thick haze over Kuala Lumpur, Malaysia, disrupting traffic and triggering health warnings, 2006. AP IMAGES.

some period of time, such as eight hours for ozone. According to the EPA, the use of a standardized measure makes it easier for people decide when to take precautions. The AQI is a "yardstick" used to measure health risks. The AQI is set so that a value of 100 corresponds to the national air quality standard for that pollutant. An AQI below 50 represents good air quality. When the AQI is higher than 100, people in sensitive groups are encouraged to limit their time outdoors. An AQI higher than 151 is considered unhealthy for the general population, in which case everyone is advised to limit their outdoor activity.

Nitrogen dioxide is no longer reported separately because the concentrations of nitrogen dioxide have remained very low for several years. However, nitrogen dioxide remains an important contributor to the formation of ozone, which is reported.

Under the Clean Air Act, metropolitan areas with populations over 350,000 are required to publicize the AQI when pollution levels are high; AQI reports are typically included in weather pages of newspapers. Some state and local air quality agencies declare "ozone action days" when the AQI reaches unhealthy levels. On ozone action days, residents are encouraged to limit automobile use, fill gas tanks only after dusk, conserve electricity, and reduce the use of air conditioners.

Record levels of smog set in 2002   Despite advances in air pollution, record smog was recorded in 2002. According to a report released by the Public Interest Research Group (PIRG), a private research organization, smog monitors in forty-one states and the District of Columbia recorded unhealthy levels of air pollution on some 8,800 separate occasions in 2002. This was a 90 percent increase over 2001. The report found that every region of the country exceeded the national health standard for ozone more often in 2002 than 2001, with the largest increases in midwestern, southeastern, and central states. California, Texas, and Tennessee led the nation in 2002 with the most smog days, which PIRG defines as days on which at least one ozone monitor in the state exceeds the national health standard. In addition, sixteen monitors at eleven national parks, including the Great Smokey Mountains and Yosemite, recorded levels of ozone in excess of the national health standard a total of 418 times during 2002.

Los Angeles: The bad news and the good news Due to its large population and high number of sunny, warm days, Los Angeles, California, has the worst smog problem in the United States. Between 1980 and 2006 the population of the city of Los Angeles grew 38 percent, to over four million. During the 1980s, the number of miles being logged by motorists increased 75 percent; however, between 1990 and 2000 the increase was only 13 percent. Los Angeles leads the nation in the number of motor vehicles with an average 1.8 registered automobiles per licensed driver. But the main problem in Los Angeles is not the number of cars, miles driven, or number of drivers. The problem is widely considered to be congestion. Los Angeles drivers do not travel an excessive amount, but due to congestion, the number of hours spent idling in traffic is much greater. As a consequence, the skyline of downtown Los Angeles is blanketed in the summer by a nearly permanent reddish-brown haze.

There were sixty-two days in 1998 in which smog levels were above the federal threshold of 120 ppb in Los Angeles. Conditions improved

What level is healthy?

The EPA uses a standard system for qualitatively reporting the health effects of each of the major pollutants, based on the AQI for that pollutant.

- Good air quality: No health impacts are expected when air quality is in this range.
- Moderate air quality: Unusually sensitive people should consider limiting prolonged outdoor exertion.
- Unhealthy air quality for sensitive groups: Active children and adults, and people with respiratory disease, such as asthma, should limit prolonged outdoor exertion.
- Unhealthy air quality: Active children and adults, and people with respiratory disease, such as asthma, should limit prolonged outdoor exertion; everyone else, especially children, should limit prolonged outdoor exertion.
- Very unhealthy air quality: Active children and adults, and people with respiratory disease, such as asthma, should avoid all outdoor exertion; everyone else, especially children, should limit outdoor exertion.
- Hazardous air quality: Government will issue health warnings of emergency conditions. The entire population is likely to be affected.

slightly in 1999, and over the summer Los Angeles passed on the notorious distinction of having the worst summertime smog day to Texas City, Texas. The respite for Los Angeles was only temporary, however. Since 1999, Los Angeles and Southern California have regained the dubious status as the smoggiest place in the United States. In 2004, the American Lung Association listed the ten worst places to live. The Los Angeles area topped the list. Four of the worst five counties were in Southern California. The Texas Gulf Coast industrial complex was bumped back down to fifth place.

1. Los Angeles-Riverside-Orange County, CA
2. Fresno, CA
3. Bakersfield, CA
4. Visalia-Porterville, CA
5. Houston-Baytown-Huntsville, TX
6. Merced, CA
7. Sacramento-Arden-Arcade-Truckee, CA-NV
8. Hanford-Corcoran, CA
9. Knoxville-Sevierville, LA and Follette, TN
10. Dallas-Fort Worth, TX

In 1967, the U.S. Congress gave California the right to require tighter auto-emissions standards than the rest of the country. Los Angeles's cars and trucks, and its industry, are now among the cleanest in the nation; yet its pollution remains among the worst. Why is the smog in Los Angeles so bad?

Ozone, the main constituent of smog, is created when ultraviolet (UV)rays from the Sun stimulate chemical reactions between nitrogen oxides and volatile organic compounds (VOCs). These photochemical reactions increase as the concentrations of nitrogen oxides, VOCs, UV, and the air temperature all increase. The climate and topography (shape of the land surface) in Los Angeles combine to make it a near-perfect candidate for smog. For half the year, Los Angeles has hot and dry weather. Mountains to the north, east and south trap the air from generally light ocean breezes. The nitrogen oxides and VOCs from traffic and industry accumulate and smog forms under the action of the famous Southern California sun. It rarely rains in Southern California in the summer, so smog is not washed out of the air.

California continues to take steps to battle smog. The EPA recently granted California's request for a "preemption" of federal air standards

Even natural areas suffer from smog

A 1999 study by a coalition of environmental groups demonstrated that no place in the United States is immune from smog. The group found, in fact, that many summer vacation places are just as smoggy as the cities vacationers leave behind. For instance, in the Great Smoky Mountains (the half-million acre park on the Tennessee-North Carolina border), like other natural areas, receive pollution from upwind coal-burning power plants (some are hundreds of miles away) as well as from visitors' motor vehicles. Due to the effects of ozone and acid rain (rain that is made more acidic by sulfuric and/or nitric acid in the air), some thirty species of plants in the Great Smoky Mountains National Park have been damaged or wiped out. Other natural areas that suffer smog in similar concentrations as big cities include the northern tip of Cape Cod; Acadia National Park on the coast of Maine; the Indiana Dunes on Lake Michigan; and the Hamptons on New York's Long Island.

On Earth Day in April 1999, Vice President Al Gore announced the goal of restoring clear vistas to our national parks by 2064. To implement this goal, President Bill Clinton's administration proposed a set of new clean-air guidelines for 37 national parks and 119 wilderness areas. On June 15, 2005, the EPA issued final amendments to its July 1999 regional haze rule. These amendments apply to the provisions of the regional haze rule that require emission controls known as Best Available Retrofit Technology (BART) for industrial facilities emitting air pollutants that reduce visibility. These pollutants include fine particulate matter and compounds which contribute to particulate formation, such as oxides of nitrogen, sulfur dioxide, volatile organic compounds, and ammonia. The amendments include final guidelines, known as BART guidelines, for states to use in determining which facilities must install controls and the type of controls the facilities must use.

for small nonroad engines such as lawn mowers. In addition, in 2005 California adopted a more stringent standard for ozone of 70 ppb averaged over an eight-hour period (the federal standard is 80 ppb averaged over an eight-hour period). From 2007 on, small engines sold in California will have to meet much stricter emissions requirements.

Temperature inversions The effects of air pollution are most intense when an inversion exists in the atmosphere. An inversion occurs when a layer of warm air exists above a colder layer of surface air. The warm air acts like a lid, preventing the surface air from rising. An inversion may last for several days.

Normally, the concentration of pollutants in urban areas is moderated by the upward motion of air, as well as the horizontal motion of winds. When an inversion forms, however, it traps air pollutants close to the ground. After several days of an inversion, the concentration of smog

Ways You Can Reduce Smog

The following list includes steps you can take, and encourage your family to take, to reduce smog.

- Instead of driving, walk, ride bikes, or take public transportation whenever possible.
- When driving is necessary, arrange car pools.
- Use a manual lawn mower instead of one that is fueled by gasoline or electricity.
- Keep your car tuned up, so it uses gasoline as efficiently as possible.
- Conserve energy. Turn off unnecessary lights and appliances.
- When filling the tank of your car, snowmobile, or other equipment, do not allow gasoline to spill; after filling, close the gas cap tightly.
- Use nontoxic cleaning supplies and paints whenever possible.
- Tightly seal the lids of household cleaners, garden chemicals, paint thinners, and other chemical products in order to prevent evaporation of toxic chemicals.

may increase to the point that cars must drive with their lights on, even during the day, and people with asthma suffer a marked increase in attacks.

Smog and human health Photochemical smog takes the greatest toll on children, people with asthma or other respiratory disorders, and people who do strenuous work or exercise outdoors. About one-third of all Americans belong to these groups, considered "sensitive groups" by the EPA. People in the sensitive groups are urged to limit their time outdoors and not exert themselves when ozone levels are high.

Ozone irritates the respiratory system, causing symptoms such as coughing, sneezing, sore throat, and difficulty taking deep breaths. Some people respond to smog with chest pains, burning eyes, headaches, and dizziness. In the presence of high levels of ozone, people with asthma are more prone to asthma attacks. One reason for this is that the allergic response to elements that trigger asthma attacks, such as dust mites, pollens, fungus, pets, and cockroaches, is heightened when ozone is strong.

Ozone also has the potential to damage the lining of the lung. When cells in the lung die after a high ozone day, the lung repairs itself by manufacturing new cells. Repeated assault on the lungs by high levels of ozone, however, can cause permanent lung damage. Ozone also aggravates emphysema, bronchitis, and other lung diseases, and sometimes weakens the body's ability to fight off bacterial infection in the lungs. If children are repeatedly exposed to dangerous levels of ozone, scientists fear that they may experience reduced lung function as adults. A 1998 study in Los Angeles found that when ozone levels are high, there is a marked increase in the numbers of people hospitalized with lung and heart ailments.

Clean-air legislation In 1970, the U.S. Congress enacted the first Clean Air Act: a law regulating the air pollutants emitted by cars, factories, and other sources. The act required the Environmental Protection Agency (EPA) to set air quality standards, to enforce those standards in every state, and to update the standards as necessary to "protect public health with an adequate margin of safety."

In 1977, when it became apparent that most states were failing to meet the clean-air standards set in 1970, the Clean Air Act was amended with new target dates for compliance. The amended law also exempted older, coal-burning power plants from many of the act's requirements. EPA officials reasoned that the plants would soon be retired, and therefore that expensive smokestack renovations would not be worth the money. However, many of the older power plants, especially those in the Midwest were still running twenty years later.

In 1997, EPA administrator Carol Browning announced a tough new set of clean-air regulations that would be implemented in 2008. The allowable level for ozone was lowered. The 1997 rules also called for a sharp reduction of harmful emissions (specifically nitrogen oxides, the main cause of smog) coming from twenty-two states east of the Mississippi River, beginning in 2003. The new rules took aim at power plants in the Midwest and East, especially those exempted by the 1977 rule.

Lawyers for utility companies sought relief from the new air-quality rules in the District of Columbia Circuit Court of Appeals. On May 14, 1999, the court ruled in favor of the utility companies and set aside the EPA's stricter emissions restrictions. The court also voided the new ozone limit of 80 ppb.

In response, EPA officials worked hard to restore the 1997 amendments, petitioning the courts to rehear parts of the case. After further legal

What do lawn mowers and airplanes have in common?

Both airplanes and lawn mowers emit a lot of air pollution. Lawn mowers, chain saws, weed trimmers, and leaf blowers emit large amounts of carbon monoxide and several smog-forming, particulate-matter pollutants. Since a lawn mower has none of the emission control systems of a car, its pollution goes directly into the air.

Using a gasoline-powered lawn mower produces the equivalent pollution of driving a car for several hundred miles. It has been estimated that backyard power tools produce 5 to 10 percent of all the nation's smog-forming pollutants. One way to cut down on this pollution is to retire old lawn mowers in favor of one of the cleaner models introduced to the market in 1996, or to use a manual push-mower.

An airplane burns fossil fuel and releases pollutants into the air from each of its several engines. In addition to emitting about 3 percent of all carbon dioxide due to human activities worldwide, airplane engines also give off carbon particles (soot), sulfur dioxides, and nitrogen oxides.

At present there are about fifteen thousand commercial jet aircraft worldwide. Industry experts expect that number to double within twenty years. Scientists from the National Aeronautics and Space Administration (NASA) are currently conducting tests to more accurately determine what quantities of pollutants are produced by aircraft.

arguments, in March 2000, the D.C. Circuit Court issued a ruling that supported most portions of EPA's rules on limits of nitrogen oxides. However, the court required the EPA to reexamine several matters before moving ahead. By 2004, the EPA had finalized all the steps it had to take in response to the courts rulings, including separating the rules on nitrogen oxides into two phases.

In 2005, the EPA established other clean-air rules—the Clean Air Interstate Rule (CAIR), the Clean Air Mercury Rule (CAMR), and the Clean Air Visibility Rule (CAVR). The CAIR limits emissions of sulfur dioxide and nitrogen oxides in the eastern United States while the CAVR limits sulfur dioxide and nitrogen oxides emissions in the western United States. The CAMR limits nationwide mercury emissions.

However, legal battles and legislative debates continue. Of particular concern to many is the EPA's handling of New Source Review (NSR). On December 31, 2002, exactly thirty-two years after President Richard Nixon signed the Clean Air Act into law, the George W. Bush administration announced provisions that many considered significant rollbacks to NSR pollution control provisions. According to critics, the new rules would allow virtually all pollution increases from old, high-polluting sources to go unregulated and communities would not have any way to know when a nearby power plant is increasing the amount of pollutants pumped into the air. The new regulations went into effect in March 2003.

The Clean Air Act remains a work in progress. Further legal and legislative actions are possible as different parties gain control of the political process and environmental laws and regulations continue to evolve.

Acid rain

A secondary effect of air pollution is the acidification of rain. Acid rain (or more accurately acid precipitation) is rain, sleet, snow, fog, or hail that is made more acidic by pollutants in the air (rain is naturally slightly acidic). This occurs as a result of acid deposition, which is the deposit of acid particles by either wet (rain or snow) or dry (dust or gas) means. The primary pollutants responsible for acid deposition, sulfur dioxide and nitrogen oxides, are both by-products of the burning of fossil fuels. These pollutants are emitted by car exhaust systems, coal-burning power plants, chemical plants, oil refineries, aircraft, and other sources. They react with moisture in the air to produce sulfuric acid and nitric acid.

Acid rain raises the acidity of lakes and rivers in sensitive areas, making them inhospitable to many species of animals. It also kills trees and has been shown to harm human health. Sensitive areas include portions of the northeastern United States, eastern Canada, and northern Europe, where the bedrock is primarily granite. In areas where the bedrock is limestone, acid rain is not much of a problem because the acid combines with the limestone to produce harmless carbon dioxide.

Acid rain corrodes the surfaces of rocks, dissolving minerals, such as aluminum, that are harmful to living organisms. Aluminum is one of the most harmful substances dissolved by acid rain. When it washes into lake and rivers, it hampers the ability of fish to absorb oxygen through their gills. Dissolved aluminum has caused the deaths of entire fish populations in hundreds of highly acidic lakes and rivers in North America (especially in the northeastern United States and Canada) and in northern Europe.

Aluminum that is washed into the soil prevents the roots of trees from absorbing essential nutrients, ultimately killing the trees. Acid rain also makes plants more susceptible to frost, insects, and disease. In some areas where acid rain is a serious problem, entire forests have been wiped out. In Europe, so many trees have been stunted or killed that a new word, *Waldsterben* (forest death), has become part of the vocabulary.

Acid rain has also been shown to harm human health. In children, exposure to acid rain (and other forms of acid in the air or water such as acid fog, acid mist, acid snow, and acid dust) aggravates asthma. Even in healthy people, acid air pollutants can cause lung damage.

Acid rain damages property, too. It gradually dissolves marble—the stone from which many statues are made. Around the world, outdoor art classics are losing fingers, toes, and noses to acid rain. In Washington, D.C., in the mid-1990s, for instance, a marble sculpture of the Shakespearean character Puck lost an entire hand.

The acid rain express   The parts of the world most affected by acid rain at present are the northeastern United States, southeastern Canada, central Europe, and Scandinavia. These locations, however, are not necessarily home to the greatest producers of acid rain-forming pollution.

Trees in the Great Smoky Mountains killed by acid rain. Aluminum washed into the soil prevents the roots of trees from absorbing essential nutrients.
JLM VISUALS.

Airborne pollutants can travel for great distances before returning to Earth. For this reason, acid rain can affect ecosystems in even remote parts of the world, far from industrial centers. It is believed that

Sweden's acid rain problem, for instance, originates in England's smokestacks.

In the United States, the primary generators of sulfur dioxide and nitrogen oxides are large electrical power plants in the Midwest. The coal used in those plants, mined from midwestern and Appalachian coalfields, is particularly high in sulfur. The pollution from the midwestern power plants rises high in the air and is carried eastward and northeastward by the wind. When the pollution descends, it may mix with precipitation to form acid rain or acid snow. In dry regions the pollution falls to the ground as acid gas or acid dust.

The acidification of lakes, rivers, and forests is a serious problem throughout the eastern portion of the United States. Some of the areas most affected by acid rain are Maine, Vermont, New York, the upper peninsula of Michigan, Virginia, West Virginia, Maryland, Tennessee, and North Carolina.

Clean Air Act takes aim at acid rain

The 1990 amendments to the Clean Air Act contained provisions for controlling emissions, especially sulfur dioxide, that cause acid rain. The amendments required a reduction of sulfur dioxide emissions by power plants to 40 percent of 1980 levels. The law specifically targeted 110 big coal-burning power plants in 21 midwestern, Appalachian, northeastern, and southeastern states.

The emissions reduction was to be achieved by issuing each plant a certain number of emission allowances, beginning in 1995. Each allowance permits a plant to emit 1 ton (0.91 metric tons) of sulfur dioxide. Plants were barred from emitting more sulfur dioxide than their allowances stated. The number of allowances for each plant was set below that plant's 1990 level of sulfur dioxide releases.

Lakes remain acidic even as sulfur emissions drop Since the 1970s, when acid precipitation was identified as the cause of dying trees and the term "acid rain" was popularized, nations in North America and northern Europe have required factories to reduce their sulfur dioxide emissions. A study released in October 1999 showed that levels of sulfur compounds (the primary components of acid rain) in lakes and rivers at two hundred sites on both continents have decreased. The study's bad news, however, was that the acidity of many of the bodies of water tested has not declined and that bodies of water damaged by acid rain show no signs of recovery.

The study, undertaken by an international team of twenty-three scientists, found reduced acidity (on the order of 25 percent) in some lakes and rivers in Vermont, Quebec, and northern Europe. The remaining portions of North American included in the study, stretching from Maine to the Midwest, had unchanged levels of acidity in bodies of water.

Trout streams suffering in Virginia

If the state of Virginia's rivers are any indication, the acid rain problem in the eastern United States remains serious. A study by University of Virginia researchers in 1998 found that 50 percent of Virginia's rivers suffer from acid rain. The trout that were formerly plentiful in those rivers have seriously declined in number. Another finding of the study was that 6 percent of the state's streams are "chronically acidic," meaning they cannot support plant or animal life.

Researchers concluded that a 70 percent reduction (from 1980 levels) of sulfur dioxide emissions would be required to prevent greater acidification of rivers and lakes, not only in Virginia but throughout the northeastern United States (the 1990 Clean Air Act law aims for a 40 percent reduction from 1980 levels). The study's authors also pointed out the need for greater restrictions on emissions of nitrogen oxides, the second-greatest contributors to acid rain.

The results of that study illustrate the difficulty of de-acidifying lakes and rivers. Researchers concluded that tackling the acid rain problem would likely require further cuts in sulfur dioxide emissions. "We've been creating acid rain for a long time," stated Dr. Gary Lovett of the Institute of Ecosystem Studies in *The New York Times* on October 7, 1999. "It may take a long time to recover from its effects."

Decline of bases adds to problem   One reason that acidity levels remain steady in lakes and rivers even as sulfur compounds decrease is that levels of calcium and magnesium are also on the decline. Magnesium and calcium are bases, that is, substances that react with acids to form salts. They neutralize acid rain, much as antacid medication neutralizes stomach acid. Calcium is also used by trees to build cell walls and magnesium is a component of chlorophyll, the substance that gives green plants the ability to photosynthesize (produce food from carbon dioxide, water, and sunlight).

The loss of calcium and magnesium has been attributed to acid rain. Acid rain removes those elements from the soil more quickly than they can be replaced by leaching from rocks. Throughout the northeastern United States, Ontario, and Quebec, magnesium and calcium levels in the soil have declined by around 50 percent since the 1960s.

Ozone depletion

While ozone in the lower atmosphere is bad, ozone in the upper atmosphere is good. Ozone in the upper atmosphere shields Earth from the Sun's harmful ultraviolet rays. The destruction of ozone by certain chemicals over the last few decades is a matter of great concern. Ozone is a colorless gas composed of three atoms of oxygen bonded together. Although ozone is commonly described as odorless, it does have a subtle and hard-to-describe odor. The "fresh" odor sometimes detected right after a summer thunderstorm may be from lingering ozone in the air.

Unlike surface ozone, which is a major air pollutant, upper-atmospheric ozone is not formed by an interaction of pollution and sunlight. The ozone layer high above Earth is formed by a reaction between molecular ozone (O_2) and atomic ozone (O), in the presence of sunlight. Ozone has three atoms of oxygen per molecule. Its chemical formula is O_3.

Earth's protective ozone layer lies between 10 and 25 miles (16 and 40 kilometers) above ground. It is in the upper part of Earth's stratosphere, a region of the atmosphere that is about 6 to 40 miles (14 to 62 kilometers) above ground. The concentration of ozone in the layer is a few parts per million. While low, this is thousands of times more concentrated than ozone near the surface. The ozone layer is important to humans and other living organisms because of its ability to absorb harmful ultraviolet radiation.

In recent years, the presence of certain chemical pollutants in the upper atmosphere has caused a reduction in concentration of ozone molecules in the ozone layer. This loss of stratospheric ozone has severe repercussions for human health, the most serious being a rise in cases of skin cancer. The term "skin cancer" refers to one of three diseases of the skin that are caused primarily by exposure to the ultraviolet in sunlight It is estimated that every 1 percent reduction in the ozone layer results in a 2 to 5 percent rise in the incidence of skin cancer. Other human consequences of the loss of protective ozone may include an increase in sun burns and eye cataracts, as well as the suppression of the immune system.

The most likely culprit behind ozone depletion is the class of human-made chemicals called chlorofluorocarbons (CFCs). CFCs can be liquids or gases, and appeared in all kinds of everyday products such as propellants in aerosol

How acidic is acid rain?

Acidity and alkalinity are measured on a scale called the pH (potential for hydrogen) scale. It runs from 0 to 14. Since it is a logarithmic scale, a change in one unit equals a tenfold increase or decrease of acidity or alkalinity. Therefore a solution of pH 2.0 is ten times more acidic than a solution of pH 3.0 and one hundred times more acidic than a solution of pH 4.0. A pH value of 0.0 is extremely acidic, 7.0 is neutral, and 14.0 is extremely alkaline (basic).

Any rain below pH 5.0 is considered acid rain. (Some scientists set the limit at 5.6.) Clean, unpolluted rainwater is normally slightly acidic, because the rain dissolves carbon dioxide as it falls through the air. In solution, carbon dioxide forms a weak acid. Normal rain and snow containing dissolved carbon dioxide has a pH of 5.6.

The acidity of rain varies according to geographical area. Eastern Europe and parts of Scandinavia have rain with a of pH 4.3 to 4.5; in the rest of Europe the rain is pH 4.5 to 5.1; in eastern United States and Canada, rain pH ranges from 4.0 to 4.6; and in the Mississippi Valley, it is 4.6 to 4.8. The rain around Lake Erie and Lake Ontario has a pH of about 4.2. The optimal pH range for most freshwater organisms is between 6.5 and 7.5.

Here are some common substances and their typical pH values:

- Battery acid: 1.0
- Lemon juice: 2.0
- Vinegar: 2.2
- Normal rain: 5.0 to 5.6
- Distilled water: 7.0
- Human blood: 7.4
- Baking Soda: 8.3
- Ammonia: 11.0

Experiment: Testing for Acid Rain

You can make your own indicator to test the acidity of rain using the following materials: three large leaves of red cabbage, white vinegar, baking soda (sodium bicarbonate), a pitcher, some rain water, and three clear glass jars.

The first step is to chop up the cabbage and simmer it gently in a pot of water for ten minutes. Do not allow the mixture to boil vigorously. After ten minutes, the liquid should be a deep reddish-purple color. The liquid is neutral (not acidic or basic). Let the water cool, then pour it through a strainer or a coffee filter into a pitcher. This water serves as an indicator liquid with which you can test the acidity of other substances.

To see how the indicator liquid works, test it with two substances: one an acid and the other a base. Pour a small amount of indicator liquid into the bottoms of two drinking glasses. To one glass, add a few drops of vinegar and to the other, a pinch of baking soda. The vinegar, which is acidic, will turn the liquid pink. The baking soda, which is basic, will turn the liquid green.

Now you are ready to test some rainwater. To do this, pour a small amount of indicator liquid into the third jar. Now pour some rainwater into the jar. Note any color change. How does it compare to the indicator liquid with vinegar added? Normally, rainwater is slightly acidic and should create a faint pinkish hue in the indicator liquid. The more intense the pink color that is created, the higher the acidity of the rain.

spray cans and foam-blowing canisters; in refrigerators and air conditioners; and in some cleaning solvents. When CFCs rise into the stratosphere, they form chlorine compounds that break down ozone molecules.

Levels of stratospheric ozone are kept in balance naturally. Ozone is produced in the stratosphere by the combination of molecular oxygen (O_2) and atomic oxygen (O). Ozone molecules are broken by the absorption of ultraviolet rays and by collisions with other oxygen atoms. The dust and gases emitted by volcanic eruptions also break down ozone molecules. By introducing CFCs into the equation, however, the balance becomes tilted in favor of ozone destruction.

The consequences of ozone depletion are not limited to humans. A decrease in ozone has also been linked to a reduction of crop yields, health problems in animals, and a loss of ocean phytoplankton. Phytoplankton are microscopic ocean plants that are a crucial link in the food chain of marine animals.

The Antarctic ozone hole Tests conducted above Antarctica in the late 1970s, at the end of the long, cold winters (in September and October), first revealed the problem of ozone depletion. In 1985, the concentration of ozone in the stratosphere above Antarctica decreased to the point where scientists began to refer to the area as the "ozone hole."

The ozone layer above Antarctica continued to thin at alarming rates throughout the 1980s, and by 1994 had been almost totally eliminated for a brief part of the year. At its worst, the ozone hole is double the size of the Antarctic continent. In many aspects the Antarctic ozone hole remains the most visible and striking example of how human-created pollution can damage the atmosphere.

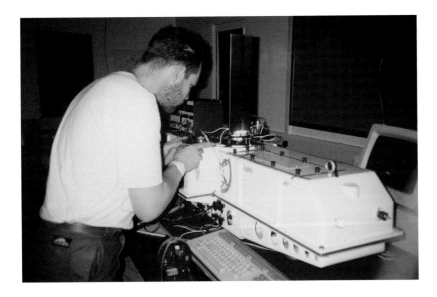

A scientist prepares to test the Dobson Spectrophotometer, a device used to measure ozone levels. ©GRAHAM NEDEN; ECOSCENE/CORBIS.

Measurements of the ozone layer over Antarctica began in 1978. In September 2006, the Antarctic ozone hole was measured at a record 10.6 million square miles (27.3 million square kilometers). At that time, the Antarctic ozone hole was also the deepest ever recorded. Near-total ozone loss was recorded at 13 miles (21 kilometers) above ground. Prior to 1997, ozone destruction did not extend higher than 9 miles (14 kilometers) in altitude. Ozone holes have also appeared in recent winters over the North Pole, northern Europe, Australia, and New Zealand.

Why does ozone depletion happen over the poles, where virtually no one lives and CFC use is practically nonexistent? It happens because both ozone and CFCs are carried around the planet by upper-level winds. The ozone layer is normally thickest above the tropics and from there it is distributed to the poles. During the cold Antarctic winter, however, a dome of extremely cold air forms, which blocks the distribution of ozone to the South Pole. At the same time, ice clouds form in the stratosphere. CFCs blown in from other parts of the world become trapped in these ice clouds. It is this combination of events that sets the stage for the depletion of the ozone layer.

Other parts of the world   The stratosphere above other parts the world has also experienced a loss of ozone. Since 1979, the ozone layer over all parts of the world except the tropics has shown a marked depletion. The World Meteorological Organization has issued a series of research reports

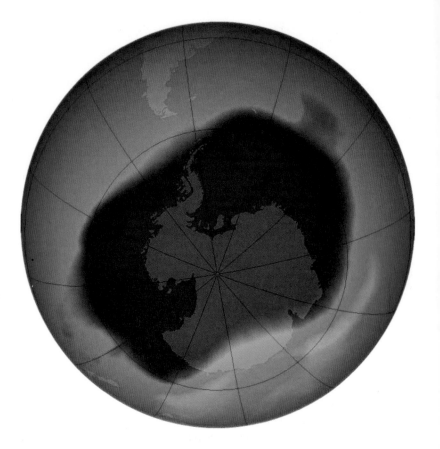

A September 2006 satellite image shows a 11.4-million square mile hole in the ozone layer over the Antarctic. The blue and purple colors are where there is the least ozone; the greens, yellows, and reds are where there is more.
AP IMAGES.

on ozone depletion. *Scientific Assessment of Ozone Depletion: 2002* confirmed that between 1979 and 1991, the ozone layer remained about 3 percent thinner over much of the Northern Hemisphere compared to pre-1980 levels. The Southern hemisphere mid-latitudes showed a 6 percent drop. The same study showed a 4 to 5 percent thinning of the ozone layer over the United States. New ozone holes also appear to be forming over the North Pole, Australia, and New Zealand. Even greater levels of ozone loss (up to 10 percent) have been found over Canada and northern Europe.

Chlorofluorocarbons destroy the ozone   The main chemicals responsible for thinning the ozone layer are CFCs. CFCs are human-made hydrocarbons, such as freon, in which some or all of the hydrogen atoms have been replaced by fluorine atoms. CFCs were formerly used in refrigerators and air conditioners; as propellants in aerosol spray cans (such as deodorants, spray paints, and hair sprays) and foam-blowing canisters; and in some cleaning solvents.

When released into the air, CFCs slowly rise through Earth's lower atmosphere and up to the stratosphere. There they are converted by the Sun's ultraviolet rays into chlorine compounds. The chlorine compounds react with stratospheric ozone molecules (O_3), converting them into ordinary oxygen molecules (O_2). The release of CFCs into the atmosphere depletes the beneficial ozone layer faster than ozone can be recharged by natural processes. These are fueled by the reaction between molecular ozone and atomic ozone, in the presence of sunlight.

Other chemicals that contribute to the destruction of the ozone layer include halons (used in fire extinguishers), methyl bromide (used for fumigating crops), carbon tetrachloride (used in solvents and the manufacture of chemicals), methyl chloroform (used in auto repair and maintenance products), and hydro CFCs (HCFCs; similar uses as CFCs but considered slightly less damaging to ozone).

Attempts to curb ozone depletion   Since the 1970s, when the world became aware the dangers of ozone depletion, there has been a flurry of national legislation and international treaties aimed at reducing the use of CFCs. In 1978, the United States government became one of the first nations to act, banning the use of CFCs in most aerosol cans.

The Montreal Protocol on Substances that Deplete the Ozone Layer, an international agreement drafted in 1987, called for the phasing-out of certain CFCs used in industrial processes by the year 2000. The protocol has been endorsed by ninety-three nations, including the major industrialized nations. In keeping with that accord, many countries have now greatly restricted the use of aerosol spray cans and other ozone-destroying chemicals. There is, however, a flourishing illegal trade in CFCs, especially in developing countries. In an effort to curb the trade, China Customs and the United Nations Environment Program launched Project Skyhole Patching in 2006. In the first six months of the program alone, nearly 72 tons (65 metric tones) of illegal ozone depleting substances were seized by authorities in China, India, and Thailand.

In the United States, the 1990 Amendments to the Clean Air Act set a timetable for the elimination of ozone-destroying chemicals. In 1993,

The global warming/ozone thinning connection

Some scientists are drawing a link between global warming and the continued reduction of the ozone layer. Increased concentrations of carbon dioxide (the main cause of global warming), which heat up the lower atmosphere, have a cooling effect on the stratosphere. This effect occurs because carbon dioxide traps heat in the lower atmosphere, preventing it from rising into the upper atmosphere.

In recent years, the stratosphere over both poles has been unusually cold. In 2006, a year of extreme cooling of the stratosphere over Antarctica, the ozone hole was wider and deeper than ever before recorded. The hole covered an area of 10.6 million square miles (27.3 million square kilometers). The ozone hole above Antarctica grows and shrinks with the seasons. Every September (the start of the Southern Hemisphere spring), increased sunlight energizes CFCs and other chemicals that destroy ozone molecules. The key stage of the chemical reaction takes place on the surface of frozen cloud droplets. Frozen droplets only form in extremely cold con-

ditions. The lower the temperature in the stratosphere dips, the more plentiful frozen droplets become. When the concentration of frozen droplets increases, ozone breakdown accelerates.

Despite the record-setting ozone hold of 2006, there is some reason for hope. In 2005, the United Nations' Intergovernmental Panel on Climate Control released a report titled "Safeguarding the Ozone Layer and the Global Climate System," which stated: "Although considerable variability in ozone is expected from year to year, including in polar regions where depletion is largest, the ozone layer is expected to begin to recover in coming decades due to declining ODS [ozone-depleting substance] concentrations, assuming full compliance with the Montreal Protocol." However, the same report suggests that the projected increases of other greenhouse gases could possibly cool the stratosphere. This cooling of the stratosphere might have the effect of increasing ozone levels worldwide, but worsening the ozone depletion in other regions, like the Antarctic.

those phase-out dates were accelerated. According to the regulations, halons were eliminated in 1994; and CFCs, carbon tetrachloride, and methyl chloroform were eliminated in 1996. The most destructive form of HCFC, a substitute for CFC that also harms ozone, was scheduled to end production in 2003, but the manufacture of other forms of HCFC will be permitted until 2030 to give industrialists time to develop less harmful substitutes. After 2030, all forms of HCFC will be prohibited.

In September 1997, on the tenth anniversary of the Montreal Protocol gathering, representatives from more than one hundred nations met to reexamine the problem of ozone depletion. They agreed at that meeting to phase out methyl bromide, a chemical used in insecticides. Industrialized nations pledged to eliminate production of methyl bromide by

2005 and developing nations by 2015. As of 2007, methyl bromide production had decreased significantly, but the EPA still made some "critical use exemptions" to the phaseout.

The international efforts to protect the ozone appear to be working. Since 1988, there has been a substantial decline in the atmospheric buildup of CFCs. Experts suggest that concentrations of CFCs reached their peak before the turn of the twenty-first century, after which the ozone layer will begin the slow process of repairing itself. CFC molecules, however, survive in the atmosphere for fifty to one hundred years. As long as CFCs are present they will continue to damage the ozone.

Environmentally friendly sources of power

It is possible for even industrialized, automobile-dependent societies to meet basic needs and remain economically strong without harming the environment. What is needed to accomplish this are environmentally friendly sources of transportation, such as electric and hybrid cars, and cleaner sources of energy, such as solar power (electricity generated from the Sun) and wind power (electricity generated from wind).

Cars are responsible for one-third to one-half of all emissions that cause global warming, smog, and acid rain. Consequently, auto manufacturers face government regulations and public pressure to design and build cleaner cars. One result of this pressure has been the development of more efficient gasoline engines. Engines of recent-model cars put out just a small fraction of the pollutants that automobile engines emitted when the Clean Air Act was signed into law. They are also more powerful and more fuel-efficient. Auto manufacturers are also producing electric vehicles, hybrid gasoline-electric or diesel-electric vehicles, and vehicles powered by fuel cells (devices that generate electricity by combining hydrogen and oxygen).

Solar power and wind power are relatively clean, safe alternatives to burning fossil fuels. While solar and wind power are not completely harmless to the environment, they cause a fraction of the damage done by burning fossil fuels. There are numerous solar and wind power facilities operating throughout the world. In the United States in 1998, solar and wind power, together with hydroelectric power (power produced by moving water), accounted for approximately 8 percent of energy consumption. Fossil fuels and nuclear power made up the other 92 percent. The United States and many European nations have stated their intention to greatly increase the use of solar and wind power through the twenty-first century.

Electric cars   Electric cars are automobiles that run on electric motors instead of gasoline-powered engines. The power that drives the electric current is stored in batteries. When the power runs low, an electric car's batteries must be recharged.

While electric vehicles are commonly thought of as a new technology, they have actually been around for a long time: They were first produced in the late 1880s. Electric cars, trucks, and buses, as well as electric trolleys and trains (with electricity supplied by overhead wires), were in widespread use at the beginning of the twentieth century. Electric vehicles were preferred over gasoline-powered vehicles because the latter class of vehicles were difficult to start, noisy, and required more maintenance.

The balance shifted in favor gasoline-powered vehicles in the 1910s, with the invention of the Kettering electrical self-starter. The starter eliminated the need for crank-starting gasoline-powered cars. By 1924, not a single electric vehicle was exhibited at the National Automobile Show.

While electric vehicles virtually disappeared in the United States, electric buses and trucks continued to be used in other parts of the world. For instance, in the latter part of the twentieth century there were thirty thousand electric vehicles in use in England and thirteen thousand in Japan.

The rise and fall of the modern all-electric vehicle   Motivated by shrinking petroleum reserves and the polluting effects of gasoline emissions, auto manufacturers in the 1960s once again began looking toward electric automobiles. The motivation to produce all-electric automobiles also came from the Zero Emission Vehicle mandate (ZEV), a law passed by the state of California in 1990. This was a radical challenge to the auto industry to produce automobiles with zero tail pipe emissions. In 2003, the California Air Resources Board reduced the regulations outlined in the ZEV mandate, but while it was in effect this legislation jump-started the automakers' development of cleaner vehicles.

In 1996, General Motors began marketing a nearly silent, electric compact car called the General Motors EV1. The EV1 could accelerate from 0 to 60 miles per hour (0 to 97 kph) in 9 seconds, which is comparable to gasoline-powered cars. It was extremely fuel efficient, and could go 140 miles (218 kilometers) between charges. Honda also produced an electric car, the EV Plus. It was the first electric vehicle to be powered by nickel metal-hydride batteries (NiMH) instead of the traditional lead-acid batteries. However, these battery-powered cars did not perform well in cold weather. Ford produced an all-electric version of its Ranger pickup truck as well. All of these vehicles were produced in very limited quantities and production has ceased.

Most other major car makers have also ceased production of their all-electric vehicles. The motivation to produce zero-emission vehicles was reduced after the revision to California's ZEV mandate. Nearly all of the vehicles have been repossessed by the manufacturers and recycled.

At present, due to the high costs and limited capabilities of batteries, electric cars are only produced and sold in small numbers. However, the development of new technologies may bring the cost and performance of electric cars in line with gasoline-powered cars in the not-too-distant future.

The future of all-electric vehicles   The primary obstacle to electric vehicle use has been the limitations of battery technology. Charging a battery can take several hours, and typical chargers can be expensive. Recent improvements to batteries and chargers, however, are making the process faster and easier. The widespread availability of NiMH batteries, which have a much better energy-to-weight ratio than lead-acid batteries, coupled with escalating oil prices in the early years of the twenty-first century, seems to have revitalized an interest in all electric vehicles. By late 2006, several companies had introduced new electrical vehicle prototypes and promised production would soon begin.

Hybrid cars   Hybrid technology cars caught on with both consumers and manufacturers during the first years of the twenty-first century. A hybrid car contains a relatively small petroleum fueled engine, with a combined electric motor and generator. Electrical energy is stored in battery packs. The gasoline or diesel engine automatically recharges the battery packs as the car is being driven or while stopped. Hybrids (and all-electric vehicles) also use a technology called regenerative braking. When the brakes are applied, the energy of motion is converted by the motor/generator back to electrical energy and stored in the battery pack.

Hybrid cars smoothly switch back and forth between gas and electrical systems. Many hybrid vehicles use less petroleum fuel than traditional vehicles. They may get up to 70 miles (109 kilometers) per gallon,

Environmental concerns about electric and hybrid cars

While the use of electricity as fuel for automobiles solves some problems, it creates others. Greater use of electricity (for vehicles) translates to greater emissions from power plants. This is a concern especially in areas where older coal-fired generators are the source of electrical power. A purely electric vehicle will be responsible for more of some types of pollution, namely sulfates and particulates, and less of others, such as carbon monoxide and nitrogen oxide emissions, when compared to a hybrid vehicle. The environmental question may boil down to whether we prefer our pollution to be emitted from a single source, typically beyond city limits (the power plant), or from many sources, concentrated within city limits (automobiles).

Another problem is in the electric power grid, which is the system of electric power genera-tion, transmission, and distribution used by the surrounding community. These grids are designed with capacity for maximum power demands, which occur at certain peak times (for example, on very hot summer days). Consumers may balk at being restricted from plugging in their cars during peak usage times.

The best solutions for the environment are to drive less and use public transportation such as trains and buses. Another alternative is the use of clean energy, such as solar energy and wind energy, to produce the electricity used by electric vehicles. In the late 1990s, two demonstration projects were installed at Boston-area commuter train stations in which solar cells generated the electricity that was used for charging electric vehicles.

making refueling necessary only every 700–870 miles (1092–1357 kilometers). In 2007, most automobile and light truck manufacturers had at least one hybrid vehicle in their production line.

Fuel cell–powered cars   Fuel cells are a promising, new source of power for vehicles. They run on liquid hydrogen or hydrogen-rich materials such as ethanol and methanol. Fuel cells work by combining hydrogen and oxygen (from the air) to produce electricity and water. The main drawback to fuel cells, at this point, is cost. In 2006, the price of constructing a fuel-cell vehicle was around $2 million. (The primary reason for the high cost is that two components of fuel cells, platinum and graphite, are very expensive.) Fuel cells are also very fragile and do not stand up well to the bumps of daily driving. Auto companies are researching ways to make a cheaper, more robust fuel cell. Fuel cells run on pure hydrogen are considered zero-emissions vehicles. The exhaust is pure water. Fuel cells that run on hydrocarbons or alcohols will still have some "tailpipe" emissions, including carbon dioxide.

Chicago, Illinois, and Vancouver, British Columbia, have prototype fuel-cell buses in their public transportation fleets. Other cities around the globe are following suit. In California, automakers, fuel companies, and government agencies are working in partnership to test fuel cell vehicle technology and are expected to produce more than sixty demonstration vehicles over the next few years. There are currently around five hundred fuel cell–powered cars in operation worldwide. They are all prototypes and are serving as test platforms for this emerging technology. A number of durability, performance, and cost issues must be overcome before fuel cell vehicles are ready for mass production.

Biodiesel

Biodiesel fuel is a renewable energy source that can be made from a number of biological substances, including corn oil and animal fat. It is most commonly made of vegetable oils, unlike conventional diesel fuel that is made primarily from petroleum. Biodiesel blends (part biodiesel and part conventional diesel fuel) can generally be used in unmodified diesel engines. With some modifications, most diesel engines can run on pure biodiesel. Pure biodiesel produces 75 percent less greenhouse gas emissions than conventional diesel fuel and is significantly less combustible (capable of catching fire and burning), which makes it safer.

Solar energy   Solar radiation is the most plentiful, permanent source of energy in the world. Energy from the Sun is nonpolluting. It can be used directly for heating and lighting, or harnessed and used to generate electricity.

The sunlight that strikes Earth provides far more power than the world's inhabitants can use. The challenge of using solar power, however, is in concentrating and storing the energy. Storage is necessary for times when the Sun is not shining, such as at night and on cloudy days. In the absence of storage capabilities, solar energy alone cannot meet all of a community's energy needs—it must be supplemented by other sources of energy.

Great strides have been made in the development of solar power technologies since the early 1970s. France, Japan, Israel, the United States, and other countries are actively seeking ways to use solar energy as a major source of power. A handful of large-scale solar power stations are operational around the world. In addition, small-scale solar power systems provide electricity to more than 250,000 households worldwide, including a growing number of isolated areas and developing countries.

One of the biggest obstacles to widespread use of solar power has been cost. At the start of the 1980s, the cost of electricity from a photovoltaic panel (device that converts sunlight to electricity) was about one hundred times more expensive than electricity from conventional power

The solar furnace in Odellio, France. © MORTON BEEBE/ CORBIS.

plants. By the end of the 1990s, the price of solar energy–generated electricity in especially sunny locations was almost the same as the price of electricity from conventional power plants. In other areas, however, solar-generated electricity was around two to five times the cost of conventional electrical power. There is also a high cost to install the systems needed to provide solar-electric energy in homes and businesses.

Despite the relatively high cost of solar-generated electrical power, demand continues to increase. The solar power industry worldwide grew at an average annual rate of 16 percent between 1990 and 1997 (in the United States the industry tripled in size during that time period). According to the Worldwatch Institute, a nonprofit organization that monitors the environment and economic development, solar power is the world's fastest growing energy source.

Passive solar collectors There are the two types of systems that collect and store the Sun's heat: passive solar collectors and active solar collectors. Passive collectors have no moving parts, while active solar collectors use pumps and motors. Passive systems are usually used for home heating and active systems are generally used for producing hot water.

Passive solar collectors operate on the simple principle that when placed in the sunlight, an object will heat up. One passive home-heating system is called a Trombe Wall. It consists a black concrete wall with air vents at the top and bottom, set on the south side of a building. A double-glazed pane of glass is placed just outside of the wall. Heat passes through the glass and becomes trapped between the glass and the wall.

Cool air from inside the room is drawn into the bottom air vents and enters the space between the wall and the glass. The air is heated, rises, and returns to the room through the top vent.

Active solar collectors   Active solar collectors use pumps and motors to heat water. A solar water heater (also called a solar thermal device) is a type of active solar heating system that used to supplement a traditional home water heater. The solar water heater consists of a network of copper tubes filled with antifreeze, placed on the roof of a house. The tubes are covered with insulated black panels that absorb the heat of the Sun.

A pump circulates the antifreeze through the tubes. The antifreeze is heated as it passes beneath the rooftop panels. It then flows through a heat exchanger (also called a heat pump), an instrument that extracts the heat from the antifreeze and transfers it to water in a storage tank. The cooled antifreeze is then pumped back to the rooftop tubes.

In some active systems a fluid is heated in order to produce steam, which is then used to spin a turbine (a machine with spinning blades) and generate electricity.

Photovoltaic cells   Sunlight can also be directly converted into electricity. This is accomplished with photovoltaic cells (also called solar cells). Photovoltaic cells contain semiconductor crystals, such as crystalline silicon, that conduct an electric current under certain conditions. When sunlight strikes the semiconductor, its molecular structure is altered: Electrons move about and an electric current is created.

The electric current runs through a wire on the back of the cell and either travels into a device for immediate use, into a battery where it is stored for short-term use, or into the local power grid.

Photovoltaic arrays (panels containing large numbers of photovoltaic cells) supplement traditional means of electricity production in some regions where sunlight is plentiful. Outside of San Luis Obispo, California, for example, an electricity-generating array of photovoltaic cells generates enough power to supply 2,300 homes.

Photovoltaic arrays cannot be relied upon as a community's sole source of electricity because they do not function when the Sun is not shining. There is as yet no battery or other system that can store enough energy to get through long periods of lack of sunshine.

A solar panel consisting of a large array of connected solar cells. ©ADRIAN WILSON/BEATEWORKS/CORBIS.

Uses of photovoltaic cells In some isolated locations (such as research stations), rural areas, and less-developed countries that are not serviced by power lines, photovoltaic cells provide the only source of electrical power. Some 70 percent of the solar cells produced in the United States are shipped to developing nations.

Photovoltaic cells are also used in the desert to power machines such as water pumps, air conditioners, and telephones. Some motor vehicles have been outfitted with photovoltaic cells, which provide a portion of the vehicle's power. There are also computers, lights, televisions, heaters, air conditioners, and video games that are powered, in part, by photovoltaic cells.

Some buildings receive all or some of their electricity from photovoltaic cells. One example is the Four Times Square building, a modern skyscraper in New York City. Photovoltaic panels that line the exterior walls of the upper levels, satisfying a large portion of the building's energy needs.

Solar shingles, first offered for sale in 1996, are photovoltaic arrays that can be placed on rooftops. It takes 20 square feet (1.8 square meters) of shingles to power a 100-watt light bulb. In sunny locations, solar shingles covering a roof that is at least 400 square feet (37 square meters) are capable of producing enough energy for an average household.

Solar power plants There are numerous solar power plants in sunny locations around the world, supplying electricity to surrounding communities. Two experimental, large-scale solar power plants, called Solar One and Solar Two, operated in Southern California (in the Mojave Desert, east of Los Angeles) between 1983 and 1999. Both plants were capable of producing 10 megawatts of electricity. (A watt is a unit of electric power; 1 megawatt equals 1,000,000 watts.)

Solar One was in operation from 1983 to 1988. A series of mirrors (eighteen hundred in Solar One and nearly two thousand in Solar Two) tracked the movement of the Sun across the sky. The mirrors intensified the sunlight and directed it onto a "power tower," which was a tower

Jump on the solar power bandwagon!

How can you go about installing solar power equipment on your home? There are a number of catalogs from various suppliers listing the wide variety of products available. Many of these can be installed by the do-it-yourselfer. There are also books that describe the solar goods available, tell where you can find them, and explain how to turn your home into an independent producer of heat and electricity. A backyard photovoltaic panel, for instance, costs around a thousand dollars. It connects to a home's circuit breaker. If the panel generates more electricity than used by the household, the local utility company is obliged to purchase the excess.

You can also invest in solar-powered items like AM/FM radios, attic fans, flashlights, battery chargers, portable ovens, and watches, to name a few.

covered with pipes. The fluid running through the pipes became heated; that heat was transferred to a tank of water and turned the water into steam. The steam drove a turbine and the turbine's rotating blades powered an electrical generator. (In a generator, a magnet is turned through a coil of wire and produces electricity.) The electricity was fed into the local utility grid and transported to homes, factories, and businesses.

In 1995, Solar One was converted into Solar Two. It operated from 1996 until early 1999. Solar Two operated in essentially the same manner as Solar One except that it stored solar energy in a tank of molten salt. That system enabled Solar Two to generate electricity continuously, even during nonsunshine hours. "We're proud of Solar Two's success," stated U.S. Energy Secretary Bill Richardson in a news release after Solar Two was discontinued, "as it marks a significant milestone in the development of large-scale solar energy projects. It takes us a step closer to making renewable energy a significant contributor to the global energy mix, while helping to make our environment cleaner."

Nevada Solar One, another solar power plant, shares a similar name to Solar One, however it is quite different in structure. It uses solar receivers, (heating tubes filled with liquid) instead of a power tower. Nevada Solar One is being built in Boulder City, Nevada, by the U.S. Department of Energy, the National Renewable Energy Laboratory, and a private company, and when completed in 2007, will generate 64 megawatts of electricity. Solar Tres, located in Spain, uses technology developed for Solar One and Solar Two. However, Solar Tres is three times larger than Solar Two.

Wind power   The use of wind as a source of energy goes back thousands of years. Since the Middle Ages, windmills have been used to pump water and perform other types of simple mechanical work. Even today, windmills are common fixtures on American farms. In the early half of this century there were around six million such windmills used for pumping water and generating electricity. However, windmills were quickly phased out as other forms of energy became available to farmers. By the end of the 1970s, there were only about 150,000 windmills still in use on farms across the United States.

In recent years, interest in wind energy has been rekindled. This is partially due to the polluting effect and growing scarcity of fossil fuels, combined with the apparent dangers of nuclear power. Wind energy, in contrast, is nonpolluting and inexhaustible (it can never be used up). Interest in wind energy has also been driven by continuous improvements in wind turbine and windmill efficiency since the 1970s. Today, a single modern wind turbine, placed in a location where winds are a fairly constant 10 to 12 miles per hour (16 to 20 kph), can meet all the electricity needs of one home. A "wind farm," consisting of hundreds or thousands of windmills in an area with strong winds, can provide enough electricity for an entire community.

The main challenge to the widespread use of wind power is its cost. New technologies, however, are continually being developed that promise to make wind power as cost-efficient as power from fossil fuels. The cost of electricity from utility-scale wind systems has dropped by more than 80 percent over the last twenty years. The price in the United States is now lower than the cost of fuel-generated electric power in some areas. The downward trend in cost is expected to continue as larger multi-megawatt turbines are mass-produced.

Use of wind power is growing quickly. As of 2003, wind power was the fastest-growing form of electricity generation on a percentage basis in the United States. Globally, wind power generation more than quadrupled between 1999 and 2005. The world leaders in wind power production in 2007 were Germany, Spain, the United States, India, and Denmark.

Wind turbines and wind farms   Wind turbines have long blades, enabling them to extract large amounts of energy from the wind. An electrical generator captures the energy of the spinning blade and converts it to electricity. The electricity travels through wires to the bottom of the tower and to an electrical substation, after which it is fed into the local utility grid.

Twenty-eight percent of the United States' wind power is generated in Texas and California. According to a U. S. Department of Energy study, the windy states of Texas, North Dakota, and Kansas could generate enough electricity with wind energy to furnish the entire nation's electricity needs.

Most of the largest wind farms in Texas are situated on high mesas in far west Texas. In this region, there is a strong prevailing wind from the west. The wind speeds up as it rises to cross these mesas, and the placement of the wind turbines along the ridge tops takes advantage of this phenomenon. Also, Texas has planned two offshore wind farms along the Gulf Coast.

Wind turbines on a hillside.
©GEORGE LEPP/CORBIS.

One of California's largest wind farms (constructed in the early 1980s) sits at the edge of a mountain gap called Altamont Pass, about 30 miles (50 kilometers) east of San Francisco. Wind is naturally funneled through the gap at high speeds. Altamont Pass contains more than seven thousand 80-foot-tall (24-meter-tall) wind turbines. Each turbine produces between 40 and 750 kilowatts of power—enough electricity for 130,000 homes (1 kilowatt equals 1,000 watts). There are also two large wind farms in Southern California, at Tehachapi and Palm Springs.

Bigger and better wind turbines Wind power developers are designing larger, more powerful wind turbines, which are able to produce electricity more inexpensively than older models. The first generation of wind turbines, produced between 1978 and 1981, had blades that were 16 feet (5 meters) long, with rotor (rotating cylindrical device consisting of blades on a shaft) diameters of 33 to 36 feet (10 to 11 meters). They were capable of producing 22 to 30 kilowatts of power. The size and capability of wind turbines has steadily increased since that time.

By the late 1990s, rotor diameters were up to 217 feet (66 meters) and turbines were generating 1.65 to 2 megawatts of power. It is estimated that wind turbines will continue increasing in size and power to the practical limit of 5 megawatts and 490 feet (150 meters) in diameter. In 2005, the largest wind turbine in the world was a 6-megawatt giant installed in Germany. It has a rotor diameter of 410 feet (126 meters).

As turbines continue to get larger and more powerful, costs of wind technology are expected to continue falling.

The future of wind power   The U.S. Department of Energy estimates that offshore wind farms alone could eventually supply all of the energy needs of the United States. That estimate is as high as 30 percent for other parts of the world. In 1999, the American Wind Energy Association, a group of wind-energy producers, predicted that by the year 2005 global use of wind turbines would have increased ten-fold and wind energy will be producing 18.5 gigawatts (one gigawatt equals one billion watts) of electricity worldwide. That estimate proved to be very low. In 2005, world wind energy production was over 65 gigawatts and growing rapidly.

In 2007, more than 46,221 megawatts of wind power were being produced throughout Europe and many new projects were in the works. Germany alone has 16,000 wind turbines, mostly in the north of the country—including three of the biggest in the world—with plans for even more expansion. Canada is also investing in wind power. By early 2007, wind power (primarily in Quebec) supplied 1,451 megawatts of electricity.

Small-scale wind power also looks promising. Wind turbines have been used for household electricity generation for many decades. Some early systems were built by hobbyists working with airplane propellers and automobile generators. Recently, small commercial systems have become widely available and are in use throughout the world. Household generator units of more than 1 kilowatt are now functioning in several countries. By using a combination of wind power, photovoltaics, and battery storage, a remote village, small island, offshore platform, or Australian ranch station can be independent of grid-supplied power.

Saving the planet

With the knowledge of the most serious environmental threats presently faced by Earth and its inhabitants comes the responsibility to find solutions. In an effort to reverse the trend of environmental degradation, scientists and environmental advocates are recommending that we, as a society, do the following:

- Decrease our consumption of coal and oil
- Develop alternative forms of energy, such as solar power and wind power

A matter of survival

There are a number of ways you can reduce your energy consumption, thereby helping to make the air cleaner and reducing your contribution to global warming. Here are a few suggestions:

- Purchase compact fluorescent light bulbs. They use 40 percent less energy than incandescent (regular) light bulbs.
- Turn off lights when you leave a room.
- Make sure your home is well-insulated. One easy way to reduce heat loss in winter is to install plastic sheeting over your windows.
- Keep your thermostat below 70°F (21°C) in the winter. Wear extra clothing to keep warm.
- Shut down your computer when it is not in use.
- Convince your family to walk, ride bikes, or take public transportation instead of driving whenever possible.
- When shopping for a new appliance, look for the Energy Star label. That label indicates that the appliance has a high energy efficiency.
- Use a manual lawn mower instead of one that is fueled by gasoline or electricity.
- Recycle paper, bottles, cans, and any other items accepted by recycling companies in your region, and purchase recycled paper goods.

- Increase the efficiency of automobiles, so they can travel for more miles on each gallon of gasoline
- Stop deforestation and replant trees on cleared lands

We can each make a difference by choosing to consume less and pollute less. That means, for instance, reusing and recycling items rather than disposing of them; minimizing our use of toxic chemicals, from lawn and garden fertilizers to household cleaning agents; and switching our means of transportation, whenever possible, from cars to bicycles or buses.

[*See Also* **Climate; Climate Change and Global Warming; Weather: An Introduction**]

For More Information

BOOKS

Botkin, Daniel, and Edward Keller. *Environmental Science: Earth as a Living Planet.* 4th ed. Hoboken, NJ: John Wiley & Sons, Inc. 2004.

Cotton, William R., and Roger A. Pielke Sr. *Human Impacts on Weather and Climate.* 2nd ed. New York: Cambridge University Press, 2007

Flannery, Tim. *The Weather Makers: How Man Is Changing the Climate and What It Means for Life on Earth.* New York: Atlantic Monthly Press, 2006

Gore, Al. *An Inconvenient Truth.* 2nd ed. New York: Rodale Books, 2006.

Wright, Richard T. *Environmental Science: Toward a Sustainable Future.* 10th ed. Upper Saddle River, NJ: Prentice Hall, 2007.

WEB SITES

"How Might Global Climate Change Affect Life on Earth?" *McDougal Littel: Exploring Earth Investigations.* <http://www.classzone.com/books/earth_science/terc/content/investigations/esu501/esu501page01.cfm?chapter_no=investigation> (accessed March 25, 2007).

"NCAR/UCAR/UOP Home." *National Center for Atmospheric Research.* <http://www.ucar.edu/> (accessed March 25, 2007).

Where to Learn More

Books

Abbott, Patrick Leon, ed. *Natural Disasters.* 6th ed. Columbus, OH: McGraw-Hill Higher Education, 2008.

Aguado, Edward, and James Burt. *Understanding Weather and Climate.* 4th ed. Englewood Cliffs, NJ: Prentice Hall, 2006.

Ahrens, C. Donald. *Meteorology Today: An Introduction to Weather, Climate, and the Environment.* 7th ed. Belmont, CA: Thomson Brooks/Cole, 2006.

Allaby, Michael. *Blizzards.* 2nd ed. New York: Facts on File, 2003.

Allaby, Michael. *How the Weather Works: 100 Ways Parents and Kids Can Share the Secrets of the Atmosphere.* New York: Putnam Group, Inc., 1999.

Allen, Leslie, et. al. *Raging Forces: Earth in Upheaval.* Washington, DC: National Geographic Society, 1996.

Andryszewski, Tricia. *The Dust Bowl: Disaster on the Plains.* Brookfield, CT: The Millbrook Press, 1993.

Anthes, Richard A. *Meteorology,* 7th ed. New York: Prentice Hall, 1996.

Arnold, Caroline. *El Niño: Stormy Weather for People and Wildlife.* New York: Clarion Books, 2005.

Bair, Frank E. *Climates of States.* 5th ed. Farmington Hills, MI: Thomson Gale, 2007.

Binhua, Wang. *Sea Fog.* New York: Springer-Verlag, 1985.

Bolt, Bruce A. *Earthquakes.* 4th ed. Salt Lake City, UT: W. H. Freeman and Co., 1999.

Botkin, Daniel, and Edward Keller. *Environmental Science: Earth as a Living Planet.* 4th ed. Hoboken, NJ: John Wiley & Sons, Inc. 2004.

Breen, Mark, Kathleen Friestad, and Michael Kline. *The Kid's Book of Weather Forecasting: Build a Weather Station, "Read" the Sky & Make Predictions!* Charlotte, VT: Williamson Publishing Company, 2000.

Brinkley, Douglas. *The Great Deluge: Hurricane Katrina, New Orleans, and the Mississippi Gulf Coast.* New York: William Morrow, 2006.

Bronson, William. *The Earth Shook, the Sky Burned.* San Francisco, CA: Chronicle Books, 1997.

Burroughs, William J., Bob Crowder, et. al. *Nature Company Guides: Weather.* New York: Time Life Books, 2000.

Campbell, N. A. *Biology.* 4th ed. Menlo Park, CA: The Benjamin/Cummings Publishing Company, Inc., 1996.

Carr, Michael. *International Marine's Weather Predicting Simplified: How to Read Weather Charts and Satellite Images.* New York: McGraw-Hill, 1999.

Chambers, Catherine. *Thunderstorm.* 2nd ed. Portsmouth, NH: Heinemann, 2007.

Chernov, Y. I. *The Living Tundra.* West Nyack, NY: Cambridge University Press, 1988.

Christian, Spencer, and Antonia Felix. *Shake, Rattle, and Roll: The World's Most Amazing Earthquakes, Volcanoes, and Other Forces.* New York: John Wiley & Sons, Inc., 1997.

Colten, Craig E. *An Unnatural Metropolis: Wrestling New Orleans from Nature.* Baton Rouge: Louisiana State University Press, 2005.

Cotton, William R., and Roger A. Pielke, Sr. *Human Impacts on Weather and Climate.* 2nd ed. New York: Cambridge University Press, 2007.

Dasch, E. Julius, ed. *Encyclopedia of Earth Sciences.* New York: Macmillan Library Reference, 1996.

De Blij, Harm J., et al. *Nature on the Rampage.* Washington, DC: Smithsonian Institution, 1994.

De Blij, Harm J., et al. *Restless Earth.* Washington, DC: National Geographic Society, 1997.

De Villiers, Marq. *Windswept: The Story of Wind and Weather.* New York: Walker & Company, 2006.

DeMillo, Rob. *How Weather Works.* Emeryville, CA: Ziff-Davis Press, 1994.

Drake, Frances. *Global Warming: The Science of Climate Change.* New York: Oxford University Press, 2000.

Drohan, Michele Ingber. *Avalanches.* New York: Rosen Publishing and PowerKids Press, 1999.

Drohan, Michele Ingber. *Floods.* New York: Rosen Publishing and PowerKids Press, 1999.

Fagan, Brian. *Floods, Famines and Emperors: El Niño and the Fate of Civilizations.* New York: Basic Books, 2000.

Ferguson, Sue, and Edward R. LaChapelle. *The ABCs of Avalanche Safety.* 3rd ed. Seattle, WA: Mountaineers Books, 2003.

Fisher, David E. *The Scariest Place on Earth: Eye to Eye with Hurricanes.* New York: Random House, 1994.

Flannery, Tim. *The Weather Makers: How Man Is Changing the Climate and What It Means for Life on Earth.* New York: Atlantic Monthly Press, 2006.

Frater, Alexander. *Chasing the Monsoon.* New York: Picador, 2005.

Geiger, Rudolf. *The Climate Near the Ground,* Cambridge, MA: Harvard University Press, 1965.

Gemmell, Kathy. *Storms and Hurricanes.* London: Usborne Publishing Ltd., 1996.

Glantz, Michael H. *Currents of Change: El Niño's Impact on Climate and Society.* 2nd ed. New York: Cambridge University Press, 2001.

Gore, Al. *An Inconvenient Truth: The Planetary Emergency of Global Warming and What We Can Do About It.* 2nd ed. New York: Rodale Books, 2006.

Hamblyn, Richard. *The Invention of Clouds: How an Amateur Meteorologist Forged the Language of the Skies.* London: Pan MacMillan, 2001.

Hambrey, Michael, and Jürg Alean. *Glaciers.* 2nd ed. Cambridge, UK: Cambridge University Press, 2004.

Hamilton, Richard. *Avalanches: Nature's Fury.* Minneapolis, MN: Abdo and Daughters, 2005.

Hodgson, Michael. *Basic Essentials Weather Forecasting.* 3rd ed. Guilford, CT: Falcon, 2007.

Hopping, Lorraine Jean. *Wild Weather: Blizzards!* New York: Scholastic Inc., 1999.

Houghton, John. *Global Warming: The Complete Briefing.* Cambridge, UK: Cambridge University Press, 2004.

Houze, Robert A., Jr. *Cloud Dynamics.* San Diego, CA: Academic Press, Inc., 1994.

Hurt, R. Douglas. *The Dust Bowl: An Agricultural and Social History.* Chicago: Nelson-Hall, 1981.

Hyndman, Donald, and David Hyndman. *Natural Hazards and Disasters.* New York: Brooks Cole, 2005.

Kahl, Jonathan D. W. *Weather Watch: Forecasting the Weather.* Toronto: Monarch Books of Canada Limited, 2002.

Kolber, Elizabeth. *Field Notes from a Catastrophe: Man, Nature, and Climate Change.* New York: Bloomsbury USA, 2006.

Larsen, Erik. *Isaac's Storm.* New York: Vintage Books, 2000.

Lauber, Patricia. *Hurricanes: Earth's Mightiest Storms.* New York: Scholastic Press, 1996.

Libby, W. F. *Radiocarbon Dating.* 2nd ed. University of Chicago Press, 1955.

Linden, Eugene. *The Winds of Change: Climate, Weather, and the Destruction of Civilizations.* New York: Simon & Schuster, 2006.

Lydolph, Paul E. *The Climate of the Earth.* Lanham, MD: Rowman & Littlefield Publishers, Inc., 1985.

McPhee, John. *Annals of the Former World.* New York: Farrar, Straus & Giroux, 1999.

McPhee, John. *The Control of Nature.* New York: Farrar, Straus & Giroux, 1999.

Merrick, Patrick. *Avalanches.* Plymouth, MN: Child's World, 1998.

Mogil, H. Michael. *Tornadoes.* Saint Paul, MN: Voyageur Press, 2003.

Moran, Joseph M., and Lewis W. Morgan. *Essentials of Weather.* Englewood Cliffs, NJ: Prentice Hall, 1995.

Murck, Barbara W. *Dangerous Earth: An Introduction to Geologic Hazards.* New York: John Wiley & Sons, Inc., 1996.

Murphee, Tom, and Mary Miller, with the San Francisco Exploratorium. *Watching Weather: A Low Pressure Book about High Pressure Systems.* New York: Henry Holt and Company, 1998.

Nash, J. Madeleine. *El Niño: Unlocking the Secrets of the Master Weather-Maker.* New York: Warner Books, 2003.

National Geographic Society. *Restless Earth: Disasters of Nature.* Washington, DC: National Geographic Society, 1997.

The National Geographic Desk Reference. Washington, DC: National Geographic Society, 1999.

National Geographic Society and Ralph M. Feather, Jr. *Earth Science.* New York: Glencoe/McGraw-Hill, 2002.

O'Meara, Donna. *Into the Volcano: A Volcano Researcher at Work.* Tonawanda, NY: Kids Can Press, 2007.

Pearce, Fred. *When the Rivers Run Dry: Water—The Defining Crisis of the Twenty-First Century.* Boston, MA: Beacon Press, 2006.

Philander, S. George. *Our Affair with El Niño: How We Transformed an Enchanting Peruvian Current into a Global Climate Hazard.* Princeton, NJ: Princeton University Press, 2004.

Pretor-Pinney, Gavin. *The Cloudspotter's Guide.* New York: Perigee, 2006.

Reader's Digest Association, eds. *Great Disasters: Dramatic True Stories of Nature's Awesome Powers.* Pleasantville, NY: Reader's Digest, 1991.

Robinson, Andrew. *Earth Shock: Hurricanes, Volcanoes, Earthquakes, Tornadoes and Other Forces of Nature.* New York: W. W. Norton & Company, 2002.

Rosenfeld, Jeffrey P. *Eye of the Storm: Inside the World's Deadliest Hurricanes, Tornadoes, and Blizzards.* New York: Basic Books, 2005.

Rubin, Louis D., and Jim Duncan. *The Weather Wizard's Cloud Book.* Chapel Hill, NC: Algonquin Books of Chapel Hill, 1989.

Simon, Seymour. *Hurricanes.* New York: Harper Trophy, 2003.

Simon, Seymour. *Tornadoes.* New York: Harper Trophy, 2001.

Simon, Seymour. *Weather.* New York: Collins, 2006.

Stanley, Jerry. *Children of the Dust Bowl: The True Story of the School at Weedpatch Camp.* New York: Crown Publishers Inc., 1992.

Stewart, Gail. *Overview Series—Catastrophe in Southern Asia: The Tsunami of 2004.* San Diego, CA: Lucent Books, 2005.

Svobida, Lawrence. *Farming the Dust Bowl: A First-Hand Account from Kansas.* Lawrence, KS: University Press of Kansas, 1986. (Originally published in 1940 by The Caxton Printers, Ltd.)

Sweeney, Karen O'Connor. *Nature Runs Wild.* Danbury, CT: Franklin Watts Inc., 1979.

Tannenbaum, Beulah, and Harold E. Tannenbaum. *Making and Using Your own Weather Station.* New York: Franklin Watts, 1989.

Tibballs, Geoff. *Tsunami: The Most Terrifying Disaster.* London: Carlton Publishing Group, 2005.

Trewartha, Glenn T., and Lyle H. Horn. *An Introduction to Climate.* 5th ed. New York: McGraw-Hill, 1980.

VanCleave, Janice. *Earth Science for Every Kid: 101 Easy Experiments that Really Work.* New York: John Wiley, 1991.

Vasquez, Tim. *Weather Forecasting Handbook.* 5th ed. Garland, TX: Weather Graphics Technologies, 2002.

Verkaik, Jerrine, and Arjen Verkaik. *Under the Whirlwind: Everything You Need to Know About Tornadoes But Didn't Know Who to Ask.* 2nd ed., Elmwood, Ontario, Canada: Whirlwind Books, 2001.

Walker, Jane. *Avalanches and Landslides.* New York: Gloucester Press, 1992.

Walker, Jane. *Famine, Drought and Plagues.* New York: Gloucester Press, 1992.

Ward, Kaari, ed. *Great Disasters.* Pleasantville, NY: Reader's Digest Association, 1989.

Waterlow, Julia. *Violent Earth: Flood.* New York: Hodder Children's Books, 1994.

Watt, Fiona, and Francis Wilson. *Weather and Climate.* London: Usborne Publishing Ltd., 1992.

Williams, Jack. *The Weather Book: An Easy-to-Understand Guide to the USA's Weather.* New York: Vintage Books, 1997.

Worster, Donald. *Dust Bowl: The Southern Plains in the 1930s.* New York: Oxford University Press, 1979.

Wright, Richard T. *Environmental Science: Toward A Sustainable Future.* 10th ed. Upper Saddle River, NJ: Prentice Hall, 2007.

Zebrowski, Ernest, and Ernest Zebrowski Jr. *Perils of a Restless Planet: Scientific Perspectives on Natural Disasters.* Ann Arbor: University of Michigan Press, 2005.

Zebrowski, Ernest, and Judith A. Howard. *Category 5: The Story of Camille: Lessons Unlearned from America's Most Violent Hurricane.* Cambridge, UK: Cambridge University Press, 1999.

Periodicals

Ackerman, Jennifer. "Islands at the Edge." *National Geographic* (August 1997): pp. 2–31.

Akin, Wallace. "The Great Tri-State Tornado." *American Heritage* (May/June 2000): pp. 32–36.

Allen, Brian. "Capitol Hill Meltdown: While the Nation Sizzles, Congress Fiddles over Measures to Slow Down Future Climate Change." *Time* (August 9, 1999): p. 56+.

Annin, Peter. "Power on the Prairie: In Minnesota, They're Harvesting the Wind." *Newsweek* (October 26, 1998): p. 66.

Appenzeller, Tim. "The Case of the Missing Carbon." *National Geographic* (February, 2004): pp. 88–117.

Appenzeller, Tim. "Humans in the Hot Seat." *U.S. News & World Report* (November 6, 2000): p. 54.

Appenzeller, Tim, and Dennis R. Dimick. "Signs from Earth." *National Geographic* (September 2004): pp. 2–12.

"Avalanche!" *National Geographic World* (January 1997): pp. 2–6.

Baliunas, Sallie. "Full of Hot Air: A Climate Alarmist Takes on 'Criminals Against Humanity'." *Reason* (October 2005): p. 1.

Beardsley, Tim. "Dissecting a Hurricane." *Scientific American* (March 2000): pp. 80–85.

Begley, Sharon. "The Mercury's Rising." *Newsweek* (December 4, 2000): p. 52.

Bentley, Mace. "A Midsummer's Nightmare." *Weatherwise* (August/September 1996).

Bentley, Mace, and Steve Horstmeyer. "Monstrous Mitch." *Weatherwise* (March/April 1999).

Bishop, Ian D., and David R. Miller. "Visual Assessment Of Off-Shore Wind Turbines: The Influence of Distance, Contrast, Movement and Social Variables." *Renewable Energy: An International Journal* (April 2007): pp. 814–831.

Bond, Kathleen. "Church Backs Poor in Drought; Brazil's Leaders Slow to Respond." *National Catholic Reporter* (August 14, 1998): p. 11+.

Brenstein, Seth. "Hottest Years Ever Strengthen the Scientific Case for an Ever-Warming World." Knight-Ridder/Tribune News Service (January 13, 2000).

Brooks, Tim. "Fire and Rain: Forecasting the Chaos of Weather." *National Geographic* (June 2005): pp. 90–109.

Brown, Kathryn. "Invisible Energy." *Discover* (October 1999): p. 36.

Carroll, Chris. "In Hot Water." *National Geographic* (August 2005): pp. 72–85.

Chacon, Richard. "The Earth Calms, and Recovery Begins." *Boston Globe* (January 19, 2001): p. A13.

Coila, Bridget. "Changing the Weather." *Weatherwise* (May/June 2005): pp. 50–54.

Currie, Lloyd. "The Remarkable Metrological History of Radiocarbon Dating." *Journal of Research of the National Institute of Standards and Technology* (March/April 2004): pp. 185–217.

De Roy, Tui. "Caught in a Melting World." *International Wildlife* (November/December 2000): pp. 12–19.

Dick, Jason. "Global Warming." *Amicus Journal* (Summer 1999): p. 13.

"Drowning: Bangladesh." *The Economist* (September 12, 1998): p. 43.

Duffy, James A. "Administration Signs Global Warming Agreement." Knight-Ridder/Tribune News Service (November 12, 1998).

Dugger, Celia W. "2-Month Flood Breeds Havoc and Diseases in Bangladesh." *New York Times* (October 10, 1998): p. A9.

Dugger, Celia W. "Monsoon Hangs On, Swamping Bangladesh." *New York Times* (September 7, 1998): p. A1, A5.

Ehrlich, Gretel. "Last Days of the Ice Hunters." *National Geographic* (January 2006): pp. 79–101.

"Enviro-Cars: The Race Is On." *Business Week* (February 8, 1999): p. 74.

Favstovsky, D. E., and P. M. Sheehan. "The Extinction of the Dinosaurs in North America." *GSA Today* (March 2005): pp. 4–10.

"Fighting Global Warming with Iron at Sea." *Newsweek* (October 23, 2000): p. 54.

Findley, Rowe. "Mount St. Helens: Nature on Fast Forward." *National Geographic* (May 2000): pp. 106–125.

"Fire Forces 200 from Homes Near Boulder." *New York Times* (September 18, 2000): p. A22.

Fox, Stephen. "For a While…It Was Fun." *Smithsonian* (September 1999): pp. 128–130, 132, 134–140, 142.

Franklin, James L. "A Season of Devastation: Atlantic Hurricanes 2004." *Weatherwise* (March/April 2005): pp. 52–61.

Gaines, Ernest J. "Home No More." *National Geographic* (August 2006): pp. 42–53.

Glick, Daniel. "The Big Thaw." *National Geographic* (September 2004): pp. 13–33.

"Global Warming May Be Beneficial." *USA Today Magazine* (June 2000): p. 10.

Gonzalez, Frank I. "Tsumani!" *Scientific American* (May 1999): pp. 56–65.

Gore, Rick. "Andrew Aftermath." *National Geographic* (April 1993): pp. 2–37.

Griekspoor, Phyllis J. "Baked Kansas: La Niña Heralds a Possible Drought for State." *Wichita Eagle* (February 2006).

Grove, Noel. "Volcanoes: Crucibles of Creation." *National Geographic* (December 1992): pp. 5–41.

Halverson, Jeffrey B. "Chasing Hurricanes in Africa." *Weatherwise* (November/December 2006): pp. 62–64.

Halverson, Jeffrey B. "A Climate Conundrum." *Weatherwise* (March/April 2006): pp. 18–23.

Halverson, Jeffrey B. "A Hurricane Is Born." *Weatherwise* (November/December 2004): pp. 72–73.

Hanson-Harding, Alexandra. "Global Warming." *Junior Scholastic* (November 27, 2000): p. 6.

Hayden, Thomas. "Super Storms: No End in Sight." *National Geographic* (August 2006): pp. 66–77.

Hebert, H. Josef. "Scientists Paint Grim View of Impact on U.S. of Global Warming." Associated Press (June 9, 2000).

Helvarg, David. "Antarctica: The Ice Is Moving." *E* (September 2000): p. 33.

Henson, Robert. "Hot, Hotter, Hottest: 1998 Raised the Bar for Global Temperature Leaps." *Weatherwise* (March/April 1999): pp. 34–37.

Henson, Robert. "The Intensity Problem: How Strong Will a Hurricane Get?" *Weatherwise* (September/October 1998): pp. 20–26.

Hertsgaard, Mark. "Killer Weather Ahead." *Nation* (February 26, 2007): pp. 5–6.

Hodges, Glenn. "Russian Smokejumpers." *National Geographic* (August 2002): pp. 82–100.

"Hurricane Havoc in Central America." *The Economist* (November 7, 1998): p. 33.

"Hurricanes Rip Through Impoverished Caribbean, Central American Regions." *National Catholic Reporter* (November 20, 1998): p. 12.

"Iceland's Trial by Fire." *National Geographic* (May 1997): pp. 58–71.

Iocavelli, Debi. "Hurricanes: Eye Spy." *Weatherwise* (August/September 1996): pp. 10–11.

Keisterm, Edwin, Jr. " Battling the Orange Monster." *Smithsonian* (July 2000): pp. 32–42.

Klesius, Michael. "The Mystery of Snowflakes." *National Geographic* (January 2007): p. 22.

Lange, Karen. "Direct Hit: Inside a Tornado." *National Geographic* (June 2005): pp. 112–115.

Larsen, Josh. "The Emergence of the Weather Blog." *Weatherwise* (January/February 2007): pp. 10–11.

Lawless, Jill. "Global Warming Threatens a Third of World's Habitats." Associated Press (August 30, 2000).

Le Comte, Douglas. "Weather around the World." *Weatherwise* (March/April 2001): pp. 23–28.

Levine, Mark. "A Storm at the Bone: A Personal Exploration into Deep Weather." *Outside Magazine* (November 1998).

Libbrecht, Kenneth G. "The Formation of Snow Crystals." *American Scientist* (January/February 2007): pp. 52–59.

McDonald, Kim A. "Unearthing Earth's Ancient Atmosphere Beneath Two Miles of Greenland Ice." *Chronicle of Higher Education* (August 2, 1996): pp. A6+.

McKibbin, Warwick J., and Peter J. Wilcoxen. "Until We Know More About Global Warming, the Best Policy Is a Highly Flexible One." *Chronicle of Higher Education* (July 2, 1999): pp. B4+.

Mazza, Patrick. "Global Warming Is Here!" *Earth Island Journal* (Fall 1999): p. 14.

Mazza, Patrick. "The Invisible Hand: As Human Activity Warms the Earth, El Niño Grows More Violent." *Sierra* (May/June 1998): pp. 68+.

Miner, Todd, Peter J. Sousounis, James Wallman, and Greg Mann. "Hurricane Huron." *Bulletin of the American Meteorological Society* (February 2000): pp. 223–236.

Mitchell, Mitch. "Wind Gusts Cause Power Outages, Dust Storm." *Fort Worth Star-Telegram* (April 2006).

Montaigner, Fenck. "No Room to Run." *National Geographic* (September 2004): pp. 34–55.

Mulvaney, Kieran. "Alaska: The Big Meltdown." *E* (September 2000): p. 36.

Nielsen, Clifford H. "Hurd Willett: Forecaster Extraordinaire." *Weatherwise* (August/September 1993): pp. 38–44.

Nuttall, Nick. "Ganges Glacier Melting Fast." *The Times* (London). (July 20, 1999): p. 9.

Pearce, Fred. "Science: Meltdown in the Mountains." *The Independent* (London). (March 31, 2000): p. 8.

Perkins, S. "Greenland's Ice Is Thinner at the Margins." *Science News* (July 22, 2000): p. 54.

Peterson, Chester Jr. "Harvest the Wind: The Midwest Could Be the Saudi Arabia of Wind-Powered Energy." *Successful Farming* (January 1999): p. 44+.

Pinna, Marco. "Etna Ignites." *National Geographic* (February, 2002): pp. 68–87.

Proctor, Paul. "Fire-Fighting Fleet Stretched to Limit as U.S. West Burns." *Aviation Week & Space Technology* (August 21, 2000): pp. 38–39.

"Rain, Rain, Go Away . . . ." *Time International* (September 14, 1998): p. 18.

Rasicot, Julie. "Locals Help Battle Fires in Montana." *The Washington Post* (August 17, 2000): p. 16.

"Renewable Energy Resources." *Current Health 2* (April 1999): p. S14.

Revkin, Andrew C. "Treaty Talks Fail to Find Consensus in Global Warming." *New York Times* (November 26, 2000).

Rosenfeld, Jeff. "Mr. Tornado: The Life and Career of Ted Fujita." *Weatherwise* (May/June 1999): p. 18.

Rosenfeld, Jeff. "Sentinels in the Sky." *Weatherwise* (January/February 2000): pp. 24–27.

Rosenfeld, Jeff. "Unearthing Climate." *Weatherwise* (May/June 2000): p. 12.

Santana, Sofia. "Remembering Andrew." *Weatherwise* (July/August 2002): pp. 14–19.

Shepherd, Marshall. "The big picture: Satellites have changed our view of the world." *Weatherwise.* (January/February 2003): pp. 24–37.

Shilts, Elizabeth. "Harnessing a Powerful Breeze." *Canadian Geographic* (May/June 1999): p. 20.

Simpson, Sarah. "Raging Rivers of Rock." *Scientific American* (July 2000): pp. 24–25.

"The State of U.S. Renewable Power." *Mother Earth News* (February 1999): p. 16.

Stevens, William K. "Catastrophic Melting of Ice Sheet Is Possible, Studies Hint." *New York Times* (July 7, 1998): p. B13.

Stevens, William K. "Human Imprint on Climate Change Grows Clearer." *New York Times* (June 29, 1999): p. 1+.

Sudetic, Chuck. "As the World Burns." *Rolling Stone* (September 2, 1999): p. 97+.

Suplee, Curt. "El Niño/La Niña." *National Geographic* (March 1999): pp. 72–95.

Taylor, Jeff. "Flood Convergence." *Reason* (December 2005).

"That Dreadful Smog Is Back." *The Economist* (March 18, 2000): p. 40.

Trenberth, Kevin. "Uncertainty in Hurricanes and Global Warming." *Science* (17 June 2005): pp. 1753–1754.

Vesilind, Priit J. "The Hard Science, Dumb Luck, and Cowboy Nerve of Chasing Tornadoes." *National Geographic* (April 2004): pp. 2–37.

"U.S. Signs Kyoto Pact." *Maclean's* (November 23, 1998): p. 93.

Williams, A. R. "After the Deluge." *National Geographic* (November 1999): pp. 108–129.

Williams, A. R. "Popocatepetl: Mexico's Smoking Mountain." *National Geographic* (January 1999): pp. 116–137.

Williams, A. R. "Montserrat: Under the Volcano." *National Geographic* (July 1997): pp. 58–75.

Williams, Jack. "Antarctica: A Land of Ice and Wind." *Weatherwise* (January/February 2000): pp. 14–22.

Wunsch, Carl. "Quantitative Estimate of the Milankovitch-forced Contribution to Observed Quaternary Climate Change." *Quaternary Science Reviews* (Vol. 23, 2004):1001–1012.

Zwingle, Erla. "Meltdown: The Alps under Pressure." *National Geographic* (February, 2006): pp. 96–115.

Web Sites

Allgeyer, Robert. "APPENDIX: The Fata Morgana Mirage over Monterey Bay." *View to the Horizon.* <http://www.icogitate.com/~ergosum/essays/vtth/viewtothehorizon.htm> (accessed June 14, 2007).

American Avalanche Association. <http://www.americanavalancheassociation.org/> (accessed June 14, 2007).

"Avalanche!" *NOVA Online.* <http://www.pbs.org/wgbh/nova/avalanche/> (accessed June 14, 2007).

"Avalanche Awareness." *National Snow and Ice Data Center.* <http://nsidc.org/snow/avalanche/> (accessed June 14, 2007).

"Cascades Volcano Observatory." *United States Geological Survey.* <http://vulcan.wr.usgs.gov/> (accessed June 14, 2007).

"Climate Change." *United States Environmental Protection Agency.* <http://www.epa.gov/climatechange/> (accessed June 14, 2007).

"Climate Change." *World Wildlife Fund.* <http://www.panda.org/about_wwf/what_we_do/climate_change/index.cfm> (accessed June 14, 2007).

"Climate Change Impacts: Feeling the Heat." *Nature Conservancy.* <http://www.nature.org/initiatives/climatechange/issues> (accessed June 14, 2007).

Cowley, Les. "Rainbows." *Atmosphere Optics.* <http://www.atoptics.co.uk/rayshad.htm> (accessed June 14, 2007).

"Do-It-Yourself Weather Forecasting." *Weather Michigan.* <http://www.weathermichigan.com/u_do_it.htm> (accessed June 14, 2007).

"Driving in Fog." *California Highway Patrol.* <http://www.chp.ca.gov/html/fog-tips.html> (accessed June 14, 2007).

"Drought." *National Weather Service: Hydrologic Information Center.* <http://www.nws.noaa.gov/oh/hic/current/drought/> (accessed June 14, 2007).

"Drought Watch." *U.S. Geological Survey.* <http://water.usgs.gov/waterwatch/?m=dryw> (accessed June 14, 2007).

"El Niño." *National Oceanic and Atmospheric Administration.* <http://www.elnino.noaa.gov/> (accessed June 14, 2007).

"Flood." *Federal Emergency Management Agency.* <http://www.fema.gov/hazard/flood/index.shtm> (accessed June 14, 2007).

"Flood Safety." *National Weather Service Flood Safety.* <http://www.floodsafety.noaa.gov/> (accessed June 14, 2007).

"Forces and Winds: Online Meteorology Guide." *University of Illinois: Weather World 2010 Project.* <http://ww2010.atmos.uiuc.edu/(Gh)/guides/mtr/fw/home.rxml> (accessed June 14, 2007).

Geist, Eric L., and Laura Zink Torresan. "Life of a Tsunami." *United States Geological Survey.* <http://walrus.wr.usgs.gov/tsunami/basics.html> (accessed June 14, 2007).

"Hawaiian Volcano Observatory." *United States Geological Survey.* <http://hvo.wr.usgs.gov/> (accessed June 14, 2007).

Helmuth, Laura. "Antarctica Erupts!" *Smithsonian Science and Technology.* <http://www.smithsonianmag.com/issues/2006/december/antarctica.php> (accessed June 14, 2007).

"Historical Winter Storms." *The Weather Channel.* <http://www.weather.com/encyclopedia/winter/history.html> (accessed June 14, 2007).

"Hurricanes." *FEMA for Kids.* <http://www.fema.gov/kids/hurr.htm> (accessed June 14, 2007).

"Hurricanes." *National Oceanic and Atmospheric Administration.* <http://hurricanes.noaa.gov/>(accessed June 14, 2007).

Jaffe, Eric. "Volcanic Lightning." *Smithsonian Science and Technology.* <http://www.smithsonianmag.com/issues/2007/february/augustine.php> (accessed June 14, 2007).

"La Niña." *National Aeronautic and Space Administration: Earth Observatory.* <http://earthobservatory.nasa.gov/Library/LaNina/> (accessed June 14, 2007).

"La Niña." *National Oceanic and Atmospheric Administration.* <http://www.elnino.noaa.gov/lanina.html>(accessed June 14, 2007).

"Local Winds: Mountain Breezes." *Danish Wind Industry Association.* <http://www.windpower.org/en/tour/wres/mount.htm> (accessed June 14, 2007).

"The Monsoon." *National Weather Service.* <http://www.wrh.noaa.gov/fgz/science/monsoon.php?wfo=fgz> (accessed June 14, 2007).

"Names of Winds." *Golden Gate Weather Services.* <http://ggweather.com/winds.html> (accessed June 14, 2007).

"National Avalanche Center." *U.S. Forest Service.* <http://www.avalanche.org/%7enac/> (accessed June 14, 2007).

"National Hurricane Center Home Page." *National Hurricane Center.* <http://www.nhc.noaa.gov/> (accessed June 14, 2007).

"National Oceanic and Atmospheric Administration Home Page." *National Oceanic and Atmospheric Administration.* <http://www.noaa.org> (accessed June 14, 2007).

"Natural Hazards—Wildfires." *United States Geological Survey.* <http://www.usgs.gov/hazards/wildfires/> (accessed June 14, 2007).

"North American Monsoon Experiment (NAME)." *NASA Earth Observatory.* <http://earthobservatory.nasa.gov/Newsroom/Campaigns/NAME_Mission.html> (accessed June 14, 2007).

"NCAR/UCAR/UOP Home." *National Center for Atmospheric Research.* <http://www.ucar.edu/> (accessed June 14, 2007).

"Official Weather Forecasts and Warnings." *The World Meteorological Organization.* <http://www.wmo.int/> (accessed June 14, 2007).

Pacific Tsunami Museum. <http://www.tsunami.org/> (accessed June 14, 2007).

"Planet Earth." *NASA's Observatorium.* <http://observe.arc.nasa.gov/nasa/earth/earth_index.shtml.html> (accessed June 14, 2007).

"Thunderstorms and Lightning." *Federal Emergency Management Administration.* <http://www.fema.gov/hazard/thunderstorm/index.shtm> (accessed June 14, 2007).

"Tornado." *Federal Emergency Management Administration.* <http://www.fema. gov/hazard/tornado/index.shtm> (accessed June 14, 2007).

"Tsunamis." *Coastal Ocean Institute.* <http://www.whoi.edu/institutes/coi/view Topic.do?o=readid=281> (accessed June 14, 2007).

"U.S. Drought Monitor." *University of Nebraska, Lincoln.* <http://www.drought. unl.edu/dm/monitor.html> (accessed June 14, 2007).

"Wave that Shook the World." *NOVA.* <http://www.pbs.org/wgbh/nova/ tsunami/> (accessed June 14, 2007).

"Weather." *National Oceanic and Atmospheric Administration.* <http://www. noaa.gov/wx.html> (accessed June 14, 2007).

"Weather Office." *Environment Canada.* <http://weatheroffice.ec.gc.ca/canada_e. html> (accessed June 14, 2007).

"Welcome to the Weather Underground." *Weather Underground.* <http://www. wunderground.com/> (accessed June 14, 2007).

"Wildfire." *Federal Emergency Management Administration.* <http://www.fema. gov/hazard/wildfire/index.shtm> (accessed June 14, 2007).

Wilhelmson, Bob, et al. "Types of Thunderstorms." *University of Illinois: Weather World 2010 Project.* <http://ww2010.atmos.uiuc.edu/(Gh)/ guides/mtr/svr/type/home.rxml> (accessed June 14, 2007).

"World Meteorological Organization Homepage." *World Meteorological Organization: A United Nations Specialized Agency.* <http://www.wmo.> (accessed June 14, 2007).

Index

Numerals in *italic type* indicate volume number. Items in **boldface** indicate main entries. Graphic elements (photos, graphs, illustrations) are denoted by (ill.). Tables are denoted by *t*.

Altocumulus castellanus clouds, *1:* 132, 134 (ill.)

Altocumulus clouds (Ac), *1:* 112–13, 113 (ill.), 114 (ill.)

Altocumulus undulatus clouds, *1:* 124, 125 (ill.)

Altostratus clouds (As), *1:* 112 (ill.), 113–14

Altostratus translucidus clouds, *1:* 124

Aluminum, acid rain and, *5:* 789, 790 (ill.)

Amateur forecasting, *5:* 664–89

    air pressure measurement, *5:* 676–78, 680 (ill.), 681 (ill.), 682 (ill.), 683, 683 (ill.)

    home weather center setup, *5:* 669–70, 670 (ill.)

    making forecasts, *5:* 684–89

    natural signs, *5:* 664–66, 665 (ill.), 668–69

    precipitation monitoring, *5:* 680–82, 681 (ill.), 685 (ill.)

    recording observations, *1:* 135; *5:* 682–84

    relative humidity measurement, *5:* 674–76, 674t, 677 (ill.)

    skilled vs. unskilled, *5:* 657–59

    temperature measurement, *5:* 670–72, 671 (ill.), 672 (ill.), 673t, 674

    wind monitoring, *5:* 678–80, 684 (ill.), 686, 687t

American Lung Association, *5:* 772

American Meterological Society, *5:* 713

American Red Cross, *3:* 368

American Wind Energy Association, *5:* 811

Anabatic winds, *3:* 433–34, 434 (ill.)

Anaerobic bacteria, *1:* 87; *5:* 732

Anchovies, threats to, *1:* 53, 54 (ill.); *2:* 284, 302

Andes

    debris avalanche, *3:* 400

    landslides, *3:* 407

    Mount Huascarán avalanches, *2:* 161–69, 163 (ill.), 164 (ill.), 170; *3:* 401

Anemometers, *5:* 680

Aneroid barometers, *5:* 677–78, 682 (ill.)

Angle of Earth's tilt, *1:* 96–97, 96 (ill.); *5:* 741–42

Angular momentum, conservation of, *1:* 29–30

Animal life. *See also specific animals*

    arctic climates, *1:* 84

    climate change history, *1:* 87–88

    deserts, *1:* 72

    earthquakes, *2:* 280

    El Niño effects, *2:* 302–8

global warming disruptions, *5:* 762–64, 762 (ill.), 764 (ill.)

    Mediterranean climates, *1:* 77

    monsoon regions, *1:* 68

    mountain climates, *1:* 85–86

    savannas, *1:* 68–69, 69 (ill.)

    steppes, *1:* 73

    subpolar climates, *1:* 80

    temperate climates, *1:* 78

    tropical rain forests, *1:* 66

    tundra climates, *1:* 81–82

    as weather predictor, *5:* 665–66, 665 (ill.)

Annual mean temperature, *1:* 59; *5:* 728

Annual Review of Ecology, Evolution and Systematics, *5:* 761

Annual temperature range, *1:* 59; *5:* 728–29

Antarctica

    global warming, *5:* 763, 764 (ill.)

    ice core analysis, *1:* 102, 103 (ill.); *5:* 747–48

    katabatic winds, *3:* 437, 453

    melting glaciers, *5:* 753, 754 (ill.)

    ozone layer depletion, *5:* 794–95, 796 (ill.)

    whirly winds, *3:* 447

Anticyclones, *1:* 22, 31

Antrim, Northern Ireland lava formation, *4:* 614

Anvil top of clouds, *1:* 121, 121 (ill.), 128; *4:* 542 (ill.)

Appalachian Mountains landslides, *3:* 405, 408

Apparent temperature, *5:* 707

AQI (Air Quality Index), *5:* 781–82

Aquifers, *1:* 48; *2:* 218, 222

AR 2 (Second Assessment Report), *3:* 333

Archaean era, *5:* 732

Archaeans, *5:* 732

Arctic climates

    defined, *1:* 64, 82–84, 83 (ill.)

    global warming, *5:* 762 (ill.), 763–64, 767 (ill.)

    steam fog, *3:* 343

Argentia, Canada fog, *3:* 342

Arid climates. *See* Dry climates

Aristotle, *2:* 274

Arizona

    hurricanes, *3:* 374

    La Niña effects, *3:* 425

    lightning storm, *4:* 633 (ill.)

Crests (waves)
    light, *4:* 495
    water, *1:* 22; *4:* 516
Cretaceous period, *5:* 738 (ill.)
Crisostomo, Yumie, *5:* 757
Critical fire protection, *4:* 627
Crockett, David, *4:* 592
Crop rotation, *2:* 248
Crown fires, *4:* 636–37
Crust, Earth's, *2:* 261–62; *4:* 596–97, 597 (ill.)
Crystal fire of 2006, *4:* 626
Cs (Cirrostratus clouds), *1:* 115–16
Cu (Cumulus clouds). *See* Cumulus clouds (Cu)
Cumuliform clouds, *1:* 107
Cumulonimbus calvus clouds, *1:* 123 (ill.)
Cumulonimbus clouds (Cb)
    defined, *1:* 120–21, 121 (ill.)
    lightning and, *4:* 522–23
    precipitation from, *1:* 138
    thunderstorms and, *4:* 505, 507
Cumulonimbus incus clouds, *1:* 120, 121
Cumulonimbus mammatus clouds, *1:* 128 (ill.)
Cumulus clouds (Cu)
    airplane view, *1:* 119 (ill.)
    with cirrus clouds, *1:* 43 (ill.)
    cloud seeding of, *1:* 145
    defined, *1:* 119–20
    mediocris species, *1:* 120 (ill.)
    precipitation from, *1:* 138
    towering, *1:* 118 (ill.)
Cumulus humilis clouds, *1:* 125–26, 127 (ill.)
Cumulus mediocris clouds, *1:* 120 (ill.)
Cumulus stage of thunderstorms, *4:* 504–5, 504 (ill.)
Cup anemometers, *5:* 680
Curly Horse fire of 2006, *4:* 627
Current leaders, *4:* 524
Current meters, *2:* 317
Currents, air. *See* Winds
Currents, ocean, *1:* 51
Cycles of El Niño, *2:* 294
Cyclogenesis, *1:* 29
Cyclones (storms), *1:* 22; *3:* 350. *See also* Storms
Cyclones (tornadoes). *See* Tornadoes
Cyprus waterspout, *4:* 553 (ill.)
Czech Republic, El Niño and, *2:* 289–90

D

Daily mean temperature, *1:* 59
Dalton, John, *1:* 10
Dams
    for drought, *2:* 227–28
    for flood control, *3:* 332
    Manchu River Dam collapse, *3:* 474, 474 (ill.)
    melting glaciers and, *5:* 754–55
DART (Deep-Ocean Assessment and Reporting of Tsunamis), *4:* 581
Dart leaders, *4:* 525
Data collection. *See also specific instruments and data types*
    for amateurs, *5:* 669
    future trends, *5:* 721–24
    international, *5:* 659, 661
    in the U.S., *5:* 661–62
Daughter nuclei, *1:* 101; *5:* 746
Day fire of 2006, *4:* 626, 636
Deaths
    air pollution, *5:* 773, 775
    avalanches, *1:* 155; *2:* 176, 180
    blizzards, *2:* 186, 188, 189, 191, 192
    derechos, *3:* 449
    earthquakes, *2:* 267, 268, 270, 271, 272, 278
    El Niño, *2:* 284, 287, 289–90
    floods, *3:* 321, 324, 328, 329, 332, 333; *4:* 532
    hailstorms, *1:* 158
    heat waves, *2:* 225
    hurricanes, *3:* 349, 350, 355, 357, 377*t*, 382, 384, 427
    Indian Ocean tsunami, *2:* 258–59
    Kashmir earthquake, *2:* 260
    landslides, *3:* 391, 398, 403, 404, 405, 407, 414
    lightning, *4:* 518
    Manchu River Dam collapse, *3:* 474
    monsoons, *3:* 460, 462, 465, 467, 468
    Mount Huascarán avalanches, *2:* 161, 164 (ill.), 166, 167–68, 170
    San Francisco earthquakes, *2:* 251
    Santa Ana wind disasters, *3:* 440
    Swiss avalanches, *2:* 169
    thunderstorms, *4:* 501

Dr. John (musician), *3:* 333

Drainage winds. *See* Mountain breezes

Drifting snow, *1:* 151

Drifting weather buoys, *2:* 316

Drinking water

    flood-contaminated, *2:* 308; *3:* 328, 463, 465, 473; *5:* 762

    threats to, *5:* 755, 756

Drizzle, *1:* 138–40, 142

Dropwindsondes, *5:* 691

Drought, *2:* **207–28**

    actions for, *2:* 222–23, 226–28

    African Sahel region, *2:* 207–13, 209 (ill.), 210 (ill.), 213 (ill.)

    causes, *2:* 213–16, 215 (ill.)

    defined, *2:* 207

    Dust Bowl, *2:* 233

    effects, *2:* 217–20

    El Niño effects, *2:* 285–87, 287 (ill.), 304

    global warming, *5:* 761

    health issues, *2:* 223–25

    human factors, *2:* 211, 220–22

    La Niña effects, *3:* 424–25

    monitoring and forecasting, *2:* 225–26, 225 (ill.)

    monsoons, *3:* 474–75

    rainmaking attempts, *1:* 144

    wildfires, *4:* 632

Dry adiabatic lapse rate, *1:* 39; *3:* 437; *4:* 505

Dry-bulb thermometers, *5:* 674–75

Dry climates. *See also* Semiarid climates

    defined, *1:* 69

    deserts, *1:* 64, 70–72, 70 (ill.); *2:* 243–44

    steppes, *1:* 64, 72–73, 73 (ill.)

    in the U.S., *1:* 86

Dry ice, for cloud seeding, *1:* 144

Dry tongues, *4:* 515

Dunes, *3:* 452–55, 454 (ill.)

Dust, in ice cores, *1:* 102; *5:* 748

Dust Bowl Diary (Low), *2:* 247

Dust Bowl of the 1930s

    clouds of dust, *2:* 232 (ill.), 235 (ill.)

    farms, *2:* 234 (ill.), 245 (ill.)

    The Grapes of Wrath depiction, *2:* 240–41, 241 (ill.)

    history, *2:* 230–35, 236

    migration from, *2:* 238, 238 (ill.)

    New Deal program, *2:* 235, 237–38, 237 (ill.)

    soil conservation programs, *2:* 239

Dust clouds, from asteroids, *1:* 98–99

Dust devils, *2:* 246, 246 (ill.); *3:* 441, 444 (ill.), 446

Dust storms, *2:* **229–49.** *See also* Dust Bowl of the 1930s

    accidents from, *2:* 248

    agricultural practices for, *2:* 247–48

    causes, *2:* 242–44

    defined, *2:* 229–30

    desert winds and, *3:* 440–41, 443, 443 (ill.), 444 (ill.)

    effects, *2:* 244–46

    human factors, *2:* 246–47

    safety measures, *2:* 248–49

Dust-whirl stage of tornadoes, *4:* 547

Duzce earthquake (Turkey), *2:* 271

E

Earth. *See also* Earth's rotation

    climate change history, *1:* 86–92; *5:* 730–36

    interior of, *2:* 260–62; *4:* 597 (ill.)

    sun's interaction with, *1:* 2–4

Earth Summit of 1992, *5:* 765

Earth survey satellites, *2:* 225–26

Earthflow landslides, *3:* 401–3

Earthquake fountains, *2:* 266

Earthquake hazard map, *2:* 277 (ill.)

Earthquakes, *2:* **251–82**

    avalanche formation and, *2:* 174

    causes, *2:* 260–65, 264 (ill.)

    effects, *2:* 265–71, 266 (ill.)

    human factors, *2:* 272–74

    Kobe, Japan, *2:* 268–69, 269 (ill.)

    landslides from, *3:* 405

    major occurrences, *2:* 255t, 257, 258–60, 259 (ill.), 261 (ill.), 272, 279

    monitoring and forecasting, *2:* 274–80, 275 (ill.), 276 (ill.), 277 (ill.), 278 (ill.)

    Papua New Guinea, *4:* 568

    Peru, *2:* 170

    safety measures, *2:* 280–82, 280 (ill.)

San Francisco, *2:* 251–58, 253 (ill.), 254 (ill.),
256 (ill.)
tsunamis and, *2:* 269–71; *4:* 579–80
Turkey, *2:* 270–71, 271 (ill.)
as volcano trigger, *4:* 590–91
Earth's rotation
climate change history, *1:* 95–97, 96 (ill.); *5:*
740–42
season changes with, *1:* 1–2
wind, *1:* 14–15
East Coast states. *See also specific states*
blizzards, *2:* 185–90, 187 (ill.), 189 (ill.), 190
(ill.), 195, 196 (ill.), 197 (ill.)
hurricanes, *3:* 381–83, 383 (ill.)
nor'easters, *3:* 446, 448
Eccentricity of Earth's orbit, *1:* 95; *5:* 741
Echo intensity, *5:* 693
Economic impact
derechos, *3:* 449
droughts, *2:* 217, 219–20
dust storms, *2:* 244
earthquakes, *2:* 279
El Niño, *2:* 284, 286, 289, 307*t*
evacuations, *3:* 388
floods, *3:* 324, 329, 332, 333; *4:* 532
hurricanes, *3:* 349, 350, 354, 355, 357, 382, 384
landslides, *3:* 391
lightning, *4:* 519
New Deal program, *2:* 235, 237–38, 237 (ill.)
nor'easters, *3:* 448
San Francisco earthquakes, *2:* 252
Santa Ana wind disasters, *3:* 440
solar energy, *5:* 803–4
thunderstorms, *4:* 501
tornadoes, *4:* 533, 539, 540, 555
tsunamis, *4:* 575
wildfires, *4:* 623, 624, 625, 627, 634–36, 642
Ecuador, El Niño and, *2:* 301–2
Education on wildfires, *4:* 651
Effusive eruptions, *4:* 600
Ekman Spiral, *1:* 53
El Niño, *2:* **283–320**
1982 to 1983 season, *2:* 306–7, 307*t*
1997 to 1998 season, *2:* 284–93, 287 (ill.), 288
(ill.), 289 (ill.), 293 (ill.)

causes, *2:* 293–98
defined, *2:* 283–84
droughts and, *2:* 215–16
effects, *2:* 296 (ill.), 298–310, 305 (ill.), 308 (ill.),
309 (ill.)
health issues, *2:* 308–10
human factors, *2:* 310–14
La Niña and, *3:* 417, 420, 421 (ill.), 423 (ill.)
monitoring and forecasting, *2:* 314–20, 316 (ill.)
monsoons and, *3:* 476
recent occurrences, *2:* 314
sinkhole from, *3:* 407 (ill.)
warning signs, *2:* 319
El Niño/Southern Oscillation (ENSO), *1:* 53–54; *2:*
296–98; *3:* 417, 420
El norte wind, *3:* 446
El Salvador earthquake, *2:* 272
El Viejo. *See* La Niña
Electric vehicles, *5:* 800–801, 802
Electricity
from dust storms, *2:* 245–46
for electric and hybrid vehicles, *5:* 802
Franklin, Benjamin, research, *4:* 518, 519 (ill.)
in lightning, *4:* 501, 521–25, 522 (ill.)
power plant pollution, *5:* 777 (ill.), 787–88, 791
from solar energy, *5:* 803–4, 805, 806 (ill.),
807–8
from wind power, *5:* 808–11, 810 (ill.)
Electromagnetic radiation, *1:* 2–3
Electrostatic induction theory, *4:* 523
Elephant seals, El Niño effects, *2:* 305
Elves (lightning), *4:* 528
Embryos, hailstone, *1:* 157
Emergency assistance. *See also* Relief projects
avalanches, *2:* 182
Hurricane Katrina, *3:* 381
search-and-rescue programs, *5:* 700
Emergency Farm Mortgage Act of 1933, *2:* 237
Emergency preparedness. *See also* Safety measures
blizzards, *2:* 204
earthquakes, *2:* 282
El Niño events, *2:* 318, 319–20
floods, *3:* 326
hurricanes, *3:* 380
tornadoes, *4:* 561

H

M

mA (Maritime arctic air masses), *1:* 23–24

"Mackerel sky," *1:* 116–17, 135

Macrobursts, *4:* 529–30

MAFFS (Modular Airborne Fire Fighting Systems), *4:* 626, 647, 647 (ill.)

Magma, *4:* 587, 597, 598, 598 (ill.)

Magma chambers, *4:* 598, 598 (ill.)

Magnesium, depletion of, *5:* 792

Magnitude of earthquakes, *2:* 274

Mahmoud, Omar, *2:* 212

Maine drought, *2:* 214 (ill.)

Majja Valley tree-planting project (Niger), *2:* 212

Malaria, *2:* 309; *3:* 328

Malaysia, significant weather events, *2:* 285–86; *4:* 566 (ill.)

Mali drought, *2:* 209 (ill.)

Malibu, California wildfires, *4:* 635

Mammals
boreal forests, *1:* 80
oceans, *2:* 304–5
steppe climates, *1:* 73
tundra climates, *1:* 82

Mammatus clouds, *1:* 127–28, 128 (ill.); *4:* 542 (ill.)

Manchu River Dam collapse of 1979, *3:* 474, 474 (ill.)

Manila, Philippines, monsoon, *3:* 450 (ill.)

Mann Gulch fire of 1949, *4:* 617–19, 618 (ill.)

Mantle, Earth's, *2:* 261–62; *4:* 596, 597 (ill.)

Manufactured housing, tornadoes and, *4:* 553–54, 556, 556 (ill.)

Maps, weather. *See* Weather maps

March of the Penguins (film), *1:* 81

Mares' tails (clouds), *1:* 16 (ill.), 125

Marin County, California, wildfires, *4:* 635

Marine animals
El Niño effects, *2:* 303–5
fossils of, *5:* 747
global warming disruptions, *5:* 762–64

Marine climates, *1:* 64, 75, 86

Marine forecasts, *5:* 721, 722

Maritime arctic air masses (mA), *1:* 23–24

Maritime polar air masses (mP), *1:* 24

Maritime tropical air masses (mT), *1:* 25

Martin, Joe "Smokey," *4:* 651

Mature stage of thunderstorms, *4:* 504 (ill.), 506–8

Mature stage of tornadoes, *4:* 547

Mauna Loa volcano, *4:* 604, 605 (ill.)

Maunder, E. W., *1:* 100; *5:* 746

Maunder minimum, *1:* 100; *5:* 746

Mawson, Douglas, *3:* 453

Maximum thermometers, *5:* 671–72, 672 (ill.)

MCC (Mesoscale convective complexes), *4:* 511

McMath-Pierce Solar Telescope, *5:* 745 (ill.)

McNally fire of 2002, *4:* 635

Mean temperature, *1:* 59; *5:* 704, 728

Media weather reports. *See* Weather reports

Mediterranean climates
defined, *1:* 64, 75–77, 76 (ill.)
levanters, *3:* 450
in the U.S., *1:* 86
waterspouts, *4:* 553, 553 (ill.)

Medium-range forecasts, *5:* 662, 664

Meghna River, *3:* 462

Melting
glaciers, *5:* 752–57, 754 (ill.)
hailstones, *1:* 157
ice crystals in air, *1:* 31, 137
latent heat, *1:* 6
road salt, *1:* 148; *2:* 201–2

Meltwater equivalent, *5:* 682

Mercalli, Giuseppe, *2:* 275

Mercalli earthquake scale, *2:* 275–77

Mercury barometers, *5:* 677, 678, 680 (ill.)

Mesocyclones, *4:* 516, 542–43, 542 (ill.), 543 (ill.)

Mesoscale convective complexes (MCC), *4:* 511

Mesoscale winds. *See* Local winds

Mesosphere, *1:* 9

Mesozoic era, *1:* 88–90; *5:* 733

Meteorologists, *5:* 655, 658 (ill.)

Meteorology, defined, *5:* 655. *See also* Forecasting

Methane emissions, *5:* 760–61, 779

Methyl bromide, *5:* 797, 798–99

Methyl chloroform, *5:* 797, 798

Mexico
El Niño effects, *2:* 286–87, 291
hurricanes, *3:* 373–74

O

Oakland, California, wildfires, *4:* 634–35
Obliquity, *1:* 96–97, 96 (ill.)
Occluded fronts, *1:* 27; *5:* 713
Ocean currents, *1:* 51
Ocean floor movement, *4:* 577–78, 597
Oceanographic satellites, *5:* 700
Oceans
    global temperature model, *1:* 52 (ill.)
    heat distribution role, *1:* 50–53; *2:* 294–95, 298–99
    monitoring systems, *2:* 315–18, 316 (ill.)
    potential asteroid impact, *5:* 744
    sediment analysis, *1:* 103–4; *5:* 742, 748–49, 749 (ill.)
    water cycle role, *1:* 47–48
Ohio
    earthquake, *2:* 273–74
    floods, *3:* 323 (ill.), 325, 329
Ohio River floods, *3:* 323 (ill.), 325, 330
Oklahoma. *See also* Dust Bowl of the 1930s
    temperature extremes, *3:* 447
    tornadoes, *4:* 535 (ill.), 540–41, 541 (ill.)
    wildfires, *4:* 625
Old fire of 2003, *4:* 636
Olivera, Ricardo, *2:* 167
Optical effects, *4:* **479–500**
    auroras, *4:* 499, 500 (ill.)
    color of light, *4:* 479, 481
    diffraction of light, *4:* 495–98, 496 (ill.), 497 (ill.), 499 (ill.)
    green flashes, *4:* 486
    halos, *4:* 490–91, 491 (ill.)
    lightning-related, *4:* 528
    mirages, *4:* 487–90, 487 (ill.), 488 (ill.), 489 (ill.)
    rainbows, *4:* 493–95, 494 (ill.), 495 (ill.), 496; *5:* 666, 668
    refraction of light, *4:* 484–86, 484 (ill.), 485 (ill.)
    scattering of light, *4:* 481–84, 483 (ill.)
    sun dogs, *4:* 491–93, 492 (ill.), 493 (ill.)
Orange lightning, *4:* 523
Orangutans, threats to, *2:* 311, 311 (ill.)
Orbit, Earth's. *See* Earth's rotation

Oregon
    Columbia Gorge wind, *3:* 436
    volcano, *4:* 601
    wildfires, *4:* 625, 628
Organized Convection Theory, *3:* 367–71, 370 (ill.)
Organizing stage of tornadoes, *4:* 547
Orion research plane, *5:* 692 (ill.)
Orographic clouds. *See* Mountain-wave clouds
Orographic lifting, *1:* 43–44, 62
Orographic stratus clouds, *1:* 141 (ill.)
Orographic thunderstorms, *4:* 509
Otzi (iceman), *2:* 181, 181 (ill.)
Overcast skies, *5:* 684
Overseeding of clouds, *1:* 145
Oxidation, in fires, *4:* 631
Oxides of nitrogen, *5:* 760, 779, 782, 788–89
Oxygen
    climate change history, *1:* 87, *5:* 732
    climate change history and,
    as fire ingredient, *4:* 631–32, 632 (ill.)
    in fossils, *1:* 102; *5:* 747
Ozone, near-surface
    health issues, *5:* 786
    odor, *5:* 792
    in smog, *5:* 779–80, 781–82
Ozone alert days, *5:* 781, 782
Ozone layer, atmospheric
    Antarctica hole, *5:* 794–95, 798
    climate change history and, *1:* 87; *5:* 732
    defined, *1:* 8–9
    depletion, *5:* 792–99, 795 (ill.), 796 (ill.), 798
    global warming and, *5:* 798
    lightning and, *4:* 520

P

P waves, *2:* 264–65, 266 (ill.)
Pacaya volcano, *4:* 608 (ill.)
Pacific Coast states. *See* West Coast states
Pacific High pressure system, *1:* 19
Pacific Marine Environmental Laboratory (PMEL), *4:* 581
Pacific Northwest United States. *See also specific states*
    La Niña effects, *3:* 426
    volcanoes, *4:* 600, 604

supercell thunderstorms, *4:* 516, 516 (ill.)
tornadoes, *4:* 543
Wind socks, *5:* 678–79
Wind speed
amateur measurement, *5:* 680
Beaufort scale, *5:* 686, 687*t*
experiment, *3:* 436
isobars, *5:* 710, 710 (ill.), 711 (ill.)
in local forecasts, *5:* 705
topography, *1:* 14
Wind turbines, *5:* 809–11, 810 (ill.)
Wind vanes, *5:* 679
Wind waves, *3:* 322, 457–58
Windbreaks, *2:* 212, 226, 247
Windchill equivalent temperature (WET), *1:* 7; *5:* 704
Windmills, *5:* 808
Winds. *See also* Local winds
blizzards, *2:* 195
convergence and divergence, *1:* 21–22
dust storms, *2:* 242, 243–44
fog formation, *3:* 338, 339–40
forecasting, *1:* 133; *5:* 668–69
global patterns, *1:* 16–18
hurricanes, *3:* 362–63, 365, 366–67, 377
in local forecasts, *5:* 705–6
monsoon regions, *1:* 67; *3:* 469–70
overview, *1:* 13–16
precipitation patterns, *1:* 60
upper-air, *1:* 19–21; *4:* 515–16
Winds aloft. *See* Upper-air winds
Windward sides (mountains), *1:* 85
Winter storm alerts, *1:* 154; *2:* 202, 204
Winter weather advisories, *1:* 154; *2:* 202
Wisconsin, significant weather events, *3:* 446; *4:* 630–31, 631 (ill.)
Witt, James Lee, *4:* 554
Wizard Island, Oregon, *4:* 601
WMO. *See* World Meteorological Organization
Wobbling in Earth's rotation, *1:* 95–96, 96 (ill.); *5:* 741
Wood, Harry, *2:* 276

Wooly Lamb (character), *5:* 715
Works Progress Administration (WPA), *2:* 237, 237 (ill.)
World Health Organization (WHO), *5:* 773
World Meteorological Centers, *5:* 661
World Meteorological Organization (WMO)
functions of, *5:* 659, 661
hurricane naming, *3:* 386, 388
ozone depletion research, *5:* 795–96
TOGA/TAO research, *2:* 315
World War I (1914–1918), avalanches, *2:* 182
World Weather Watch (WWW), *5:* 659, 661
World Wildlife Fund, *5:* 762
WPA (Works Progress Administration), *2:* 237, 237 (ill.)
Wuchner, Jan, *3:* 332
WWW (World Weather Watch), *5:* 659, 661
Wyoming
flood, *3:* 329
landslide, *3:* 404–5
wildfires, *4:* 628, 638 (ill.)

Y

Yellow lightning, *4:* 523
Yellow River flood, *3:* 331, 331 (ill.)
Yellowstone National Park
steam fog, *3:* 343
wildfires, *4:* 638 (ill.), 641 (ill.), 642–43, 643 (ill.)
Yosemite National Park landslides, *3:* 410, 410 (ill.)
Yungay, Peru, avalanche, *2:* 170

Z

Zebras, *1:* 69 (ill.)
Zero Emission Vehicle mandate (ZEV), *5:* 800, 801
Zhang Heng, *2:* 274
Zonda winds, *3:* 438

2/13/08 $ 300.00

LONGWOOD PUBLIC LIBRARY
Middle Country Road
Middle Island, NY 11953
(631) 924-6400
LIBRARY HOURS

Monday-Friday	9:30 a.m. - 9:00 p.m.
Saturday	9:30 a.m. - 5:00 p.m.
Sunday (Sept-June)	1:00 p.m. - 5:00 p.m.